Water, World & Weissmuller

A BIOGRAPHY BY
NARDA ONYX

VION Publishing Company, Inc., Los Angeles

To G.J.V. and Maria

ACKNOWLEDGMENTS

Grateful acknowledgment for assistance kindly and generously given is made to:

The White House.

Helms Athletic Foundation and especially W. R. "Bill" Schroeder, Managing Director.

George T. Davis, Los Angeles Herald-Examiner.

The Motion Picture Academy.

Hulbert Burroughs, Edgar Rice Burroughs, Inc.

Sy Weintraub, Banner Productions, Inc.

Sol Lesser.

Metro-Goldwyn-Mayer, Inc.

Columbia Pictures Corporation.

Charles Sweet, Los Angeles Times.

And to those whose names appear in connection with newspaper articles and with the photographs in this biography.

CONTENTS

PREFACE

"THE MAIN issue in life is not the victory but the fight, the essential thing is not to have won but to have fought well."

When Baron Pierre de Coubertin, founder of the Modern Olympic Games, first embraced the spirit of the Olympiad in these words, men and women athletes from the five continents had gathered under a Grecian sky in Athens, 1896, to compete and win recognition for individual achievement, not on mercenary terms but in honor of country, fair play, clean living, hard training, integrity, and sportsmanship.

CITIUS, ALTIUS, FORTIUS — "quicker, higher, more strongly" — these three words frequently appear under the Olympic symbol and are indicative of the competing athlete's endeavor to run faster, jump higher, and throw more strongly. Thus, years later under different skies, in two different countries, but under the same symbol recognized throughout the world, its five different colored circles linked together on a field of white, Johnny Weissmuller brought home to the U.S.A. the spoils of his victories — five Olympic gold medals.

In his competitive career as a sprint swimmer, Johnny held almost every record in the book, 174 individual and 21 relays, making a total of 195! So completely did the tall, deep-chested Weissmuller dominate the aquatic sport in the 1920's that a quarter of a century later the Associated Press, the nation's sports writers and broadcasters, voted him by an overwhelming margin of 132 against 102 over all the other swimmers and divers of the 1900-1950 era combined the "Greatest Swimmer of the Past Fifty Years." In recognition of this honor, Helms Athletic Foundation was invited to present a trophy to Johnny Weissmuller, but recalling that he had been recipient of so many awards in the past, the officials came up with an idea to create a "Swimming Hall of Fame Trophy" in his honor, with his name deeply engraved upon it, at the same time giving credit to all those who had been cited as "Swimmers of the Year" for the period in question. Today, this trophy graces Helms Hall in Los Angeles. The same chamber holds the wall plaque quoting the Baron's never-to-be-forgotten words. Yet inasmuch as these words give essence to the world of swimming which engulfed the early part of Johnny's life, they apply even more to the second phase of his existence, Hollywood, where he fought well in spite of a different kind of competition, equally spirited but by far less honorable.

When the silver screen introduced Johnny Weissmuller as the first speaking Tarzan, a new world of entertainment became known to young and old alike; it spelled thrills and chills to movie fans everywhere, especially to the young . . . and the young in heart . . . and again Johnny, the champion, set a record in this role of Edgar Rice Burroughs' famed hero of the jungle, unmatched in portrayal to this day. While movie studios since have pawned off other actors in the role, and exhibitors widely publicized several new faces in the part, none ever managed to capture the imagination of the public as completely as Johnny's Tarzan.

Even as the maze of television antennas began to spread across the country, the people kept on tuning his pictures into the privacy of their homes, still captivated by his perilous feats and accompanying famous yell on early or late-late shows.

Three generations have known Johnny Weissmuller as the swimmer, the Olympic champion, Tarzan, even Jungle Jim, but while his name appeared in print in headlines, in by-lines and even between the lines, little was said about Johnny — the Man. Nevertheless, it was in this private life in his own realm of thoughts, loves, tragedies, faith, that he has had to fight the most significant battles of his life. When his dual career took the athlete out of sheltering waters, and placed the actor onto naked earth, he, perhaps, truly learned the meaning of ". . . the essential thing is not to have won but to have fought well."

And so the readers of this biography, some old friends, some new acquaintances, are invited to take a closer look at both the sunny and the dark sides of Johnny's terrestrial globe, a globe he knows so well, having traveled circles around its lands and seas, cheered onward along the way by the multitude. Alone.

PART ONE

The Weissmuller Clan.

*Peter John
and John Peter*

EARLY IMPRESSIONS

1

"BEFORE SWIMMING, there was nothing — only surviving." Scattered throughout Johnny's mind, carefully hidden behind shielding partitions, some of them locked with invisible keys long since lost in the passage of time, linger the memories of his childhood . . . somber memories of poverty-stricken days blotted out in the process of growing up . . . carefully sealed scars of early hurts which still mar some tissues within his heart. Time has covered most with oblivion. Only fleeting impressions, episodes of inconsequence are left to spell out a boyhood where one major instinct prevailed, that of survival.

According to the statistics, Johnny was born on June 2, 1904. En route to Chicago, in a small coal town named Windber, in Pennsylvania, immigrant Peter Weissmuller's wife, Elizabeth Kersh, had to interrupt her journey which was to reunite the couple with her parents. She gave birth to a ten-pound boy child. This first-born was christened in the Catholic faith and named Peter John Weissmuller.

Eight years later, on a sunny day at Fullerton Beach, in Lincoln Park which bordered on Lake Michigan's shore, a short distance from downtown Chicago, their son experienced the beginning of his true existence, more so than the shock of birth which had cast him into the world. At the moment Johnny came in contact with the warm wavelets that played inside this protected bay, life surged through the skinny kid whose tall, lanky frame resembled a shapeless stick, and whose anemic, pale complexion seemed as transparent as the shallow water itself.

Donning a pair of water wings his mother had bought from meager savings, the boy waded into the bay and took to the water with ease. No one taught him how to swim.

"I guess, it came sort of natural." Johnny related once.

And when the boy began to splash around, he wondered why he had not been permitted to do this before. Getting wet presented something that meant fun, a sport which not only challenged Johnny's strength but imagination as well. Only his mother knew that this particular exercise had been prescribed by their family physician as "the only thing that can save the sickly lad from an early grave."

Thus, the water wings soon wound up underneath his one-year-younger brother's arms. This second addition to the clan was born when his parents finally made Chicago, and was given Johnny's name in reverse, consequently called John Peter. But Peter John liked 'John', and John Peter — plain 'Peter'; henceforth, Johnny had a brother answering to his first given name.

The brothers spent their 'tadpole' days at Fullerton Beach. Whenever their mother managed some free hours, she took the boys to the water both liked so well. As they grew older, the children began going alone or with other youngsters, and the beach became a regular hangout for these early-day "surfers." Soon, growing bolder and more cunning in their sport, the boys strayed over to the lake itself to a section called "The Rocks," a broken-down breakwater with huge boulders strewn about. There the water was deep and cold, often rough, way out in the open with rollers sweeping in off Lake Michigan and dashing against the rocks. The breaking waves held a strong fascination for the boys. The brothers learned how to dive off these very rocks, and do all sorts of stunts that were impossible to carry out at the shallow Fullerton Beach. By that time, they knew enough about swimming to plunge right in and keep going, right on out through the surf, skilled enough to join some races held by older boys. However, let us go back to the beginning.

The unavoidable expenses that followed Johnny's birth had to be paid by his immigrant father. In Windber, coal mining was the only livelihood that brought in desperately needed income. With the daylight left above, the elder Weissmuller was forced to toil in darkness, gathering the black gold hidden within the earth's crust. A far cry, indeed, from his past affiliation with Franz Josef's army in Vienna, where he had served as captain of German-Austrian origin.

Mystic folklore forbade any coal miner to remain below the surface of the earth when the clock struck midnight. It was murmured that at this fatal hour the ground shifted and demons invaded its layers of dirt, changing the living who dared defy their rule into dust. A strange, old superstition carried onward with many generations to which Peter Weissmuller, Sr., paid little attention. Deep beneath he labored overtime, heedless of warnings by fellow workers. He challenged the spirits of the dark for almost a year, until the elements united against him. He caught tuberculosis. The disease was diagnosed incorrectly at first; however, years later, at the time when the world celebrated the end of World War I, Peter Weissmuller died in the aftermath.

It is inevitable that the beginning of a biography runs a gamut of dull, colorless shades. Yet, woven into the early pattern of the first few years is the starting point of a lifetime that becomes a brilliant color. The formation of character begins as soon as the seed is sown. Similar to the process of planting, some seeds are sown on purpose, whereas others fall accidentally along the wayside. Some plants grow strong and healthy while others wither on nearby soil. No gardener has ever ventured to pick the fittest for survival in an early stage of growth. Equally, man has little to say in a progress which involves nature's paradoxical whims. The choice of fertile or barren breeding ground is removed from his reach until the moment when he begins to consciously think, and his first thought hesitantly touches the verge of maturity, fumbling along its brim, blindfolded by juvenility and accompanying Weltschmerz customary to the very young.

"One has to be mature, before one can think," Johnny remarked when he talked about his tender years. "I guess, I didn't much at first. I was a punk kid who went to nickelodeons, and made a habit of grabbing ice cream cones from ladies wearing feathered hats."

He saw five shows in a row, and fearing that the usher

would throw him out, he moved during each intermission, winding up in the front row, eyes bulging against the screen, his nose pressed almost against it. His favorite stars were Pearl White, William S. Hart, and Douglas Fairbanks, Sr., whom he later met, and whose friendship he won. Action always appealed to Johnny, and he often tried to copy swashbuckling adventurers by jumping over picket fences, tearing countless pairs of trousers, much to the dismay of mother Elizabeth. To this day, Johnny cannot pass a picket fence without experiencing a certain wicked urge to leap across; nevertheless, he admits that reason has lately triumphed over foolishness.

At home, his mother worked hard to keep the brothers from want. Regardless of weekly budgets, the boys always ate well. And as an additional treat, mother baked apple strudel, sometimes homemade 'Kaesekuchen', which temporarily kept Johnny's sweet tooth from getting him into further mischief at the movies. She never let the boys help her in the kitchen, because she believed, in Old Country tradition, that a woman wore the apron, and that her menfolk better keep their fingers out of her soup. For obvious reasons, mother's golden rule was sanctioned threefold.

Elizabeth was employed as head cook in Chicago's famous Turn-Verein, while her husband became entangled with Keeley's Brewery Company, and opened a beer saloon which later went bankrupt because Peter, Senior, lacked the qualifications a businessman had to possess in order to profit, squandering money on needy friends and strangers alike. She managed to pay forever accumulating debts long after her mate had signed away his enterprise as a total loss.

17

The German neighborhood where they lived was adjacent to other nationality quarters. Each street harbored a juvenile gang. And every corner meant segregation as vicious as some kept alive in parts of our country these many years hence. Yet these kids were all white of skin, however their parents had immigrated from alien environments.

Johnny's address was 1921 Cleveland Avenue, a street lined with brick houses, two or three stories high, with attics. There were tiny walk-in gardens surrounded with fences. Toward evening, sidewalks were alight with electric street lanterns which the gangs would knock off come Halloween. Pedestrians thus could not see the wires strung across and, in darkness, stumbled or fell down at short intervals, much to the amusement of the safely hidden, howling brats.

The brothers Weissmuller went along with the gangs for a while, until someone called Peter a "Hunyak" — a name which meant "dirty Magyar." Austrians are by nature proud of their neighbors, the Hungarians, and even more touchy when the insult happened to be extended to someone of kin. Johnny was a good runner. Besides, he had picked up the art of leg work, the sort that is required in boxing, after having collected enough beer-bottle tops in his father's saloon to win a pair of gloves, offered as a prize. He decided to teach the riff-raff a lesson they would not so easily forget.

Dressed in his customary short pants, long black stockings that always itched when worn, and a sailor's broad-collared shirt, he picked a fight with the whole bunch. The skinniest kid of the lot, Johnny used strategy as he tackled all the bigger guys single-handedly, and advanced as the victor. He simply spread them over a large area by slowly retreating . . . and sharpshooting.

When he, later, ran into Officer O'Malley on his beat, he had to explain to him how he happened to walk three blocks backwards during the melee. Johnny quickly put the officer straight. In fighting the boys, he informed him, he had felt more secure knowing their angle of assault and, backing up, applying the quick dance of his legs, his punches landed on targets to the left and right, leaving bloody noses to bear witness of a job well done. O'Malley, apparently, thought it was a nice accomplishment, too. His Irish spirit thoroughly approved of Johnny's actions and the undeniable fact that he had managed to lick the lot. But Johnny fared less favorably after confessing his brawl to the Catholic Father at Saint Michael's Parochial School.

Checking some of the evidence of black eyes along a line-up of his pupils, the Father quietly ordered Johnny into the chapel where the child usually served as altar boy.

His sore knees hugged the cold stone floor for hours, and after countless dozens of "Hail Marys," Johnny soon learned that confession, whatever it did for the soul, certainly brought little of physical comfort. And the boy gradually decided that whitewashing one's sins completely in this manner seemed a martyrdom a trifle too severe. Henceforth, he decided to censor his confessions just enough to escape the ultimate punishment.

While between the ages of five and twelve, Johnny remained at Saint Michael's. Every morning he attended mass before school hours, and often fainted when a Brother decided to keep him suspended on his knees indefinitely, despite his actual innocence in pranks the class had played without letting "the skinny one" take part in their activities. In his condition, the strict abuses the holy Brothers constantly inflicted upon "the little devils" became unbearable for the boy. Hit on the fingers with the sharp edge of a ruler, and punished by forever endless kneeling sessions, Johnny remained at Saint Michael's until, at last once too often, he passed out again. Thereupon, his parents removed him from the parochial school and registered him with Menier Public School, a mixed tutoring place for boys and girls alike.

Johnny, at the age of twelve, did not care for the weaker sex at all. "I wish I could have stayed a middle-of-the-roader between my early apprehensions toward girls, and my later infatuations. It might have saved a few fireworks," Johnny mused, remembering. "Anyway, at Menier School I thought only about swimming, and went to bed with my pair of boxing gloves."

After Johnny's father failed in his business venture, things became increasingly worse at home. With his health deteriorating, the once disciplined-to-die captain tried to drown his miseries in liquor, and unable to control its effects, often gave vent to his bitterness by berating his wife and sons. A sensitive child, Johnny could not bear seeing his mother hurt, so ran away from home. He slept overnight near his house, under an elevated railroad, covering his shivering young body with discarded newspapers. In the morning, he returned to face the inevitable violent beating his father reserved for, and never failed to administer to his son after similar occurrences.

But the tides swirled onward and the lad began to earn extra money by working as a delivery boy for a church supply company which sold artificial flowers, religious statues and crosses. Often, he had to carry enormous packages from one part of the city to the other and, trying to ease the weight of his load, he made frequent use of streetcars. However, he soon found out that he was not a welcome passenger. He took up too much seating space with his parcels. In desperation, the over-bundled kid stood in front of the streetcar until its motorman had to halt the vehicle for fear of running the boy down.

Other heartaches plagued the youngster's early memories, and remained locked within the adult's subconsciousness. One winter's morning, Johnny finally managed to buy a second-hand sled which he had wanted for many long years. In a moment of impulse and daring, he fastened it to a truck for a fast ride through the glistening snow. It was a ride on the wind! A few joyous moments until the driver of the vehicle yelled out, "Get lost!" Johnny began to loosen the rope of his skimming chariot, but to his horror discovered he could not free his sled from the speeding truck, as they went faster and faster. Johnny hung on to his precious sled as long as he could, his fingers stiffening and turning blue in the icy wind and snow spray. He had just about managed to break the holding knot . . . when he fell off! He sat in the snow.

He watched his sled disappear into the distance.

The tears became frozen on his face. He never again

21

during his early youth saved enough money to replace the first jingle-bells-transportation he had so briefly called his own.

But there were the happy times when the family joined the mother's parents who owned acreage on Chicago's rural outskirts, where they kept a sturdy horse, a friendly cow, and a flock of noisy chickens. The German-born neighbors joined in a community picnic which, yearly, was highlighted with a pig-roasting ceremony, or 'Schlacht', as the picnickers used to call it. Incorporated into such a social gathering was the ever-popular laugh-provoking potato-sack race of the era, as well as a yodeling contest.

In a Germanic neighborhood, equal amounts of beer are mixed with equal amounts of song. Young Weissmuller's love for singing had been inspired by occasional visits to the opera, the performances his mother patronized and where she fondly took her boys. Johnny's melodious, projecting tenor voice was noticed by the local vegetable peddler, whose rustic time-worn pipes malfunctioned when shouting out his wares. The old man made a deal with young Weissmuller: In turn for voicing commercials along a daily route, his horse-drawn cart would get Johnny halfway to school. He also promised a small basket of vegetables and fruit if the boy called "Tomatoes! Potatoes! Fresh beans and cabbages!" loud enough to attract the attention of the neighborhood housewives. It paid off. Johnny's take-home basket soon increased in size proportionately to the growing volume of his voice.

Then came the yodeling contest. Learning to sing with frequent changes from the ordinary voice to falsetto

and back again, in the manner of Swiss and Tyrolean moun-
taineers, the boy perfected his yodel. And thus from the
icy wastes of the Matterhorn came the inspiration and the
beginning of Johnny Weissmuller's famous Tarzan yell which
was later recorded in Hollywood, five octaves higher and
twice over, to become Tarzan's song of the jungle, the
theater-goer's best-known call of the wild. With the exception
of one actor, all others who have since appeared in the part
have used Metro-Goldwyn-Mayer's soundtrack of Johnny's
voice. "Oo-uh-hoo-uh-woo" originally sounded more like
"yodel-lay-e-o", but given the material Hollywood's sound-
men soon "mixed" the difference.

The year of the yodeling contest was also the year when
Johnny joined the swimming team at the Stanton Park Pool,
and, together with two chums, "Hooks" and "Hank" Miller,
won all the junior competitions held there. Next, the boys
migrated to the North Side Y.M.C.A. on Larrabee Street,
but that move took a bit of finagling on Johnny's part. To
be admitted to the "Y", a guy had to be fourteen, but Johnny
was only twelve at the time. So he took the only way out
and practiced a bit of deception about his age. Anyway,
have we not all at one occasion or another, perhaps, been
inclined to deduct — instead of add to (Confucius say:)
— honorable years in question. Johnny's height supported
the validity of his claim and no further inquiries were made.
He and his pals became regular members of the "Y" team.
But since these workouts took place only twice a week, it
was not enough to appease the fish-like creatures of the
waters the boys were turning out to be, and they soon went
on the prowl for other indoor pools with greater challenge.

But the Y.M.C.A. had left its mark and had exerted a positive influence for the better on the boy who once liked to take cables off streetcars so that his pals could jump on and get a free ride, and who would collaborate in the purchase of potash and sulphur, the basis of gunpowder, and put the mixture into Bull-Durham tobacco pouches to be placed on the tracks. No one was ever hurt in these childish pranks, but many a streetcar came to its own particular end of the line as the tracks were blown up by these miniature block-busters. These joys were strictly reserved for the 4th of July celebration, and in the months ahead weary store owners tightened down on their sales of the ingredients contained in these potent firecrackers. When all precautionary measures passed without preventing the preparation of the land mines, the streetcars stopped running rather than cope with the hazard, and none were seen during the Independence holiday on the deserted, bomb-laden tracks running in parallel lines through the streets of Johnny's neighborhood.

Then there came a day when Johnny began to ask himself what all this nonsense was about. The boy had become a teen-ager, with all its serious problems about life. To come home with a head split open by some lead-pipe-packing delinquent, just because a gang war had broken out and a certain code demanded the defense of his gang's honor, seemed somewhat ludicrous all of a sudden. He began to know right from wrong, to know the real meaning of the Golden Rule, and a clear picture about past actions and their effect on the future emerged through the mists that had confused his youthful outlook on life.

"It's the way you start," Johnny ruminated and slowly settled backward as a thoughtful frown appeared on his forehead, during an interviewing session. "All through the years one always knows that nothing good will follow something evil. One might call it conscience, but I think it's more than that — it's an inbuilt heaven or hell."

When summer came, the boys ran out to Oak Street Beach, a long sweep of sand on Lake Michigan's shore at the south end of Lincoln Park. The Miller brothers were his constant companions, and then there was Fred "Pal" Lauer, who eventually became one of the greatest goal tenders in water polo in the United States. Lauer was a big, handsome youth with black, curly hair, a regular giant of a boy, a physical attribute which undoubtedly served as his best asset in guarding the polo nets. He was later made a member of the Illinois Athletic Club which sponsored Johnny into championships, and made two trips to the Olympic Games with American water polo teams.

Johnny's pronounced love for animals finally found an outlet when he managed to obtain a Dachshund he called Hans. The dog accompanied his young master everywhere; well — almost, for Hans simply would not take to the water the way Johnny had hoped, no matter how thoroughly the teen-ager and his friends trained the pup. Hans stubbornly refused to be associated with fish, until, carried away with a chase after a flirtatious butterfly, he fell into the lake. Typical of the Dachshund's aversion to swimming, his little body sank like a rock and, as the coldness of the water closed in, he remained below. With Hans sitting tight on the bottom of the lake, Johnny had to act fast. He jumped into the water, wearing his Sunday best, and brought out a mortified but grateful dog who had expected nothing less than just such a perfect rescue from his master. Johnny's ten-mile hike homeward in wet clothes, with a drenched Dachshund paddling alongside, eventually paid off when Hans decided to become a warm-water champ on his own merits, beating all the mongrels along the beach during the last, hot days of summer that followed.

On such a day, swimming around at Oak Street Beach where all the lifeguards had tasted mother Elizabeth's apple strudel as a bonus for admitting her sons free of charge at any hour of the day or night, Johnny caught the attention of the assistant coach of swimming at the nearby Hamilton Club. The coach recognized Johnny's potentials and urged him to call at the club's pool for a tryout on their team. Johnny swam there for several months. His speed and stamina were building up. Soon he could do a hundred yards in about fifty-eight seconds, which was pretty solid timing for a boy who had never been properly disciplined or trained in the art of sprinting. But the club's possibilities were limited in as far as getting into big-time competition was concerned.

Meanwhile, Johnny had lost his job with the church supply outfit, but had found new employment as bellboy at the Plaza Hotel in Chicago, where he was later promoted to serve as elevator operator. Years later, when Johnny's fame had spread across the North American Continent and into every part of the world where movies traveled, he visited the Plaza on several occasions. Strangely, none remembered a puny kid riding up and down the elevator, busily opening doors at floor levels. Or, perhaps, not so strangely, for fame in itself lasts only while the illusion prevails and an aura of imaginary affection is placed around the momentarily idolized object. Or have we yet reached another stage of birth, that of popularity born through success?

As Johnny spent more and more hours each day in perfecting his style and rhythm, training himself to slice through the rough waves of the lake, or sprinting across smooth waters in pools, the teen-ager's dreams of becoming a champion swimmer increased, and his desire to achieve something worthwhile in life reached a high peak of determination. He was on his way!

"I had to quit school after my father died. You know, your guts get so mad when you try to fight poverty and its constant inevitable companion — ignorance. (Johnny was reaching way back, trying to recapture his thoughts of the past.) I told myself, I'm going to get out of this neighborhood, if only because he's got a quarter and I haven't. I fought my way out of the 'Dunkelheit'. Maybe it is this drive to better oneself and one's surroundings that makes a champion out of the less-fortunate boy, instead of the one born with a silver spoon in his mouth, as the saying goes. With but few exceptions, like Jack Kelly, Jr. (brother of Princess Grace of Monaco), it is always the underdog who wins through sheer will power."

It may be of general interest to note here that young Kelly followed in his father's footsteps and won the highest rowing award — the Diamond Sculls. Yet he failed thrice in the Olympics of 1948, 1952, and 1956 to bring back the Single Sculls his illustrious sire had won in 1920 at Antwerp, as well as the Double Sculls Jack, Sr., picked up twice with Paul V. Costello.

When Jack B. Kelly, Sr., started out as sculler, his profession was that of bricklayer. In those days, merit alone did not qualify a man for enrollment in competitive sporting events; however, old Kelly was such a great rower that he had to be admitted in spite of the taboos society had inflicted upon sportsmen.

What Walter Hagen did for golf, Kelly did for rowing; the combination of these two great talents and their easy good manners managed to overcome the ostracism of the elite. As the story goes, Walter Hagen had — once upon a time — attended the open golf tournaments in England. As he drove up in his Rolls-Royce, he changed clothes inside this fashionable automobile, because no golf pro was permitted to enter the sanctified threshold leading inside the clubhouse; then played, and won. The Prince of Wales soon made friends with the champion, and invited him for lunch. Thereafter, by royal command, all golf pros were admitted into the dining area of the club, whereas, hitherto, they had supped with servants in a back room.

Kelly's final answer to Boston came when his rowing feats were followed by a second talent, that of quickly accumulating wealth. But father Kelly never forgot about his humble start in life and, therefore, he taught his son well the value of a broad outlook . . . and the dangers of too many riches, too early . . . or too late.

At sixteen, with no proper outlet in sight to further

his burning ambitions, Johnny accidentally ran into "Hooks" Miller whom he had not seen for a while. Hooks had made the Illinois Athletic Club team as he was able to do the hundred-yard crawl in about fifty-six seconds, a little faster than Johnny had managed to that date. The friend spoke glowingly about their coach "Big" Bill Bachrach, and Johnny did not need more than a hint of an invitation to accept a proposal to swim the next day.

Membership in the Illinois Athletic Club beckoned as the great chance Johnny had been looking forward to find. And now all depended on a performance that would convince Bachrach that Johnny possessed championship potential and caliber.

The hours between dragged on indefinitely.

TRAINING UNDER BACHRACH

2

THOUGHTFULLY, William Bachrach watched the boy's tall, lean body plunge into the I.A.C. pool and take off, plowing through the water with extraordinary speed, but showing no style . . . just an incredible awkwardness, and the worst stroke Bachrach had seen in his entire career as a swimming coach.

He chewed on his unlit cigar, and without taking his keen eyes off Johnny, he acknowledged Miller's rooting, fingers-crossed, presence. "John Weissmuller is his name, you say, eh? He's got the world's lousiest stroke!"

Bachrach never minced words. Only too familiar with that fact, Hooks never dreamed of arguing with this giant of a man standing six-feet-two and weighing no less than 340 lbs., whose reddish smoke-stained mustache matched the color of his sparse hair. Young Miller knew that Bachrach had trained the best of them, and no one had ever surpassed his inbuilt knowledge of handling a swimmer. At the same time, he noticed a certain steady gleam in the instructor's calculating gaze; it meant that the coach saw more than he cared to admit.

Big Bill Bachrach had accompanied the Olympic team

to Antwerp earlier in the year, where he had guided Duke Kahanamoku to his second victory in consecutive Olympiads. His swimmers had always followed the long, slim line like fishes, sandpikes and pickerels, snaky in motion. Champions like Robert Skelton, John Faricy, Ethel Lackie, Sybil Bauer and Paul Samson. This boy, Weissmuller, seemed ideally endowed for crawl sprinting. But he had a lot to learn . . . and more to forget.

"You come down tomorrow and I'll start you on a real course of training." Bachrach said, as Johnny shook the water from his hair. "I'm going to change your stroke all over, and I want you to do everything I say to the letter, without questions. Okay?" And he handed Johnny the membership card to the Illinois Athletic Club without awaiting the sanction of the athletic committee.

Johnny stood there, dripping, gingerly holding a little bit of cardboard, trying not to get it wet . . . just a little bit of cardboard.

Johnny's training began in October, 1920, and continued through the following August. With the exception of two preliminary tryouts, Bachrach kept his prize pupil out of competitive swimming in these months, nevertheless racing him against a watch.

"First forget all you've learned. It's all wrong! So what if you can stay afloat? That's no miracle! All fish swim. Look at your stroke! You cross over with your arms in front, and fumble up in the air; your legs move like a mongrel's. You have no system in breathing. What kind of body position is that? Relax, boy, relax!"

The workout started with the arms only, and continued

31

for months and months without the slightest hint about the use of the legs.

"The secret about the arm stroke is a pull and a push. Get that — a pull and a push! Not a thrash or a sweep or a chop or anything else!" Bachrach kept exclaiming, repeating, while showing the young swimmer just how to go about the pursuit of perfection.

The pull part came first. After making the catch of the hand in front, not reaching too far out, but reducing the reach by bending the elbow, and keeping the elbow and shoulder higher at all times than the hand, he made Johnny pull almost straight down in the water on a line with the shoulder. When the hand came under the shoulder and to the breast, the pull ceased and became a push.

"At this point the hand is about eight or ten inches separated from the breast, and the elbow is pointing out. From here you carry on the stroke, pushing backwards and out. The push ends at the hip and then you relax your arm. You bend your elbow still more . . . yes . . . now recover your upper arm and carry it parallel to the water, the lower arm and hand flopping loosely at an angle of forty-five degrees. Do you feel the lower arm, wrist and hand relax? As the arm arrives to the forward position, it straightens somewhat, and here you get your relaxation in the upper arm and shoulder."

While Bachrach talked, Johnny thought about getting this relaxation, keeping easy and loose all over. He tried to forget about his legs as much as possible, and while they dragged along in the water, rather changing his position, he developed his arm stroke, slowly mastering it, bettering it endlessly, continually, as his physical structure also changed.

And while Johnny swam, Bachrach watched.

"What are you thinking about?" He would ask the boy.

"Well, I'm thinking about not crossing over with my hands out in front. About keeping my elbow bent . . . not reaching too far out."

"All right," Bachrach said. "Go ahead." But pretty soon he would stop Johnny again: "What are you thinking about?"

"About how and when to bend my elbows. I am thinking about not holding my arms straight; about keeping my shoulders flat, not dipping down with either shoulder on the arm I am pulling with; about keeping the shoulder and elbow higher than the hand when I'm making the catch of the hand; about keeping my head up."

"How about relaxing?" questioned Bachrach. "Aren't you thinking about that, too?"

"Yes, that, too!"

Relaxing was one thing above all others that the coach forever impressed upon the youth's mind. And it became the secret of Weissmuller's success — relaxing at the same time as he swam at maximum speed.

Practicing in the pool, Johnny often placed his feet into an inflated rubber tube and not using them at all, he employed only the arms. He soon found that he was able to keep going indefinitely without tiring; not so if he had used his legs. This method he still uses whenever he feels in need of a workout.

Finally, Bachrach decided to start Johnny on the leg kick. He explained to the teen-ager the difference between the Australian-crawl leg beat versus the American one. The

Australian is a hangover from the scissors kick of the trudgen stroke, thrashing the legs straight up and down, operating from the knee. Whereas the American-crawl beat works from the hip. The leg, while not held stiff at the knee, is used more as a unit from hip to toe, a method which gives twice the length of leverage, and the superior power obtained from the thigh muscles. Furthermore, a knee thrash has the tendency to raise the feet out of the water and, consequently, many Australian swimmers break the water with their feet, thereby losing traction. Keeping the legs lower in the water gives a superior propelling power.

Arguments about how many leg beats had to be taken with each revolution of the arms, straight six- or eight-beats, left Bachrach laughing and waving aside the issue. The coach taught Johnny that the arms were the main force in the crawl stroke, and that the legs had to be subordinated. He acknowledged the power of the leg beat, but chiefly to maintain a high body position. Otherwise, all attention had to be concentrated on arm action.

"Anything that goes fast has to go above the water."

Johnny arched his back and swam high, applying his newly learned technique; his legs remained well below the surface. One day, Bachrach noticed him exhaling bubbles.

"Why do you inflict that punishment upon yourself, holding your breath until you're ready to come up for more air?" he asked.

"Because I need my wind for the final snort out of the water to clear my nose of any drops that might trickle down to my windpipe." Johnny retorted promptly.

"This is what you should do," said Bachrach. "Keep

a flow of air either going or coming at all times, the same as you do on land. Don't blow it out so fast that it will be all gone. Let it out slow. Let the exhale be a 'slow-motion movie', taking four or five times longer than the inhale. The inhale is a quick bite, a gulp through a wide-open mouth. Then at once start the slow exhale, and keep just enough material for the final snort."

Johnny found it hard to break the former habit. However, he kept at it until, finally, the new way became the natural thing to do. This experience served to prove to him the importance of acquiring the fundamentals of breath control. He went into them in great detail, repeating elementary exercises over and over until, thoroughly mastered, they became his second nature.

Coach Bachrach insisted from the very beginning that Johnny was a sprinter, not a long-distance swimmer. He felt that the youngster's speed at shorter distances assured victory, while longer ones offered some room for doubt. Bachrach also believed that sprints presented less of a strain on the growing body of the boy. Longer grinds were for older, more mature men. Seeing in Johnny the makings of a champion, he one day voiced his thoughts to his eagerly listening pupil.

"How would you like to be a world's champion?"

"When?" asked Johnny.

Bachrach's good-natured face broke into a grin. "As soon as I say you are ready."

He told the young Weissmuller to stick to the 100-yard distance, to get it into his blood. "You can try others later," Bachrach said, not once, but many times, "but 880 should be your limit."

During these months of training, the coach never permitted Johnny's speed to exceed 65 percent of his capable output. And he impressed upon the teen-ager the importance of swimming for form. "Form counts," he said repeatedly. "You can't beat it, and without it, you can't truly expect to become a champion."

Bachrach finally allowed Johnny to swim in a couple of preliminary tryouts in the early part of 1921, one in the men's junior 100-yard event. In the excitement of the moment, young Weissmuller made three false starts, jumping into the water each time, which, with his somewhat erratic swimming, gave proof of his overanxiety. He might yet have won the race, had he not worn a swimming cap over his longish hair, a cut fashionably styled after the mode of the day. Splashing through the pool, the cap slipped, covering both his eyes, and consequently, he finished the race blindfolded, yet coming within a second of the world's record in practice only. The defeat he suffered in this, his first preliminary tryout, ironically was caused by his own bathing cap to which he bade farewell the moment he climbed out of the pool. Thereafter, he quickly cut his hair short in front, and it has remained that way forevermore. That was Johnny's only and single defeat, and since it occurred during a tryout and not in actual competition, the claim that Weissmuller never lost a race in his entire career as a sprinter stands true to facts. Bachrach let him swim in a second preliminary event, where he won the open hundred-yard free style at the Central A.A.U. championships at the Great

Lakes Naval Training Station on March 17, 1921, defeating Abe Seigel, a teammate.

After that, the coach withdrew his pupil from further tryouts. He kept the boy to lone training but now, swimming under Bachrach's watchful supervision, Johnny had to break a world's record every single day. Many of Chicago's leading manufacturers and businessmen ate lunch at the I. A. Club. Bachrach took advantage of this and approached them on behalf of his protégé. "Would you like to see a world record broken?" he would ask. "Pick any one you fancy from fifty yards to half-a-mile. Bring your own stop watch or choose any of ours. I'll furnish the record timetables." When most enthusiastically accepted the invitation, Bachrach sprung his catch. "Nothing for nothing is given here. The boy likes to eat, so when he wins, you buy him a lunch." Or when Mr. Netcher from the Boston Clothes Store wandered in: "Johnny needs a suit, you get him one providing his timing fulfills your expectations." He got to various haberdashers, owners of shoe stores, and soon young John was fitted out with more clothes than he had dreamed of owning, and his stomach was filled every day with a nourishing meal at the expense of some bettor involved in Bachrach's honest scheme. From then on, when Johnny paraded down his street in all his new finery, his ears often caught the words: "Look, boys, there goes Beau Brummell!" But the young swimmer was too happy to pay any attention to teen-age ribaldry; he knew that he had finally discovered the better side of the tracks . . . and how to stay there.

On August 6th, the same year, at the Duluth Boat Club, Johnny Weissmuller made his actual debut in competitive swimming. He won his first National A.A.U. championship at fifty yards free style. His time in this event was twenty-three and one-fifth seconds, just one-fifth of a second short of the world's record.

Later that year, in September, Johnny established his first world record in one-hundred and fifty yards, at Brighton Beach, N.Y. He swam it in one minute, twenty-seven and two-fifths seconds, taking two and one-fifth seconds from the mark held by Ted Cann of New York.

From then onward, Weissmuller's victories became part of the national scene.

In the first year of swimming in competition, Johnny's physique improved. He remained slender but no longer bony; he weighed one-hundred-and-sixty pounds. Meanwhile, he also grew an inch taller, standing six-feet-three in height. Constant practice in the water, long workouts by the young champion brought an insatiable craving for food at all hours of the day, and if Bachrach had permitted it, Johnny would have soon become a record-breaking eater, matching his aquatic feats along the line. "He thinks there's nothing but meat and ice cream in the world," the coach told reporters.

When Bachrach awakened from a siesta, he often found Johnny sitting nearby, reading a newspaper while munching on some food. Coming out of his hibernation, the coach grunted, "Hey, what are you doing? Get back into that pool!"

"Don't feel like it," Johnny swallowed the last morsel, and yawned.

"Get undressed and get in there!" came the command.

"But I've ordered another club sandwich!" Johnny protested.

"Never mind that sandwich." Bachrach remained firm. "You get out of those clothes and into that water." And Johnny knew that Bachrach's word was law, not to be questioned or trifled with further.

Once in the pool, young Weissmuller began to swim with all the classical form his instructor had taught him, pleasing the old master to the extent where he bellowed out his favorite expressions: "Hooray! Eldorado! Eureka! I'll make a swimmer out of you yet. Don't let those victories fool you, my boy; you've got a long way to go!"

Bachrach believed that keeping his swimmers in perfect athletic condition required practically no change from their personal habits and normal routine. He constantly advised a diversified diet, with emphasis on greens, vegetables, and fruit. A rigid or freakish diet often recommended for other types of athletes has no beneficial effect upon a swimmer, for the simple reason that swimming is an all-year-round racing sport. To ask a swimmer to keep up a continuous twelve-months regime of self-denial would only serve to make him irksome under the strain. There are some coaches who believe proteins such as meats, fish, and eggs are harmful since they are highly acid foods and apt to increase fatigue, whereas fruits and tomatoes commonly thought of as acid-containing are really alkaline or basic in their chemical action on the body. Bachrach believed in permitting his pupils a full range of foodstuffs, however, balancing the intake with the necessary nutriments of grown edibles.

Swimming is a sport apart from all others with a standard of values almost foreign to the other sports. Many great, all-around athletes have excelled in various kinds of competition, only to fare poorly after a jump in the pool. After swimming a few lengths, they quit, breathless and exhausted. On the other hand, a swimmer should not participate in certain other sports, since such action could easily prove harmful. Johnny, who later became fond of playing golf and in which he has accumulated over a hundred trophies throughout the years, was not permitted to indulge in the game during his amateur status, for reasons that too much walking was bad for a swimmer.

Under Bachrach's constant guiding Johnny developed a position in the water which enabled him to maintain hydroplaning, like a speedboat, reducing water resistance to a minimum. He swam higher in the water than anyone had to date, with shoulders and chest high, back arched. It took speed to get up and stay there without strain, but once he had mastered it, the position became a cinch to hold, increasing his speed with the same effort as swimming lower at a slower pace. While his powerful arm stroke propelled his way forward, his legs thrashed through the water like separate whips, employing each foot like a lash but in a pigeon-toed set fashion, thus relaxing the ankles and achieving a proper motion that yielded force. A regular "whiplash," as Bachrach called it. Once this training was perfected, it was equally important to forget all about the feet, allowing them to function naturally within the pattern.

After the false starts at the early tryout, Bachrach started Johnny on the plunge and push-off bit.

"You have to overcome your anxiety, Johnny," he said. "By nature your reflexes are slow. You can't make up for it by jumping ahead of the gun. While you stand there, waiting, prepare yourself mentally. When the others jump — you jump! You'll soon find you're even with your rivals, or ahead. Imitate an arrow. The minute you hit that water, bring your arms down with a powerful slap, at the same time let your legs down with a strenuous plop. Look at the water so as to time it exactly at the moment of impact. The result will keep you above, while the other swimmers take a deep plunge in, losing valuable seconds."

Next Bachrach explained the importance of the number of strokes used in going a given distance. For instance, in a sixty-foot tank, he underlined the necessity of using but five revolutions of the arms, and not more than six, possible through powerful push-offs and proper turning at the end of the tank. For a while Johnny remained a poor turner, making up the lost time penalized by this handicap through sheer physical effort and a forced drive. Even Bachrach's explanation did not seem to light the bulb of sudden recognition, until along came Perry McGillivray.

Perry was skilled in sprinting, was known to be one of the best in his day. He saw Johnny's difficulty and urged his fellow athlete to try his system.

"You're trying to turn flat on the surface; that's wrong for sprint swimming," Perry instructed the listening younger colleague. "As you swim up and touch the end of the tank with the tip of your right hand, turn your left ear down and go deep into the water. Do not touch the end of the tank with your left hand, but use it as a paddle in the water to aid the body in pivoting on that left ear. Go deep and make your push-off, and as you shoot away, plane upward until you hit the surface just at the right place to begin your arm action. You see, this is different from the starting plunge, which you make shallow, whereas the push-off should start deep."

Perry's advice sank in, and Johnny soon mastered the turn which was to contribute fractions of seconds, or more, to the many records he was to break in the future.

Yet, in spite of everything Johnny learned about form and method, the sundry tricks that helped him increase his speed and propelling power, he experienced one other great need once he was thrown into the race: The fine ability and finesse of swimming within his power and retaining that little all-important extra reserve to win at the end. It is easy to use up one s energy in the early stages of sprinting . . . only to tire at the finish. Violence in effort can cause a loss of relaxation as well as efficiency in the long run. Holding back too long also can be fatal; equally, a prolonged speeding ahead with sudden exhaustion has the same result. It's that elusive happy compromise that finds the winner's circle.

Whenever Johnny swam, once he had learned the art of using all his faculties through constant, vigorous train-ing, he tried to keep ahead of the other swimmers at a com-fortable distance, making secure the victory, relaxing within that knowledge, and using the last stretch to break his own record over again. Applying this rule to his system, he gained in confidence, winning race after race with an ease which astounded his opponents and fans alike. Soon the name of Johnny Weissmuller was followed throughout the swimming-records book and almanacs with ditto marks.

The newspapers that had once dismissed him as "just another promising young swimmer discovered by Bachrach" soon began to label Weissmuller as "Prince of the Waves"; "Flying Fish"; "Aquatic Wonder"; "America's Greatest Waterman"; "Human Hydroplane"; "King of Swimmers"; and other such lofty-sounding titles, exceeded by one common acclamation, that of the undisputed term of "Champion".

BETWEEN LORELEI AND KAHANAMOKU

3

JOHNNY'S HOME remained at 1921 Cleveland Avenue whenever his aquatic meets kept him in Chicago. Money remained scarce, since his amateur standing forbade him to accept any funds, and his meager income at the Plaza Hotel was spasmodically interrupted through travel to various swim events. Thus, his earnings covered only the essentials. Meanwhile, his mother still practiced her culinary art at the Turn-Verein, and Peter continued in school.

The Weissmullers lived a quiet, secluded life, letting the neighborhood and its people pass them by. Little had changed there since the early days of childhood; however, Johnny's inner outlook had altered to an extent which had left nothing in common with his one-time playmates. Some of his former companions had wandered with the tide, had become regular hoodlums. Nevertheless, they respected Johnny's newly acquired claim to fame with silent envy and a quiet awe, wishfully placing themselves into his shoes, but none possessing an equal drive to change their fortune toward something more positive.

Johnny nowadays was ever in a state of transition, adjusting to his opportunities, constantly becoming more and more a part of the I.A.C. scene, guided by his fellow athletes who taught him how to dress, and he was developing a taste for the conservative. Whenever his sparse income permitted, the now eighteen-year-old rushed to Capper & Capper, THE place for men's clothes, and ordered a tailor-made suit of the finest material, carefully choosing a tie and other accessories to match. Some items still came free of charge through Bachrach's clever planning; others cost him a pretty penny, but he found pride and satisfaction in these newly purchased symbols of success.

Winning and, then, defending championships kept the young swimmer forever on the move; "under pressure," the pros call it. And the temptation to relax in practice was great, indeed. But the wily, cunning ol' Bachrach came up with a remedy.

"Have you heard of the San Blas Indians?" Big Bill casually asked, one day.

"No." Johnny answered. "What do they sand blast?"

Bachrach suppressed a smile. "They may blast you right out of your swimming trunks, come the right time. These Indians beat boats in a harbor, outdo crocs, and brother — they wear derbies just to keep the sun out of their eyes while swimming; besides, these derby hats never get wet 'cause they hydroplane above the water just like you. And there's always one in every race! So watch out!"

"Ach, du lieber Strohsack!" Johnny exclaimed in German and, slightly nervous, his training habits improved a hundred-fold.

His spreading popularity as a champion obviously attracted much attention from the fair sex, but Johnny remained cool and distant against the lures of sirens, until a blond-tressed Lorelei hit the right note to his fancy.

Johnny kept working out at the beach whenever the weather permitted it, and on one of these occasions, his eye caught a slender girl coming out of the water. In all his shyness as a teen-ager, his confidence as a swimmer managed to wangle an introduction and, soon, Johnny was taking the girl to the nicest places in town, like the College Inn where Isham Jones and his fifteen musicians played invitations to the dance.

To young Weissmuller dancing came naturally, possibly on account of his early leg work at the time when he had still preferred his pair of boxing gloves to romance. It was not long before he and his Lorelei entered popular dancing competitions and won a total of five cups for this effortless amusement. Among the places they patronized was the Trianon, where Paul Whiteman's eighty music-makers entertained. But while Johnny fell head over heels in love with his maiden-of-the-lake, coach Bachrach sensed disaster.

"So you want to marry the girl, eh? That'll be a nice mess to get into! Here I'm trying to train you for the Olympics, make a national hero of you, and all you do is moon about the first girl who crosses your path. What'll you live on? Air, water, and love? An amateur athlete gets seven bucks a day when he is on tour, and expenses. Besides, you're only a kid! Still out-growing your trunks," Bachrach scolded. "Don't be a goof!"

"She'll wait for me." Johnny stubbornly persisted.

"Like heck she will! I've never met a dame yet that

did not forget a guy the moment he passed out of sight. And there'll be plenty of times you'll be out of sight in days to come."

Johnny was not convinced. The romance continued. He was introduced to the girl's parents. Then Bachrach took Johnny to Hawaii.

In 1922, the Shriners' Convention was to take place in Honolulu. Chicago's participants wanted to see how their boy, Weissmuller, would do in competition against the invincible Duke Kahanamoku, as both were considered likely contenders for the coming 8th Olympic Games. In return for this entertainment, they promised to pay all expenses to get Johnny and his coach to the island. Bachrach accepted at once. As it happened, the entire I.A.C. team eventually went along to participate in the National A.A.U. championships held in Hawaii.

This voyage presented the longest trip Johnny had taken till then and, the excitement of the venture mounting, it overshadowed his youthful infatuation toward Lorelei. He kissed his girl temporarily "good-bye", and boarded the train to San Francisco, accompanied by his smiling coach and I.A.C. teammates.

Bachrach had arranged a swimming meet in San Francisco before taking the boat to Hawaii, where Johnny defeated George Schrot and a few others by such a considerable margin as to create a sensation in swimming circles, and send word ahead to Honolulu, and Kahanamoku.

The boys had a rough crossing, so rough in fact that during their daily workout, the ship's pool emptied overboard, leaving the swimmers like fish on dry canvas. It was Johnny's first encounter with salt water, which he found more buoyant; therefore, he needed his legs much less to keep his body in the high, hydroplaning position. He soon learned that by varying his leg beat, the result became extremely gratifying for distances over a hundred yards.

Everyone in Honolulu anxiously awaited the unofficial swimming contest between the gold medal winner, Kahanamoku, and this new kid, Weissmuller, whose swimming reputation had preceded him to the islands. The meet was to take place between two huge barges in the harbor lying some hundred meters apart. The day before the event, Bachrach called on Kahanamoku.

"Duke," the coach said, "will it mean anything to you if you're beaten in Honolulu? Unofficially speaking, of course!"

"What do you think?" Kahanamoku's darkly-tanned brow lifted in a frown, but then, he bared his teeth in an amused smile. "You are kidding, my friend! Who can beat me?"

"John Weissmuller," came the reply.

Kahanamoku gave a pensive smile, and settled back in his chair.

"I'm telling you, the kid is great!" Bachrach continued. "Come and see for yourself. Bring your stop watch. No one need know."

Johnny was working out in the 25-yard Punahou pool when Bachrach told him to swim a hundred yards against the watch. As his powerful arms cut through the water with the greatest of ease, Kahanamoku, wearing dark glasses, sat nearby timing the young swimmer, as did Bachrach. Both stop watches clicked at the given moment.

"Okay, Johnny!" Bachrach called after the swim, and leisurely strolled over to Duke's side. Kahanamoku was looking at his watch.

"Must be broken," the native Hawaiian said. "It stopped at fifty-two and two-fifths seconds."

"Sorry to disappoint you, Duke. Look at mine!" Bachrach's time registered a fifth of a second more, fifty-two and three-fifths. "I remember, you swam the same distance in 54 seconds."

"I can't believe it!" Duke got onto his feet and started pacing up and down. "I can't believe it!" he muttered anew.

"I told you that kid was great."

After a long pause, Kahanamoku halted in front of the other man. "Too bad we won't find out before the Olympics . . ." he commented.

What about tomorrow's race in the harbor?" Bachrach wanted to find out.

"What race? Didn't you hear? I'm leaving Honolulu in an hour . . ."

"No . . . Why?" Bachrach interjected.

"A friend of mine needs me!"

"But the Shriners . . ." Bachrach tried.

"The hell with the Shriners!" Kahanamoku said. "Friendship comes first!" And Kahanamoku took off.

In spite of the fact that leading newspapers hereafter often carried stories of other proposed races between the two great sprint swimmers, such an event never occurred

49

until their paths briefly crossed at the 1924 Olympic tryouts in Indianapolis and, afterwards, under Parisian skies, when the two met face to face in an Olympic match the world would not soon forget.

However, to return to Honolulu and the Shriners: Thirteen world records were broken on this trip by Big Bill Bachrach's valiant team, with Johnny reaping most of the laurels.

When Johnny returned to Chicago, his Lorelei was waiting at the station with open arms. Bachrach winced, seeing her on the platform, and quickly started cleaning his pair of spectacles to escape his pupil's triumphant look of righteous indignation. Little did young Weissmuller foresee the future, or know that a woman's heart might well reserve a double-cross. And the blond Lorelei proved no exception to this likely rule, acting out the part of her fabled namesake to the letter.

CASE OF THE AILING HEART

4

THE "Star of the Illinois Athletic Club" picked up a handful of gold watches and one by one dropped each into the outstretched hand of a teammate.

He kept one as a souvenir.

Johnny had just won the hundred, two-hundred, quarter-mile, relay and water polo contests, and for every event he received one ticking, solid-gold timepiece. What the young athlete lacked in available funds certainly seemed provided for by an excess of prizes, trophies that wound up in a place of honor at the club, and watches he gave away to his pals. In time there were more gold watches and more giveaways, until each member of the I.A.C. proudly displayed one on a wrist or inside a waistcoat with its chain visible to the naked eye. In fact, Johnny collected so many that their supply lasted for years to come.

However, while winning for his team, Johnny fared somewhat badly at the same time. It was 1923, and the Olympic tryouts loomed only seven months away when he experienced a weakness, a slight fever and fatigue, something he had never known before as a result of swimming. A hearty eater especially after a race, he had no appetite at the table, which caught the attention of Bachrach, who advised him to go to bed.

"I told you not to play water polo!" The coach scolded. "I told you it's the roughest, toughest sport of all! But you wouldn't listen! Now look at you . . ."

Johnny protested weakly. He had learned how to stay underwater for slightly more than three minutes; it had taken him two months of vigorous training, but he had mastered it. On this particular afternoon his newly acquired skill had come in handy. One of the roughnecks playing against him had caught him and, keeping a hold on him, pulled him down.

In water polo, seven players compete against an equal number; elimination of one could mean victory for the opposing team. There are no replacements and often a player singled out as the fastest swimmer is grabbed and forced to remain under eight feet of water until he loses consciousness. It happens as fast as switching off a light bulb. And it could be fatal!

The player who took Johnny down had acted with fanatic determination; he was going to get that ball from Johnny or drown him. He hung on. But Johnny kept the ball and, innerly amused, held the fellow in a tight grip as well. The seconds passed. One minute went by, then another — still the strange embrace lasted beneath the surface. As the third minute was nearing its end, the other player's grip weakened; he became panicky, but Johnny had decided to teach him a lesson; he held him under. After he finally brought him up, it took twenty minutes to revive the other player. A lot wiser, the victim of his own plot never ventured to play it quite as rough again. But Johnny, too, was aware of repercussions, a slight dizziness, a touch of nausea. Skin divers nowadays call it "oxygen starvation."

"Will you get into bed?" Bachrach said again. "You look terrible."

The team was leaving Decatur at midnight, and Johnny spent the rest of the night in a sleeping-car berth. It took about four hours to reach Chicago. A car rushed the patient to the club from where Bachrach called a doctor. The latter immediately arranged for an ambulance that took the swimmer to a hospital. A quick checkup revealed something wrong with the action of his heart. Two days later, the doctor reported his diagnosis as an acute dilation of the heart, but since he felt not absolutely certain, he advised that a specialist should be called in to determine more accurately the cause of Johnny's trouble.

When an old, bespectacled specialist arrived from Albany, he and the other doctor listened to Johnny's heart for two full weeks. The medical practitioner from out of town made a habit of glancing at Johnny across the brim of his bifocal lenses, shaking his head, and muttering something indistinctive. Whereupon, the local physician quickly placed his stethoscope onto the patient's chest, puzzled frowns lifting first one, then the other of his hairy eyebrows as he gave ear.

"Ja, ja . . ." the specialist observed, scratched his grayish-white mane, and clicked his tongue, "Tch! Tch! Tch!"

"Ah-hmmm ---" the local doctor agreed.

"Perhaps, we must send him to a sanitarium . . . the one in Tennessee."

Johnny got tired of just lying around on his back, serving as a guinea pig, hearing such consultations, and all the while thinking that a doctor who was as blind as a bat, and toothless besides, had better retire before setting medicine back a century. If anyone knew his heart, he thought, he ought to, himself.

"What will happen if I get up and run around this bed?" he inquired, politely at first.

"I will not be responsible for you. I must ask you to refrain from such nonsense. You are a sick person, as a specialist . . ." He got no further, before his spectacles dropped off in horror.

"Eureka! Eldorado! Here I come!" Johnny shouted, and jumped out of bed, running around it like a madman, scaring both distinguished sons of the medical profession out of the room. Coach Bachrach arrived just in time to prevent the hospital's musclemen, the staff of orderlies, from getting into a brawl with the patient.

"You go back to bed, and stop this foolishness," the coach scolded. "Remember, I'm paying for your cure."

"You're wasting your money," Johnny said, but obliged.

The same day, Bachrach checked Johnny out of the hospital, paying some $500 for his release, and took him to see a physician who practiced at Chicago's university, taking care of the health of its football team. The doctor carefully listened to Johnny's heart.

"Get up!" he told the young man. "Get up, and if you feel dizzy, sit down any place, on the carpet if you must. All that is wrong with you is that you've spent too much time in bed. And, damn it, I wish I had a heart like yours!"

On the following morning, the university doctor accompanied Weissmuller to the I.A.C. pool where Johnny swam two lengths. Thereafter, the physician again checked his heart. It was beating perfectly, as it has ever since.

What had actually caused Johnny's ailment had been a case of grippe or influenza. Someone in the hospital had given him an overdose of drugs to put him to sleep and this had temporarily affected his heart. Luckily, Johnny was far removed from hypochondriacal tendencies, or the U.S.A. would have lost one of her greatest Olympic winners.

Six weeks after his illness had begun, he was back swimming in competition.

En route to Indianapolis to participate in the 1924 Olympic tryouts, Johnny remembered the time when he had witnessed the same event four short years before. Unable to afford fifty cents admission, the boy discarded most of his clothes in a thicket at Lake Michigan's shore, then plunged into the water and swam out to the Lincoln Park Lagoon where the tryouts were held. Chicago's law enforcers soon spotted the teen-ager, swimming outside the enclosed part; however, there was little they could do as long as the water remained between them and the intruder.

By force of habit, Johnny's hand touched the wooden ring on his finger. He always touched wood before every race, a small idiosyncrasy he had acquired somewhere, some time ago, without truly recalling when or where. Mostly, it was hard to find trees or any kind of wood near a pool a split second before the gun went off; so he had a ring made of this hard, fibrous substance.

The young man was tense, but confident. He knew he was ready for the challenge that lay ahead. Yet, swimming in the Olympics presented something much deeper, far more demanding than had all his former victories combined. It personified the ultimate goal any athlete is inspired to reach, together with a responsibility to be carried on his shoulders, to win for his land. Just to conquer one medal at the Olympic Games, to beat the world for his country, meant more to him than had anything ever in the past. And in his mind, he saw the Star-Spangled Banner waving high above the other flags, and he felt proud to be an American.

The three-day swimming carnival was held at Broad Ripple Pool, in Indianapolis, Ind., on June 6th, 7th, and 8th; it was known as the Final Olympic Tryouts. Men swimmers from all over the United States attended the meet and many came from Hawaii. It was obvious that Weissmuller and Duke Kahanamoku qualified, so did Duke's brother, Samuel. However, at that time, Johnny's time beat the Duke's. After the selection had been completed, the chosen team was ordered to report at the Park Avenue Hotel, in New York City, not later than on June 15th, and as no one was missing, the team sailed for France on the S.S. America, on Monday, June 16, 1924.

Coach Bachrach and some of his boys. (Photo by John Williams — Courtesy of the Illinois Athletic Club.)

Between Johnny and Arne Borg, the swimming lovelies include (from left) Helen Meany, Sybil Bauer and Ethel Lackie (sixth.)

Six world record holders after competing in the greatest water carnival, 1923, at the Broadripple Pool, Indianapolis, Ind. (Left to right: Lundy Langer, Charlotte Boyle, John Weissmuller, Norman Ross, Robert L. Pearson, Ethel Bleibtrey. (Photo by Coburn—Courtesy Helms Athletic Foundation)

Johnny Weissmuller at
the 1924 Olympics in
Paris with Andrew Charlton.

The "star" of the
Illinois Athletic Club.

Katsuo Takaishi

*hnny leading the U.S. Olympic
*am in the march-past. Photo:
*gemeen Fotobureau (Ltd.) Am-
*rdam (Courtesy of Helms Ath-
ic Foundation.)

*hnny carrying the identifying
*ndard for his country at the
*28 Olympics in Amsterdam.
*oto: Algemeen Fotobureau (Ltd.)
*nsterdam (Courtesy of Helms
hletic Foundation.)

*Johnny in private life demonstrates his famous
Swan dive. (Photo by Tom Evans, MGM)*

Johnny demonstrates his backstroke.
(Photo by Tom Evans, MGM)

Working out, Johnny, with his feet placed into an inflated rubber tube, uses only his arms.

How it was done at Pickfair. (Douglas Fairbanks Sr. and Johnny.)

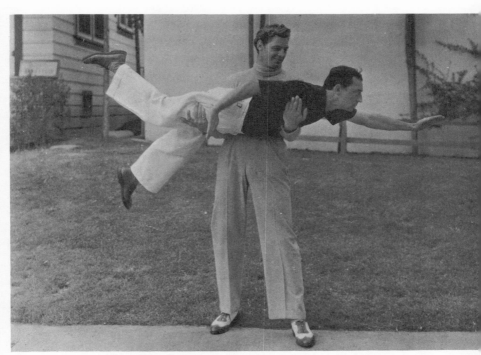

"She went that-a-way!" Says Buster Keaton. (MGM photo)

The brothers Weissmuller.

Eight World Champions in a Common Mold. (Left to right: Babe Ruth, Gene Tunney, John Weissmuller, Bill Cook, William Tilden, Bobby Jones, Freddy Spencer, Charlie Winter.) (International Newsreel Photo.)

VIVE L'AMERIQUE

5

T HE HUGE S.S. America was chartered for a round trip when she left New York harbor on the bright June morning, in 1924, her destination Cherbourg, France. As she sailed past Liberty Island, she proudly winked at the "Lady with the Torch," her mission clearly spelled out in large, painted letters on each side that read "American Olympic Team"; and, bidding farewell to the statue, she joined the 320 athletes and officials aboard in asking a blessing for a safe, victorious voyage across the Atlantic, and back.

Bound for the Paris games were 110 track and field men, 66 swimmers, 20 fencers, 15 oarsmen, 25 boxers, 11 gymnasts, 16 wrestlers, 12 coaches, 10 team managers, 10 trainers, 6 massagers, and the various officials in charge of the expedition. This impressive number, however, did not yet represent the full American force. The Yale crew, selected for the eight-oared race abroad, did not sail with this group because of their annual race with Harvard. The Eli oarsmen went over later on another liner. And the Navy, as in 1920, sent its athletes on a battleship.

But this illustrious gathering of sports men and women

did not complete the passenger list. Along went wives, some husbands, children, relatives and friends of athletes and officials, numbering more than 250 in their collective ranks. The president of the American Olympic Committee was Colonel Robert M. Thompson. The manager — John T. Taylor, from Pittsburgh. The head swimming coach — none other than William Bachrach. The women's swimming coach was L. de B. Handley, and the diving coach, Ernst Brandsten.

Manager Taylor gave the following description in the official "Report on the 8th Olympiad": ". . . the greatest swimming and water polo teams ever gotten together in the history of American swimming." And they were, these sixty-six that sailed aboard the S.S. America. The Illinois Athletic Club was well represented by such names as Weissmuller, Robert D. Skelton, Fred Lauer, John Faricy, Oliver Horn, Jam Handy (formerly of New York), and femmes first class like Ethel Lackie and Sybil Bauer. Hawaii presented the Kahanamoku brothers, as well as Warren and Pua Kealoha. Then there were Harry Glancy from Pittsburgh; Ralph Breyer, Richard Howell of Northwestern University; Adam Smith from the Erie YMCA; Jack Robertson and Lester Smith of the Olympic Club; Wallace O'Conner — Venice A.C.; Martha Norelius. A. C. White, Caroline Smith and Elizabeth Becker brought the divers into the game. Too few names chosen by far, merely because each of the above mentioned played an immediate part in the adventure to unfold during the Olympic heats, touching Johnny's competitive swimming, or winning gold medals for the honor of their country, and the glory of sport.

In the ancient odes of Pindar (circa 522-442 B.C.)

celebrating the victors at Olympia in Elis long before the modern Olympic games returned to Athens, the Greek poet said, "Water is best." And so, indeed, it seemed to those sixty-six swimmers, divers and water polo players as they took one last, long look at the French lady in New York's harbor, the lady sent across the ocean for a similar purpose of peace and good will between the point of their destination and that of their return.

Once clear of the harbor a fresh sea breeze cooled Johnny's heated brow, as he watched the towering waves like weird giants lifting their white manes of foam in never ceasing motion, crushing against the ship's bow, being atomized into a spray that dampened his skin and entered his nostrils. For a brief moment he remembered home, his mother's blessing when they said farewell, and his girl's embrace. He had told Lorelei they would be married upon his return.

Then the wind that tousled his hair blew his thoughts toward the foreign land that lay ahead, where soon he would see the Olympic flame being carried into the stadium by a runner. A flame that had been brought from Elis, Greece, where the games had begun more than 2,500 years ago. A flame, rekindled by a Frenchman twenty-eight years ago, and this same Frenchman, Baron Pierre de Coubertin, was going to be present in Paris at the time he, Johnny, competed.

His thoughts were sharply interrupted by Fred Lauer's voice. "We've come a long way from Oak Street Beach," his boyhood playmate remarked as he viewed the restless ocean.

"We've got a long way to go." Johnny said, glancing into the distance without seeing the horizon.

During the nine-day crossing, arrangements had been made for the athletes to continue their training routines. For the swimmers a special canvas tank had been rigged, but since it was relatively a small one, they practiced their strokes while being virtually anchored from above by a rope or sticking to the inflated rubber tube method, first working out the arms, then the legs. Due to the restricted area, two men at a time went through the motions of swimming and the exercise lasted half an hour, repeated at intervals throughout the day. As well as training for competitive events there were daily gymnastics, walks along the ship's deck to keep the athletes physically fit, and other recreational activities such as shuffleboard.

Cabins usually accommodated four double-decker bunks, but there was plenty of space left over for each occupant, and none felt crowded. The stewards co-operated in every possible manner to make their passengers content with close attention to even the minor items, such as laundry.

The cuisine was excellent, a great morale builder. Coaches and managers, in all cases, ate with the swimmers, and Bachrach saw to it that only certain dishes, though quite ample and tasty, were served at the table, as ever, with emphasis on greens and lots of fruits. Not much mixing occurred between the opposite sexes. Watchful eyes were ever turned towards the athletes inasmuch as the team represented all the physical and moral virtues embodied in the spirit of the Olympiad. Moreover, all were far too preoccupied, too engulfed in their future in the games to become involved in shipboard romances. But there was one dance held on Saturday night. The strict regimen set bedtime for ten o'clock sharp and none rebelled against the rules dictated by the committee.

The Rev. Ralph Spearow, pole vaulter from the University of Oregon, conducted Sunday services during the voyage.

Everything went according to plan and schedule, with the exception of one incident that caused Coach Bachrach a few anxious moments. Johnny and friends accidentally discovered a stowaway, a Nebraska hurdler, who had failed to pass the final tryouts, but was nonetheless determined to compete in the Olympics at any price. The youngster was half-starved and scared to tears, begging Johnny, Fred and company not to give him away. So the young swimmers smuggled the boy from one room into the other but, in the end, he was spotted by the ship's crew and reported. Even though the officials paid his passage and took him along to Paris, he was not permitted to join the games. The I.A.C. mates were threatened with disciplinary action . . . but it only remained a threat.

As the days passed and Cherbourg moved closer, they grew continually more engrossed with their goal. The circled date on the calendar loomed ever larger. Nerves became tense, and even the lulling effect the surrounding sea normally instilled in those who traveled the crests of her waves did not succeed in slowing the rising excitement which possessed the young athletes. The men of the Illinois Athletic Club team kept closely together during this period, their friendship making it easier to communicate individual thoughts. Long before anyone sighted a first lonely sea gull off the shores of France, suitcases were packed and ready for disembarkation.

All the athletes had taken along their Olympic outfits, navy-blue jackets embroidered with the Olympic crest, with several pairs of white trousers for change. Johnny had brought along half-a-dozen swim suits, a couple more than required, and a few personal items like a sports jacket and a scarf his mother had given him for his twentieth birthday, just two weeks prior to sailing time.

And then the sea gulls, flapping their wings, increased in number. The birds dove onto the decks of the floating athletic argosy until, on June 25th, the S.S. America docked at Cherbourg. She was greeted at the pier by many Americans and more newspaper correspondents. The U.S. team was ushered to a special train that took them to Paris, arriving in the French metropolis at 4 p.m., where a tremendous crowd of well-wishers greeted them.

No accidents had happened on the sea, but when the train arrived in Paris, John Faricy of the I.A.C. sprained his ankle getting off. He was disabled for the duration of the games and, regretfully, Coach Bachrach had to keep him out of the Olympics. Two other incidents happened en route to Paris, one when a diver disobeyed an official and kept running behind the train, claiming he needed the exercise. He was disqualified. And Johnny almost got into trouble with the Olympic Committee when his hot temper flared at a heckler riding a bicycle alongside the railway tracks. He shouted insults at the Americans, underlining his words with accompanying gestures of contempt and with grimaces. The swimmers withstood this unabashed rudeness for a while, finally drew straws to determine which one would teach the uncouth person some manners. Johnny was elected. He quickly jumped off the train and before the heckler knew what had hit him, he found himself on the ground with his bicycle covering him. The officials took a dim view of Johnny's action. Some were worried about the act's causing an international incident. Johnny's friends tried to explain the circumstances: "We are all keyed up in antici- pation of the games. No one ever sleeps properly anymore at night, swimming along in fitful, harried dreams. And then someone like that came along, and bingo . . . !"

Bachrach, too, came to Johnny's defense. He explained to the Olympic Committee that without Weissmuller the United States had little chance of winning the 400-meter event, or the men's relay, as well. "You must understand these kids," Bachrach said. "They are human, high strung. Living by the book doesn't always work out under such circumstances. You can't expect them to be athletes, diplo- mats, gentlemen all rolled up in one, and then go out and break records. Besides, Johnny is basically an even-tempered fellow, and the heckler received what was coming to him. I'd have done it myself." The members of the committee listened. Johnny won out. All was quiet on Mt. Olympus.

The annoyances of the train ride were soon forgotten in Paris, where the athletes emerged from the Gare St. Lazare to climb into seventy waiting cars that took them up boulevards lined with wildly enthusiastic crowds, and out to Rocquencourt, an estate that had once belonged to Prince Joachim Murat, Napoleon's dashing marshal.

Rocquencourt had been adopted by the American Olympic Committee a year before as headquarters for their men's team in Paris, and eleven concrete barracks had been erected to house them. Officials of the team were quartered in the historic chateau itself. While it was a beautiful place, it was also nearly inaccessible. The shortest routes from there to Colombes, where the games were to be held, were an uncertain 21 miles, round trip. Traveling in busses with hard tires made the ride twice as long and far from relaxing. Everyone concerned complained of the jouncing he received. It was generally conceded that this was not in the best interest of the athletes in training, but there was little anyone could do to change matters. Sort of . . . c'est la guerre!

During the first night at Rocquencourt everyone was aroused by a fire alarm. Ten or twelve small houses in the vicinity burned down and the Americans were literally breaking their backs trying to aid French firemen in their rescue work. For a guy like Johnny, fire was a long way removed from his habitat, the water, but he, with the other swimmers, did his best to save the townspeople and their properties. One Frenchman lost his life in the holocaust. The United States athletes promptly took up a collection on behalf of the widow and children and raised some $200, a commendable sum from the men whose earnings of a few dollars a day often were sent back home to assist their families. But the natives appreciated this generosity deeply.

The popularity of the team from "les États-Unis" spread and doubled itself overnight.

It had been expected that swimming would be conducted at the pool at Colombes, but it was found that this pool would not hold water and so the swimming was held at La Tourelle in Paris. The tank at La Tourelle was 50-meters in length, 100-feet in width, and 4 to 15 feet in depth. The diving tower and springboard were of the very best . . . as was mutually agreed. Mr. Henry Musnick was in charge of the swimming stadium and, whereas morning and afternoon practice periods were ordered at first, they were later cut to but one a day, the swimmers being permitted to spend the rest of their time at Colombes, watching the other athletes perform.

The crowded conditions at Rocquencourt prompted the committee to send the men's swimming team to Colombes, where enough beds were obtained. Not that it helped in the transportation problem. On the contrary! The trip from Colombes to La Tourelle was made through the heart of Paris and was even longer, twenty-four miles a round. It also presented additional expenses, since meals were paid for in Colombes but the swimmers rarely indulged in more than breakfast which was taken at 8 a.m. Luncheons and dinners were served in Paris at extra cost.

Practice hours were from 11 a.m. to 1 p.m., and again from 3:30 to 5 p.m., the rest of the time being taken up by other competing nations, who shared the pool.

Shortly after dinner, quick walks were taken along the boulevards of Paris, and then the square-wheeled bus ride to Colombes ended the timetable of daily routine. The aquatic members of the team amused themselves for a brief hour or two with occasional card games or reading, but as soon as the clock struck ten, lights went out and everyone was supposed to be tucked into his barracks cot.

"They kept us locked up, under constant guard, and all the guys called Olympic Village a high class Boy Scout camp," Johnny recalled. "We younger men did not mind it too much, but some of the older fellows complained. Still, no one tried to sneak out. We knew that our officials had some spies running loose in the bars, and if one happened to spot you taking a champagne cocktail, or something — pow! You were thrown off the team without mercy. We were carted around like tourists, never allowed to separate, always in groups of twenty-five or so. Most of us wanted to see the Moulin Rouge but we all wound up on top of the Eiffel Tower. That was that! Anyway, most of the time we were too nervous to care much for anything except the games. We had come to the Olympiad to do a job and training for it was foremost on our minds. There was an atheist in our crowd who used to preach to us at night, just when all of us needed a few strong prayers. He eventually swam in one of the first events, got last place, and immediately opened a 'speak-easy' under his mattress. How he smuggled the booze in, no one apparently knew, but he sure became a popular guy. Anyhow, he left off preaching, much to my relief. I guess I was one of the few swimmers who had to compete in so many events that I never got a breather until I left Paris."

And so, the watermen closed their eyes nightly and fell into a restless slumber, crowded with nightmares of jumping ahead of the gun, missing the jump, making a slow turn, seeing an opponent in front; all of this mingled with sub-conscious struggles to retain religion and fight damnation in spite of it all. And this was summer . . . along the Seine. . .

THE OLYMPIC FLAME

6

THE OPENING ceremony of the 8th Olympiad took place in perfect weather. Colombes Stadium was encircled by the flags of all the nations taking part in the games as the stands, capable of holding sixty-thousand people, were packed with spectators. It was Saturday, July 5, when the teams, in alphabetical order, entered the arena by the Marathon Gate. They were headed by South Africa, the United States paraded as the "États-Unis," and last came Yugoslavia. America provided the greatest and most imposing team in numbers, Haiti the smallest. They were played around the track by the bands of the Garde Républicaine and the three Regiments-of-the-Line. As each unit passed the Tribune of Honor the standard-bearer lowered the flag of his country in salute to the President of the French Republic, M. Gaston Doumergue, who was seated with their Royal Highnesses the Prince of Wales and Prince Henry, the Crown Prince of Roumania together with the Crown Princess; Prince William of Sweden and all the ambassadors and members of the Corps Diplomatique, including Their Excellencies the Earl and Countess of Crewe, His Grace the Duke of Sutherland and Her Grace the Duchess, the Earl and Countess of Cadogan, Lord and Lady Campden, the Rev. R. S. de Courcy Laffan, Brigadier-General R. J. Kentish, the Earl of Caledon, the Earl Fitzwilliam, Sir Emsley and Lady Carr; and many other notables and members of the nobility.

Only the standard-bearer of the United States kept the Star-Spangled Banner straight and waving high; for, adhering to custom, the American flag shall not be lowered or dipped before any foreign power or potentate. There was, however, some speculation amid the crowd that wondered why a single flag remained upright, and some remarked that the American who carried it was stiff in shoulder and back!

At the conclusion of the march-past, and having completed the circuit of the track, the teams formed up in their appointed positions in the middle of the arena facing the tribune. M. Le Comte Clary, president of the French Olympic Committee, with Baron Pierre de Coubertin, a slight, heavily mustached figure at his side, called upon the President of the French Republic to declare the games open, and M. Doumergue did so in a loud, clear voice. But not before cheers rang out as a swift runner carried the blazing torch into the stadium that had been brought in endless relays from the foot of Mount Olympus to light the Olympic flame.

Then the Olympic flag bearing the insignia recognized throughout the world, showing the five different colored circles on a field of white, representative of the five continents linked together to denote the sporting friendship of the peoples of the earth whatever their creed or country, rose to the mast-head to the strains of "The Marseillaise" while the guns roared the traditional Olympic salute and a great flight of pigeons was released from the traps to carry the news to every corner of the country. It was only the second time (first in 1920, at Antwerp) that the Olympic flag had been hoisted above a stadium. The colors of the rings — blue, yellow, black, green, red — were chosen because at least one appeared in the flag of every nation in the world.

All at once, the strains of Saint-Saëns' "La Marche Héroique" played softly as it was sung by l'Institut de Prague. The standard-bearers of the nations moved forward and lowered their flags as Georges André, the French hurdler who represented the athletes of all nations by proxy, mounted the rostrum to recite the Olympic Oath. And at this time, the Stars and Stripes humbly dipped, paying tribute to men's aspiration toward friendship and good will between nations.

As André's voice rang out for all men to hear — "We swear that we come to the 8th Olympiad animated by a respect for the regulations which govern it, and desirous of participating for the honor of our country and the glory of sport." — Johnny mentally visualized the small figure of de Coubertin, and he wondered at the dedication of this man's spirit which had made possible all this. From all the corners of the earth they had come. Men of different races, colors, religions, aspirations, to meet in a mighty concourse of peoples under one common sky. Possibly, the First World War had helped the Baron to spread the gospel of athletics around the world, but more likely, it was the people themselves who preferred the white dove of peace to the red cloths of blood upon the arena of life.

Germany was not represented at the 8th Olympiad,

and had been conspicuously absent in 1920 as well, for the same reason that had forced the Olympic Games to retire in 1916, with history repeating itself later in 1940, and 1944. And, as ever before and since, peoples the world over found it in their hearts to hope and pray that the Four Horsemen of the Apocalypse would never return, and that the omitted 6th (12th and 13th) Olympiad would remain the last insofar as placing a stoppage onto the passage of time which had been counted in Greece hundreds of years B.C. according to the ancient Olympic calendar and which made the first year of the 195th historic Olympiad correspond with the first year of Christ.

The golden sun cast long shadows across the stadium when the teams filed out through the Marathon Gate whereby they had entered, and the games were on. But not before the following day did actual athletic competition begin.

The last day of the track and field competition took place on Sunday, July 13, which also marked the beginning of the swimming events that were conducted entirely at La Tourelle throughout mornings and afternoons.

In order to eliminate contestants in the 100-meter free style, Johnny swam against Pycock, Great Britain; Vanzeveren, France; Christie, Australia, and Pinillo, Spain. He had been placed in the fifth heat, and won easily.

At this stage, Bachrach's coaching to a major degree consisted of merely looking after the physical fitness of his team and giving the boys all the encouragement they needed. "You don't have to worry, Johnny," he said, talking to his favorite till the last minute before a race. "It's just another contest. Only don't throw your stroke off by going too fast in the first fifty yards. Toward the end leap ahead. You are the world's champion! Remember that! And remember to relax!" Bachrach knew that his protégé suffered from high strung tenseness; he also knew that the slightest provocation could result in an angry outburst between the athletes. He kept a forever watchful eye on all his wards but especially on Johnny, whom he wound up like a watch . . . with care not to overwind, damage or recoil the spring. "Just don't get lazy in there," was his oft-repeated remark.

In the semi-final heats Johnny's victory came with even greater ease, with hardly any effort at all. He had been placed in the second heat against Arne Borg, Sweden; Henry, Australia; Pycock, Great Britain; Stedman, Australia, and Zorilla, Argentina. For a long time it appeared that Henry would be second in the race, but Borg got up to qualify for the finals by inches only.

Bachrach, favoring his "snaky" swimmers, always maintained that Arne Borg's performance matched that of a steamboat with only ten percent "snake" thrown in. Nevertheless, he had great respect for the Swede who later became a member of the Illinois A.C., and who seemed to be the favorite of the Europeans before competitions began.

After Johnny had won the semi-finals, he looked as always to Bachrach, who had lifted up his hand with his forefinger and thumb forming the letter "o", a sign meaning "well done!" As in O for okay! The swimmer then stayed in the water, moving about slowly for some ten minutes, to let his heart action and breathing return to normal, to allow the intensity of the excitement of the race to be replaced by soothing relaxation. Climbing out of the tank too early meant expanding his chest action too violently. Water pressure eased the strain whereas the contact with air exerted and fatigued, as Bachrach had been careful to point out at every occasion.

Then came the harrowing finals! Johnny's opponents were of the highest caliber: The Duke, and his younger brother Sam Kahanamoku, Arne Borg, and Katsuo Takaishi from Japan.

"Don't get your head too high, breathe on both sides and don't forget to blow the air out," Bachrach warned. "It's like flooding a carburetor when there is too much gasoline and not enough air. It simply doesn't work."

Slowly, Johnny strolled over to his mark. His hand touched the wooden ring on his finger as he waited for the starter's gun. Outwardly, he seemed calm and collected, a big grin on his face. Inwardly, he felt as if a swarm of bees had invaded his intestines, busily buzzing about and organizing a club in his stomach. He was to swim between the brothers and, as he stood on his mark, he glanced at Duke on his right and Sam at his left. "Which one of these two guys will run in front of me to let the other win?" he wondered.

As Johnny flexed his knees for the racing-dive crouch, he thought back of his bad experiences, especially in the 50-yard events when his competitors had united against him, blocking his path, letting the third man over sprint ahead. Johnny had won . . . but only after considerable effort. Bachrach had warned him, then, to keep his eye on the fastest swimmer in the meet and jump as soon as he moved, with or without listening to the gun to outdistance any blockade. That had been back home, and only in the 50-yard competitions, which had been eliminated on account of too many identical scandals.

But the hushed exclamations of the spectators now sounded foreign. And these were Olympic contenders, not to be confused with some "backwoodsmen" swimmers elsewhere. Nevertheless, he felt an uneasiness hard to shake, as he curled his toes over the edge of the pool.

As if Duke had read his thoughts, he leaned over. "Johnny," the great swimmer said, "Good luck!" And he showed his white teeth in a big smile. "The most important thing in this race is to get the American flag up there three times. Let's do it!"

A tremendous relief passed through Johnny as he shook the Hawaiian's outstretched hand, innerly feeling apologetic about his former doubts. No time was left for further consultation. The starter called out in French what Johnny knew meant, "On your mark!" Johnny slipped into the coiled-spring crouch. "Get set!" That long, breathless moment when eternity stands still. . . ! And then, "Bang!" The gun sounded and five swimmers hit the water like five torpedoes. The race was ON!

The official report of the race stated as follows:"Weissmuller started at a great speed, and was soon clear of the brothers Kahanamoku, who were racing close together with Arne Borg. Weissmuller increased his advantage to win easily, breaking the previous Olympic record. The two Kahanamokus fought out a great finish for second place with Duke leading on Sam. Arne Borg was about two meters

74

behind, and Takaishi (having qualified for the final by being the fastest third of the semi-final heats) a meter behind him again." Thus, the results read: Weissmuller, U.S. - 59 s.; Duke P. Kahanamoku, U.S. - 1 m. 1.2/5 s.; Samuel Kahanamoku, U.S. - 1 m. 1.4/5 s.; Arne Borg, Sweden - 1 m. 2 s.; K. Takaishi, Japan - 1 m. 3 s.

Johnny Weissmuller, whose world American record was 57.4/5 s. broke Duke Kahanamoku's previous Olympic record of 1 m. 1.4 s., shaving 2.4 s. off the time. And, proudly, three American flags were hoisted to the masts of honor as the winners stepped onto the presentation blocks, with Johnny highest in the center. The young Olympic champion accepted his first gold medal for winning the 100-meter free style event, with the silver and bronze going to the Kahanamoku brothers.

Johnny soon became the idol of the spectators who witnessed the games, and he was greeted with acclamation wherever he went.

The comedy stunt performed on several occasions at the Paris stadium by him and a teammate was one of the features, and the French public could not get enough of this act. On one occasion the water polo contests were delayed because the audience, wanting to see more of Johnny, kept throwing derbies into the pool. As stated in the official report of the 1924 Olympiad, the friendly feeling of the French people toward the Americans was clearly demonstrated when an audience of close to seven thousand stood up and called for Weissmuller for two or three minutes; this was after the American had won the 100 meters.

They sat down only when it was announced that Weissmuller would appear again later in the afternoon.

The comedy routine, among other stunts, included four dives in which Johnny demonstrated his talent on the platform. First came the swan dive in which he, while in air, assumed a position with arms outstretched to the sides like the wings of a soaring gull or swan, legs straight and together, back slightly arched, entered the water headforemost. Next, he did the jackknife in which the diver assumes a folded position of the body like a closed knife while moving through the air, and straightens out before entering the water. Third, the one-and-a-half somersault, an acrobatic, aerial spin of the body forward in which it describes a complete revolution, heels over head, with an extra half turn. Last, the full gainer, a type of dive in which Johnny took off facing forward and performed a complete back somersault before entering the water, perhaps the most difficult but easily one of the most spectacular in a diver's repertoire. While Johnny performed with style and skill, he was mimicked by his partner who, dressed like a clown and acting out typical slapstick, jumped with one or both eyes closed, running in mid-air, and hitting the water with a big splash in the most ridiculous of positions!

When the exciting series of the 400-meter free style event began, Johnny swam in the third heat against Charlton, from Australia; Peter, Great Britain; Pellegry, France, and Kohler, Holland. It was obvious from the start that he would come in first. The semi-finals started off with Johnny competing in the first heat. Breyer, U.S., did not start for some unrevealed reason. Weissmuller won rather easily, but Charlton gave the impression of being content to finish an easy second and qualify. There was some speculation among the crowd as to whether he would come on stronger in the finals and threaten the American's superiority, but these guesses remained unfounded. Others in the race were Smith, U.S.; Vernot, Canada, and Antos, from Czechoslovakia.

The end saw Weissmuller, Charlton, Arne and Åke Borg, as well as Hatfield who had qualified as fastest third for the finals. How these five swimmers looked moments before the starter's gun hurled them from the side of the tank into the flat dive of the racing start was told by Grantland Rice, in his article entitled "Loose People," printed in Collier's Weekly: "There were, among others, Arne Borg and Charlton, the great Swedish and Australian stars, keyed up and ready for the big test. They were all set and eager to get away. Suddenly another entry, who had been talking and laughing with a nearby group, threw aside his bathrobe and strolled into line. He still had a broad grin and his hands were also dangling at his sides as if hung there by strings. There was only a second or two before the starter's gun would bark. And yet this latest arrival was about as tense as a loose towel. Just before the gun cracked he turned and said, 'Come on, fellows, let's go!' And he hit the water with the loosest-looking body and the loosest-looking pair of arms one could ever expect to see. His name was Johnny Weissmuller. On that occasion he won another Olympic championship and broke another world's record as he outsped Borg and Charlton through the last few yards. Weissmuller knew the competition he faced. He knew that he had to break another world's record to win. And yet there wasn't a single sign of nerve strain or tautness or physical stiffness either in arm or body. He remained loose and willowy and elastic on his way through the air into the pool."

(And years later, there would be a great war . . . and when the heat was on, sergeants would talk quietly to their tense or frightened men . . . and say, "Stand loose!")

And so Johnny had finally mastered what Bachrach had taught him, namely, that nothing equals relaxation once a heat was on. And, in a way, Duke Kahanamoku had done his share in aiding the young champion to victory by reassuring him of fair competition.

When the race was over, Weissmuller had won in 5 m. 4.1/5 s., beating the previous Olympic record held by Norman Ross of the U.S. by as much as 22.6 seconds. The world American record for this event stood at 4 m. 57 s. Arne Borg came second with 5 m. 5.3/5 s.; A. M. Charlton was third, his time registering 5 m. 6.3/5 s.; Åke Borg lagged behind with 5 m. 26 s.; and J. Hatfield was last, his time 5 m. 32 s. The race was recaptured in the report as follows: Weissmuller led from start to finish, breaking the existing Olympic record. Charlton was a close third to Arne Borg who came second, and Åke Borg only just beat Hatfield for fourth place.

Once again Johnny's country saw her flag waving from the tallest spar as the second gold medal was placed into the hands of one of her brave sons.

They made a fine showing, these fabulous Neptunian children of Uncle Sam. The 100-meter backstroke went to Warren Kealoha, U.S. The 200-meter breaststroke to Robert D. Skelton. Springboard diving was won by A. C. White as well as the fancy high. The women held their own as Ethel Lackie won the 100-meters. Martha Norelius got the 400-meters for herself. The 400-meter Women's Relay was won by the U.S. As were the 100-meter backstroke by Sybil Bauer, plain high diving by Caroline Smith, and fancy springboard diving by Elizabeth Becker. All shining golden medals! All keeping Old Glory proudly flying on the highest center pole!

Charlton, of Australia, made a good showing winning the top honors for the 1,500 meters, as did Richard Eve in plain high diving for the same part of the Commonwealth. And Lucy Morton, from Great Britain, won the laurels for the 200-meter breaststroke in the women's finals. France walked away with water polo, wherein the United States placed third, winning the bronze prize.

But in the 800-meter men's relay it was the U.S. again all the way. Four swimmers competed in the team, each sprinting two-hundred meters, with Johnny as anchor man. In the first heat the United States came first, Italy second.

In the semi-finals the American team raced in the second heat against Sweden, Japan, Italy, and won quite easily, beating the previous world's record by no less than 5 seconds.

In the finals, the United States started off by getting a lead on Australia in the first relay. Charlton, who swam second for Australia, made up the deficit, but in the last two relays the Americans went ahead again and won easily, beating their own world's record by 6 s., and the record previous to the Olympiad by the enormous margin of 11 seconds. The swimmers for the U.S. according to their relays were Ralph Breyer, Harry Glancy, Wallace O'Conner, and John Weissmuller. Their victory was won in 9 m. 53.2/5 s. Australia won the silver medal with 10 m 2.1/5 s. Sweden got the bronze with 10 m. 6.4/5 s. Japan was fourth, coming in 10 m. 15.1/5 s., and Great Britain fifth and last, timed at 10 m. 29.2/5 s.

Johnny accepted the gold medal on behalf of his team.

As he stood crowned for the third time an Olympic victor, hearing his national anthem played, his eyes beholding the sight of his flag, his hands clutching those of his teammates, his heart was filled with happiness and pride. His eyes became moist and a deep sigh escaped his innermost being. "Veni, vidi, vici." Indeed! He had come, he had seen, he had conquered. Not like the Romans had done when they had destroyed and made a mockery of the ancient Olympiads once they came, saw, conquered. But in the light of truth and athletic skill he, a boy born to nothing, had in a matter of a few short years reached their culmination in the last days, won the friendship and recognition of the world . . . the American way. Gratefully, the new Olympic champion glanced over at his coach just in time to see Bachrach wiping away a tear, self-consciously hiding his emotion before someone happened to notice his sentiment caused by the fatherly affection he carried in his heart for the tall, lank young man he had taught to swim and become the pride of his land.

When the swimming events closed on July 20th, the United States team had reaped the greatest honors. To sum it up, the British Olympic Association issued a statement in their official report which read as follows:

"Our friends the Americans again dominated the situation, both in the men's and ladies' competitions, and their men's team led by such magnificent swimmers as Weissmuller, the Kahanamoku brothers, Kealoha, Skelton, etc., and the ladies by the Misses Bauer, Lackie, Ederle, Wehselau, Morelius, Geraghy, etc., carried off practically every event; and not only this, but they took most of the second and third places as well — indeed, a wonderful performance."

The President of the French Republic presented Johnny with a special medal in token of his appreciation of the athlete. It could easily be said that the stars of the 8th Olympiad were the peerless Paavo Nurmi from Finland, winner of four races from 1,500 to 10,000 meters in the track and field events, and John Weissmuller, winner of three races in the swimming events. The all-around popularity of these two men clearly supported their individual meteoric rise to fame in the firmament of sports.

CRISSCROSS EVENTS

7

A FTER THE closing of the Olympic Games, the American Athletic Union accepted an invitation for Johnny to go on a prolonged tour of Europe. Several countries had requested the champion to give exhibitions, and were anxious to try him out against their own swimmers at local levels. The Germans especially showed eagerness, having been left out of the international meeting, and maintained that there might still be found a better sprinter than the "human fish" Weissmuller. Meanwhile, the A.A.U. had also accepted an invitation for the entire team to compete in Belgium on July 22, at the Royal Circle of Natation of Brussels.

Johnny's greatest kick during his European junket came when he watched the royal family attend the exhibition and saw the king laugh like a schoolboy at the antics of his comedy routine. Albert I, King of Belgium, honored him afterwards at a dinner party where he presented Johnny with a medal for his meritorious aquatic achievements. And, as His Majesty shook the swimmer's hand, he winked at him with a twinkle of mirth, mixed with deep-rooted appreciation for the athlete's performance shining in his eyes.

When the team left Brussels, they shook hands with

the trio that remained to tour. Coach Bachrach predicted a successful trip but Johnny frowned, not the least impressed with his promotion as an ambassador of good will for a probable duration of more than a month. He yearned to return to Chicago and his girl, Lorelei, who had not written to him since he had sailed from home. During the past exciting weeks of competition he had had little time to fully concentrate on her and on their planned nuptial. Sometimes, at night, he had thought of her and then written wishful letters reminding her of their private vows. Now that everything had calmed down considerably, he found ample time to worry about her silence, unable to comprehend what had caused it and if he had been to blame.

At home, too, the honorary president of the 8th Olympiad, President of the United States, Calvin Coolidge, together with Chief Justice William H. Taft who had been elected honorary vice president for the duration of the games, were giving a rousing welcome to the returning athletes, and he would miss all the fun and the honors that had been planned for the American Olympic Team. Nevertheless Johnny, Coach Bachrach and a comedy diver boarded one of the many "choo-choo" trains that followed a hectic schedule, with Johnny swimming, eating, sleeping, and continuing the route of travel with little time left over for actual sightseeing wherever he went.

Cities flashed by — Hamburg, Magdeburg, Dresden, Berlin . . . Berlin, where Johnny saw his first artificial waves created in the shallow water of a pool, a make-believe image of the sea. He was accustomed to the overall swimsuits fashionable then; so upon seeing German swimmers don nothing but jockstraps to compete in front of an overwhelmingly female audience, he became slightly embarrassed. What he did not know was that all the ladies' eyes were mainly centered on his own by now six-foot-four physique, and that Bachrach had his hands full keeping the adoring feminie away from the pool. Bachrach even had to hire some local help to guard his champion from the advances of the weaker sex, for if they had succeeded in breaking through the barrier in numbers, they might have easily reduced Johnny's modest swimming attire to mere sample shreds. For female admiration knows no barriers except that of skin and, likewise, it often remains only skin-deep.

Vienna came and passed, and Johnny remembered only that it had rained and that someone had stolen one of his shoes. He hobbled to the hotel, frustrated by his loss and the rain that kept pouring down. The next day saw him competing against Bárány, European champion swimmer from Hungary, who challenged Johnny, but lost. And on went the journey to Budapest on the Danube, and to Prague, the golden city on the banks of the Moldau.

Alike many places the champion visited and where he constantly found a doubting Thomas in the crowd who wished to be convinced about the great Weissmuller's invincibility, there was one found in Prague and he happened to be a Czechoslovakian swimming coach. This man approached Bachrach. "I want to see how your boy will swim up that river," he said, his eyes holding a sarcastic gleam. "I will make you a bet of $100 that he cannot conquer the Moldau!"

Bachrach wanted to know how far up and for how long.

"That does not matter," he answered, imitating a smart aleck, "just as long as he will swim up the river." The Czech knew that no one had ever made headway in the turbulent, rushing torrent. Going down the river was simple, but up — impossible!

Bachrach talked to Johnny. "Do you think you can make it?"

"We'll see . . ." Johnny said. He rehearsed that night, had a try at the river. The swim was to take place along the length of a 50-yard bathhouse. He swam and swam, the speed using up all his physical strength, but discovered that he had not moved very far. After a short minute, he felt absolutely worn out. He tried again. This time he made no effort in speed, just relaxed and kept swimming evenly and soon found that he slowly moved forward, reaching a nearby cabaña pole. When he stopped all motion he was carried back to his starting position.

"I've just learned," he told Bachrach, "that I can't sprint ahead. It's too tiring! I've got to take my own time, work at it and then I'll be able to make it. So take him on! But make sure that pole is all I have to aim for."

The following morning Johnny swam to the pole and won the bet. It upset the Czech to such an extent that he screamed that he had been taken for a ride, accused Johnny of accepting money, thus forfeiting his amateur status.

"I made the bet, not Johnny!" said Bachrach. "Don't try to make a pro out of my boy, I've got witnesses." And the sly, old fox procured the statement of an American tourist who had witnessed their conversation the day before. With the sour face of a poor loser, the Czech paid up. The golden domes of Prague grew gray in the dawn of yet another day and the Moldau disappeared from the sight of the small troup.

Wherever Johnny went he was greeted by enthusiastic crowds of spectators who followed his rehearsed routines that covered the evolution of swimming that started with the dog paddle and ended with the backstroke. When he swam the American crawl he demonstrated his capable speed, unwittingly breaking his best records time after time and, always, the show ended with its inevitable climax, the comedy-diving stunt. Sooner than he realized, the tour had been completed and he was homeward bound.

Once again at sea, on the S.S. Rotterdam, Johnny found time for reflection — and, meditation. The after-effects of the great adventure were starting to set in on Johnny. The responsibility he had vaguely recognized before he had entered the past Olympiad now bore down on him. The thought to carry on the real and approved amateur ideals, with the inner hope of giving to the younger generation an opportunity for self-expression, honest endeavor and determination for a better physical goal, impressed itself on his mind. An acute awareness of the fact that he no longer represented just another swimmer in the eyes of the world but an ambassador of sports with no language barrier to prevent its message from spreading to all interested parties filled his being. He promised himself to set a good example to all aspirants in this field and live up to expectations. Simultaneously, a foreboding of another nature, a melancholy that divided and crept into his brain, took part of him. He still had not heard from his girl, and could not understand what had happened. His brooding did not go unnoticed by Bachrach's ever-watchful eyes. The coach gave his two performers leeway, permitting them to train at their leisure, allowing them to indulge their appetites in whatever looked palatable on the menu, and instead of the customary Seltzer water, he ordered wine for dinner. Still he saw Johnny gloomily staring into space.

When Bachrach tried to joke, "What ails my prima donna?" Johnny walked away without a reply, and the coach knew something deeper than fatigue had to be blamed. Later that day, he witnessed a change in Johnny, who had picked a conversation with a pair of shapely, long-legged fillies. He took him aside to ask him if he still planned to go ahead with the wedding to Lorelei. The young man's attitude left no room for doubt as to where his unhappiness rested. Bachrach did not repeat his earlier counseling, nor did he reveal his lack of surprise. However, his paternal spirit prompted him to keep a closer lookout. The moment he felt that Johnny was ready to ease his lonesomeness with a casual romance aboard ship, he clamped down on his boy, putting him back to regular training hours and an early bedtime. Shortly thereafter, Bachrach himself took over and was seen parading along the decks, escorting both willing damsels, one on each arm, his broad face aglow with contentment, his mustache hidden behind an aromatic smoke cloud as he puffed on his cigar.

As Johnny's calendar moved on, the year ended with two postscripts. Upon his return home, Johnny was invited to the White House and an audience with President Coolidge. Since he had missed out on the formal ceremonies that honored the Olympic team, the President of the United States presented young Weissmuller with a citation for his outstanding athletic achievements in the Paris-held Olympiad, and accompanied it with personal sentiment in wishing the swimmer much success in future ventures. When Johnny left the privacy of the Presidential office, he returned to Chicago and immediately telephoned Lorelei.

There were several rings on the receiving end before the voice of Lorelei's mother answered. "She doesn't live here anymore," came the cold reply to his palpitant question, "she's home with her husband. Leave her alone!" The line became disconnected . . . as did Johnny's heartbeat.

Months later, months that he had spent in a stupor which even the applause to his victorious swimming events did not remedy, Lorelei called. "Johnny!" The familiar sound crept across the wires, making them burn with lost emotion. "Johnny, I want to see you. Will you meet me in Lincoln Park tomorrow afternoon at four?"

She was waiting when he arrived and he sat next to her on the bench, keeping his look fixed into the distance away from her face. "Johnny," she said, "I wasn't going to wait until I became an old maid. You're like a sailor, a traveling salesman, a pursuer of trophies! You are ambitious! I picked a husband who'll remain at home with me and not go gallivanting around the globe. I want a home, children, security! You can't ever give me those things; you can't ever afford to . . ."

"Couldn't you have given me an ultimatum?" Johnny's voice sounded rasp and hoarse, as if he were suffering from a sore throat. His eyes were still centered on a distant elm tree where he thought he saw two squirrels chasing up the bark. "Didn't you remember your promise?" That last word seemed to hang in his throat.

Lorelei got to her feet abruptly. "I'm sorry, but my decision suits me just fine!" The sound of her swift footsteps faded into the late afternoon. To Johnny it seemed that one squirrel had fallen dead beneath the elm as a huge hawk took flight across the trees and hovered momentarily over the bench on which he sat, then spread its wings across the waters of Lake Michigan and, soon, no longer belonged to the horizon, as his own footsteps carried him into the mists that settled along the lakeshore.

Johnny took the end of his first romance very hard. For several years thereafter he shied away from girls, afraid of being hurt again. Thus Lorelei started the line of bitter experiences in love that followed Johnny through most of his life and, in a sense, she became personally responsible for the mistake of his first marriage. However, there is nothing unique in the claim that fame and happiness seldom are blissful bedfellows.

Time ticked on. Johnny's keenest competitors were men like George Kojac and Walter Laufer, yet he held his championships proudly intact, defending them, surpassing his own records in indoor and outdoor meets, while keeping in constant training. "If I kick him out of my pool he goes to another." Bachrach thought, feeling concern. "If I'd cut his head open, I know I'd find a swimming tank inside. It is very commendable but I wish he'd meet another dame for his own sake."

Two of Johnny's most noteworthy performances happened within the four years between the Olympic Games, one in swimming against Kojac in the 100-meter straightaway, a feat still unbroken in 1963; the other in churning a hundred yards in 49.5 s. to set a world's example in free style sprinting. This latter effort equaled only 4.01 m.p.h. but even so, it was faster than the normal speed of many fish.

Chicago's marvel began giving advice to future swim aspirants, and he enveloped more hands in his huge mitt and smiled more winning smiles on countless excursions across the country when he happened to stop at the star-studded film capital where he met his childhood hero of the silent movie era, Douglas Fairbanks, Sr. The latter prided himself on his long line of friends in the sports world and, taking an immediate liking to Johnny, invited him to watch the filming of "The Black Pirate," which was being produced at the Goldwyn Studios in Hollywood. When Johnny was first admitted into the enclosure of sound stages and dressing room bungalows, his eyes practically popped from their sockets in wonderment and awe. A red-skin, leaning against a cactus made of papier-mâché smoking Indian Weed and leisurely toying with his tomahawk, turned out to be a Swede with not even a trace of English in his conversation, let alone any tribal lingo. On the next-door set the grand dame a Russian cossack escorted across the plaza was a honeysuckle babe from way down South and her guardian, in reality, a Spaniard. The director, however, left little doubt as to his national origin, for, dressed in knickerbockers and a beret, he hardly minced his phraseology, "Kommen Sie schon, Sie alte Kuh! Schnell, hier gibt's keine Zeit zum herum wackeln!" When Johnny finally reached Doug's side, he found him seated in a regular barber chair in his spacious bungalow while an artist of the trade was putting on his make-up. "Step right in, old boy, get comfortable!" Douglas called to him, "You'll find some liquor at the bar."

"Thanks, but I don't drink," Johnny said, looking around with eyes as big as melons. All he had known about dressing rooms in the past was some corner wherein to perform a quick change. This bungalow seemed fit for a king!

He accompanied the star of the pirate film to his stage where he watched scenes unfold before the camera. Later, he joined him at lunch. A gentleman was waiting at their table whom Fairbanks introduced as Sol Lesser.

"Have you given some thought to playing Tarzan?" Lesser began the conversation and leaned closer to Fairbanks. "It's time to revive the character. Why, with the combination of the public's urge for untamed jungle adventure and your interpretation, it'll be the hottest picture ever made. What do you say, Doug?"

Fairbanks wrinkled his brow and shook his head. "No, Sol. It's not my cup of tea. You should get a new face to play your hero." Thoughtfully, he glanced at his young guest. "Now there's a lad who'd be sensational in the part. He looks like Tarzan, and he's a marvelous swimmer besides."

Lesser turned, and for the first time scrutinized Johnny closely, then shrugged. "The kid's all right, but we need a star!" And he continued plugging the importance of Douglas Fairbanks' taking the role.

At night when the star retired to his private steam room, he began to shave his chest. "Tell you, Johnny — if you ever get into movies, be sure to shave every bit of hair from your body. Looks dirty on the screen. Always catches attention and steals the scene in a smelly kind of way," he advised and, finished with his task, took a plunge in a cold water tub before surrendering himself once again to steam heat.

He invited Johnny to "Pickfair", his and Mary Pickford's beautiful home, where he served tea at the side of the pool, and asked Johnny and a diving pal to perform their comedy act which he filmed. When the print was shown in the privacy of his home, he had used trick photography in reverse where he, Douglas, jumped out of the pool completely dry and served tea. When Johnny left Hollywood to return to Chicago, Fairbanks presented him with the film, in token of his friendship.

Hooks Miller had quit the I.A.C. team and gone into business. Johnny's brother, Peter, had tried his luck in swimming and won second place in his first national contest; nonetheless, he never competed again because he felt that his physical stamina was not equal to such strain. He told Johnny that he simply did not have the stomach to be champion and, perfectly contented, settled for a job as lifeguard at Oak Street Beach. The nineteenth annual Chicago River 3-Mile Marathon loomed in the near future, a race Johnny had already swum a year ago, winning this first invasion into long-distance realms but failing to break the record. This time he meant to succeed in both.

Peter borrowed a boat that belonged to the lifeguards, and as he rowed up Lake Michigan a mile and back, Johnny swam alongside, faithfully sticking to daily workouts despite frequent changes in the weather, which seemed unusually severe and turbulent for this summer season of 1927.

With the river marathon just around the corner, Johnny and Peter increased their distance, going for one and a half miles each way and becoming somewhat a part of the sight-seeing cruise of the Favorite, a double-decker excursion boat with an approximate passenger capacity of eighty, that came from Lincoln Park and circled to the Navy Pier and back.

It was a lovely day when the women and children aboard the Favorite waved to the swimmer and his escort, shouting greetings and well wishes. Johnny had just completed his one-way track and Peter was about to turn the boat back, when suddenly the heavens turned pitch dark and a storm cloud appeared, spitting flashes of lightning followed by loud thunderclaps. Such freak atmospheric disturbances, well known to lake people, were known to occur at certain times of the year. The squall made the people on the Favorite scurry to the lee side of the boat, where more shelter was available. As the hurrying feet transferred the weight to one side, the ship heeled over. It went right on over, grotesquely, coming up in a moment with the top practically clear of the surface but the bottom of the boat leveling with and resting on the bottom of the lake. It all happened so fast that the noise caused by the accident was lost in yet another thunder-bolt and Johnny, swimming, did not hear it. He was unaware of the tragedy until his brother touched his back with the tip of the oar.

At once, the two rushed to the sight of the catastrophe, reaching the Favorite in a few minutes. All seats on the upper deck were empty with no one in view except a seated captain smoking a cigarette still lit, holding onto the hand of a little boy.

"Do something!" Johnny shouted, as he closed in on the scene.

The stunned captain came out of his horror-stricken trance. "I can't swim!" he babbled. "My God! The people — they're all below . . ."

Johnny dived. He plunged down into the depths of the lake, his arms grabbing human beings without hesitation or selection. He brought up a couple of kids first. Peter was right behind him, bringing up two others.

"Start pumping them out," Johnny called before taking another dive, "or they'll die!"

Feverishly, Peter kept trying to revive the victims as fast as Johnny kept bringing up more. Johnny dived and dived. They worked alone for what seemed an eternity, but merely covered some fifteen minutes, before help arrived. Johnny had brought up about twenty individuals, children and some adults. Out of these twenty, eleven lived. When the rescue squad arrived it was too late to do anything except recover more of the bodies of those who had perished in the disaster.

By that time, oil was flooding over the surface of the water. Johnny's eyes were nearly blinded. His arms were heavy with exhaustion. He slowly pulled himself into the rowboat. "I've had enough," he told Peter. "Let's go back. There's nothing we can do anymore." He said a silent prayer as his brother rowed away, leaving fellow athletes from the I.A.C. and the lake patrol to continue the ghastly search.

As suddenly as the squall had hit, stillness set in. Johnny collapsed into one corner of the boat, his eyes closed, his arms folded across them. He thought, "I'm going to teach kids how to swim! Those poor little rascals never had a fighting chance, but I'll give them one so help me . . ." He swallowed hard. He felt sick.

Three days later a telephone call was placed from the Mayor's office to the Weissmuller home. The brothers received a scroll citing their rescue work. The City of Chicago hailed them heroes. The I.A.C. gave them each a gold watch at a ceremonious dinner affair. But these honors that were bestowed upon them by civic leaders never matched a letter which Johnny received many, many years later in 1962, from a girl he had saved. "I have seven children," the woman wrote, "and one day, my seven children will have their young ones. This circle of life will continue forever or as long as God grants this earth to remain fertile within the atmosphere. But only you, Mr. Weissmuller, are responsible for this vast miracle that has come to touch my life, because it was you who rescued me from certain death, and enabled me to marry and have my children. I shall always impress upon the minds of my young ones to say a prayer of thanks on your behalf and, God willing, these prayers will last through a part of eternity."

The Chicago River 3-Mile Marathon race was on!

Thousands of spectators were packed upon barges, bridges, and the two levels of Wacker Drive. More crowds lined the sides and ends of the pier, massed upon the breakwaters and upon the docks. Hundreds followed the course of the marathon in excursion boats, undaunted by the shadow of the tragedy of the Favorite. Sirens shrieked, bells clanged, horns tooted, and people yelled themselves hoarse on this Saturday, the second to last day in July.

Chicago's classic river spectacle started at the north side shore line of the Municipal (now Navy) Pier and ended at Wells Street Bridge and was performed before some fifty-thousand spectators, by far the greatest crowd that had ever assembled prior to 1927. They had come to watch the long arms of Johnny Weissmuller flash through the murky, green water to a record breaking finish. And Johnny, fulfilling all expectations, trimmed nearly ten minutes from the old record set for the course. He finished the three miles in 54 m. 29 s.

Fourteen times in the nineteen years that this event had been held, the I.A.C. swimmers had brought home the cup under Coach Bachrach's management. Among others, Perry McGillivray had won it four times and W. L. Wallen thrice, twice before joining the I.A.C. Norman Ross also twice. This was the second victory for Weissmuller and once again, the thousand-dollar William Hale Thompson Trophy belonged to the club.

Piloted by his brother who rowed the escort boat, Johnny assumed the lead from the start. He battled his way through a mass of driftwood brought in by steamers docking at the pier where the water, roughened by a fresh breeze from the northeast that sent waves crashing, and caused considerable backwash, bothering the swimmers. The champion employed a leisurely modification of his famous crawl stroke, slowed down the leg beats and indulged in a more restful roll from side to side. When he rounded the corner of the Municipal Pier, three-quarters of a mile on his way, he had built up a 100-yard lead on his closest opponent, Adler. He swam south half a mile to the end of the breakwater, which extended east into the lake almost as far as the pier itself. When he turned west around its end, he further increased his lead by fifty yards more. Under the south lee of this breakwater, Johnny found smoother water, and he made splendid time westward in the direction of the mouth of the river. As he approached it, he sprinted for about two-hundred yards and, hitting the current which flowed into the river from the lake, Johnny stretched his lead over Adler to three-hundred yards. Such a lead left no chance for Adler, who recognized the futility of trying to make it up. From this point on, it was Johnny all the way.

The Weissmuller victory chant was picked up by a boatload of Hawaiian ukulele players and singers, who added much to the gaiety and color of the occasion. These island natives were there to root primarily for their countryman, John Kaaihu, of the Healani Boat Club, Honolulu, but since the Hawaiian swimmer had been left well back in the race, they sang about the winner instead. "Clap hands — here comes Johnny!"

When the champion climbed out of the river, his first thought was not of the marathon he had just won, but of Bachrach who had taught him to swim high in the water. Never before in his entire career had he experienced more need for hydroplaning. To anyone who is familiar with the Chicago river this must seem self-explanatory because the river, alas, was used as a city sewer! And even though his body was literally covered with refuse that emitted an offensive odor he, at least, had kept his head up at a safe altitude.

Surrounded by an enthusiastic entourage of reporters and photographers — (for news knows no smell but that of roses!) — he was pushed into his mother's waiting, outstretched arms. "Mrs. Weissmuller! Will you please pose with your son!"

Mother Elizabeth took one sniff of her offspring. "Don't you dare come near me, Johnny!" She shrieked in German. "You stink!" And the little lady quickly hid herself behind some of the amused onlookers; Peter became convulsed with laughter. The champion merely stood there, dripping, while the cameras clicked on.

AT AMSTERDAM AND TOKYO

8

WHEN THE S.S. President Roosevelt docked in the Dutch harbor at Amsterdam, she was used as a floating hotel for the athletes who had won in the Olympic tryouts at Detroit, and had ventured forth to compete in the Ninth Olympiad.

The games were officially opened on July 28, 1928, by Prince Hendrik of Holland, acting for Queen Wilhelmina, who was away on a visit to Norway. Some 40,000 spectators filled the stadium to capacity with an estimated crowd of another 75,000 outside trying vainly to get in. The parade was smart and colorful, and noteworthy for the fact that for the first time after World War I, the Germans and their allies of the Central Powers were allowed to take part in the international athletic meeting. It also marked the first celebration of the games at which women athletes were represented, although they had had their part in other branches of sports such as swimming in former years. During the assembly of the flags, H. Denis, a Dutch athlete, spoke the Olympic Oath on behalf of all competitors. Only France was not represented in the parade. The French had on the previous day attempted to enter the stadium and had been prevented by a gatekeeper. The team was so outraged by this audacity that they were ready to quit the games and Holland without further notice but, eventually, matters were straightened out and, following official apologies, France remained one of the competing nations.

The United States on this occasion was far back in the alphabetic ranks, marching as the "Vereenidge Staten." Johnny had been chosen to carry the identification standard for his country, leading the team in the march-past. This honor was reserved for someone who had already proven his worth in past Olympic contests, and considered a task of high favor and esteem. Following him, Bud Houser held the Stars and Stripes as ever upright, and the Europeans, as in Paris, found subject for conversation in the odd behavior of the Yankee and the arthritis in his joints.

While general accommodations seemed superior to those they had experienced in Paris, Manager Taylor and his assistant, Dr. M. Francois D'Aliscu soon found that the two designated practice pools at Amsterdam were as totally unfitted as those they had found in Paris, four years ago. The only desirable pool was located after a few days of frantic search at Haarlem, a distance of sixteen miles, which required too much travel each day. Swimming competitions were actually conducted at the new Swimming Stadium, its foundation stone laid a little more than a year ago. The basin in this stadium was reinforced concrete and measured 50 meters long by 18 meters wide. At the deepest part, near the diving board, it was 5 meters. Stands had been erected on both sides and at one end to accommodate about 6,000 spectators. At the other end was a building with two wings containing twenty men's dressing rooms, sixteen ladies' dressing rooms, a room for those directing the contests, an apartment for the jury, a depository, and an auxiliary post office. Over this building were the stands principally reserved for official visitors, contestants and the press. In the yard between the two wings containing the dressing rooms was a small building in which the water from the municipal mains was heated to 19° C. and then pumped into the basin.

The track and field events preceded as ever and closed on August 5th, just one day after the swimming events had begun. These lasted through the 11th and drew a total paying attendance of 50,826. Strength in field events had made certain the American victory, but the United States had, in effect, bowed to little Finland, for considering the vast difference in the population of these two countries, Finland ran away with major honors. Whereas the United States gathered an overall total of 24 first places, 21 second places, 17 third places, and 131 points; Finland was second with 10 first places, 11 second places, 10 third places and 62 points; all other nations followed.

Douglas MacArthur, then a major-general and president of the American Olympic Committee in 1928, also the official directly in charge of the United States team at Amsterdam in the "Olympische Spelen" of that year, quoted a passage in Plutarch wherein Themistocles, being asked whether he would rather be Achilles or Homer, replied: "Which would you rather be, a conqueror in the Olympic Games or the crier who proclaims who are conquerors?" — Nevertheless, it happened that de jure the United States won the competitions, and de facto we conquered, too; but the national pride in our genius for athletics suffered in the setback on the track.

While these games were now quite familiar to Johnny, he still felt tense during the preliminaries, and Bachrach, again acting as head coach for the swimming team, once more treated the swimmer with the psychological touch, with understanding, handling him like a temperamental thoroughbred, careful not to let him run himself out, to burn up his energy before the last leap to victory.

In the first contest, the 100-meter free style, Johnny won the third heat followed by W. Spence, of Canada; N. S. Brooks, Great Britain; H. Heinrich, Germany; in that order. In the semi-finals, he won again in the third series, leading E. Bárány, the Hungarian swimmer whom he had previously met on his European tour following the last Olympiad. Third came A. Heitman of Germany; then K. Olsen, Norway, and E. Polli, Italy. It may be of interest to note here that Johnny's time in the semi-finals equaled his victory in the finals to the split second; he won in 58.3/5 s., breaking his previous Olympic record by 1.3/5 s.

Johnny had this to say about the race which had seemed smooth sailing to the crowds of spectators. "I had always dreaded swallowing a mouthful of water. I knew the lights would go out and I wondered what I'd do if it ever happened to me. Sure enough, my time arrived as I did the turn, the only turn in the race! I dipped down and came up with a throatful of water. We were all even. I felt like blacking out. I swallowed the stuff and lost two valuable yards. Lucky for me, we still had some forty meters left to go, with only ten or so I'd never have made it. But — well, I guess I had to win for the States, to come in first."

In winning the gold medal he defeated Bárány who got the silver award for swimming the event in 59.4/5 s., and Takaishi, his former rival, who swam the hundred meters in one minute flat. Kojac and Laufer, both of the U.S. and Johnny's foremost rivals for national and world's records, placed fourth and fifth. A Canadian, W. Spence, came in sixth with his time clocked at 1 m. 1.2/5 s.

However, George J. Kojac secured top place in the backstroke, Walter Laufer came in a shining second, and P. Wyatt with his third prize made it unanimous for the United States.

Others on the team who gave credit to Uncle Sam's land through personal achievement that won them the highest recognition were men like Pete Desjardins, hailing from Florida, for springboard and platform diving; he reaped two gold medals as his reward. And naturally, the strong, masculine fellows on the 800-meter relay team performed with vigor and dedication. Johnny, as in 1924, swam anchor. Six alternated in the preliminary and final effort. In the first heat it was the U.S. all the way with Paul C. Sampson of the I.A.C., A. R. Clapp, D. K. Young, and Weissmuller timed at 9 m. 38.4/5 s., against Japan's second, Sweden's third, and the Argentine. In the finals, the United States team was represented by Clapp, Laufer, Kojac and Weissmuller. They came in even faster, setting their victory at 9 m. 36.1/5 s., beating their past Olympic record by a margin of 23.2 s., and heading Japan by 5.1/5 s. Neighboring Canada qualified for the bronze medal, followed by Hungary, Sweden, Great

Britain, and finally Spain, in seventh place, leaving no mark upon the official report. Johnny accepted the honors for the team, at the same time rounding his total Olympic victories to three individual and two team efforts, totaling five gold medals. To the relay, he had added more than his share because four years later, in the Olympics of 1932 at Los Angeles, after he had retired from amateur competitions, the highly coveted 800-meter relay was no longer won by the Americans. Japan had taken over the aquatic honors for this event and held onto them for the span of yet another Olympiad. Only after wars had besieged the children of the kingdoms of God and the Idols of the Far East, did the United States once again show two successive triumphs in that meet.

Johnny did not compete in the 400-meter free style race. Bachrach kept him out. "Too much is too much!" the coach proclaimed. "We need you in the relay but also to strengthen our water polo team. Total points count!" Thus Albert Zorilla from the Argentine won, and broke Johnny's previous record which Johnny knew he could have walked away with. He had, in 1924, defeated Zorilla in the semi-finals of the 100-meter event. But Johnny's attention was focused somewhere else at the time . . . like watching Helen Meany win the fancy springboard diving.

Helen — brown-haired, doe-eyed, the Mona Lisa of the femme divers . . . but with a smile that left no doubt by comparison. She was a girl-athlete like no other girl-athlete Johnny had ever encountered. She knew about water, and she knew about friendship. And she carried herself with an air of honesty and modest womanliness which Johnny had forgotten existed after Lorelei. She hailed from New York and they had met aboard the Roosevelt. There was nothing romantic in their behavior toward each other except, perhaps, a deep sense of mutual attraction which made it easy to communicate. Thus Johnny found himself rooting in her corner, watching her small, yet muscular, well-trained body fly through the air, in tight spins, in snap rolls, twists, with the split second timing of the champion, to the applause of all who beheld her perfect form and style. And he found himself cheering for her victory, proud to be present as she climbed into the center of the presentation block, her head slightly bowed, a streak of her brown hair clinging stubbornly against her forehead, to receive a golden token for her beautiful performance.

As valiantly as the fair Helen conquered, her athletic sisters also served the same cause well, and again the American women reaped recognition and top honors. Albina Osipowich won the hundred meters, Martha Norelius triumphed as she had in 1924, in the 400-meter event. The women's relay was again captured by the U.S., and the ladies managed to keep on winning it even in 1932, at the time when the men lost out to the Japanese. And Elizabeth B. Pinkston competed successfully in platform diving for the first time in ladies' events. But the 100-meter backstroke went to a native through the efforts of Marie Braun, and the 200-meter breaststroke, formerly won by Great Britain's darling, Lucy Morton, found a new mistress in Hilde Schrader of Germany.

Arne Borg became an undisputed champion in winning the 1,500 meters for Sweden. In the 200-meter breaststroke, Y. Tsuruta showed what Japan held in store for the future.

Then nothing was left except the fatal hour that struck once the water polo teams ventured to submerge. What a disaster that turned out to be!

The I.A.C.'s husky Perry McGillivray was coach for the American water polo squad, a fine-looking assembly of tall menfolk such as hardly any female could by-pass without some inclination to swoon. They were all young, handsome and, unfortunately, too cocksure for their own good! Next to Johnny, the I.A.C. had Samuel Greller, who competed, and Wallace O'Conner and Ogden Driggs, who did not, but stood by in case. In addition, there were H. C. Daniels, G. F. Mitchel, G. E. Schroth, R. J. Greenberg and H. R. Topp. In the second round, Great Britain defeated Holland 5 to 3; Germany defeated Belgium 5 to 3; and then came Hungary — and defeated the United States 5 to 0! Afterwards no one on the American team really cared whether France defeated Malta 16 to 0. . . The finals were won by Germany defeating Hungary 5 to 2. By this time, the Yankee boys who remembered the Paris Olympiad were wishing that they had another atheist in the crowd with a "speak-easy" under his mattress where they might drown their sorrow and their loss.

The official report of the manager of the men's swimming team, the by now well-known John T. Taylor, read as follows: "In water polo America had the misfortune to draw Hungary, which had won the European championships, for our first match and we were defeated decisively. Two outstanding faults are evident in American water polo; first there is very little competition in this country and secondly our national championships and Olympic tryouts are held in small indoor pools. Consequently our players are handicapped when placed in a large outdoor pool. Unless leading athletic clubs foster outdoor water polo and provide more competition, it would be useless for us to enter another water polo team in the Olympics."

This statement held true to the facts along an unbroken line of defeats.

Toward the end of the Ninth Olympiad, Queen Wilhelmina, who had returned to her realm a little over a week after the games had started, stood in the royal box at the stadium, behind a railing covered with a lush oriental carpet with a brilliant multi-colored design that brushed against the leaves of specially planted palms, and handed out the gold medals to the winners, while Prince Hendrik delivered the silver ones, and Count Henri Baillet-Latour, president of the International Olympic Committee, gave out the bronze medals for third places.

Johnny was honored with a special award from the Queen. And when the benevolent monarch placed her personal medal into the outstretched hand of the young swimmer, she smiled the tender smile of a woman who liked what she saw in the tall American with the European name and, strangely, Her Majesty reminded Johnny of the mother he had left waiting at home.

At the conclusion of the games, the report of the assistant manager of the swimming team, Dr. D'Eliscu, stated: "Every swimmer was considered a gentleman or a perfect lady, respectively. They all won a place in the hearts of officials and spectators, and it is sincerely hoped that some day when they return to these United States, that we can

107

demonstrate, prove and express the same appreciation as they have manifested throughout our entire meetings."

The full team left Amsterdam on August 13th, and upon return, the athletes were given a typically all-out New York welcome on their debarkation.

Johnny received his second Presidential citation, but on this occasion it was attended by all the pomp and circumstance that are lavished on Olympic victors, including a ticker tape parade down 5th Avenue, followed by a formal reception where New York State's Governor Smith presented yet another medal, and His Honor the Mayor, Jimmy Walker, handed out keys to the city that harbored the Lady with the Torch.

It was not long before the swimmer again left his homeland. His globe-trotting feet followed the arrangements of the American-Japan Society that sent him on an International Swimming Contest into the Far East. These contests duplicated the events of the Olympic Games, except that they were held in the month of October, and in a considerably cooler climate. All winners and runners-up who had competed at Amsterdam were invited, but not all the former contestants were able to attend.

The S.S. Taiyo Maru carried Johnny and Helen Meany, among others, into Tokyo Bay, where they caught their first glimpse of the beautiful, snow-covered symmetry of Mount Fujiyama. Throughout the voyage they had been an inseparable couple, holding hands, posing for photographs which were to be placed in a single album to serve as a memento of their joint adventure on land and sea.

On their arrival, they were met by Takaishi, whose friendly greeting warmed the heart of his former rival, and Arne Borg, who had traveled from his native Sweden, bringing with him his fiancée, whom he planned to marry in Japan before taking her to the United States. Diving Coach Ernst Brandsten from Stanford University in Palo Alto, California, had arranged this visit which later became extended into permanent residency for Arne and his bride. Borg asked Johnny to be best man at his wedding and the latter accepted, with pleasure. On their way to the hotel where accommodations had been reserved for Bachrach's party, Takaishi leaned closer to Johnny.

"I must talk to you," Takaishi whispered.

"Go ahead!"

Takaishi put a finger to his lips, uneasily glanced about and leaned closer. "Not now, later, in private. It is very important!" His secretive attitude left Johnny wondering what this was all about. When they arrived at their destination, he took the Japanese swimmer aside.

"Johnny," Takaishi began, "I like you. We have always competed in all fairness under the Olympic code, so I feel it my duty to tip you off. There is a conspiracy against you. When you swim, the water temperature in the pool will be near freezing, you will get a cramp in your muscles and lose."

Johnny gave the other a look of disbelief. "What about your own swimmers? You, for instance. I'm not going to be in there alone!"

"We are all used to swimming in very cold water. We have been trained for it."

"But why? What's the gimmick? I've been invited here and . . ."

Takaishi interrupted. "It is the work of one man. A very powerful man. Only few people know of it and they will not speak up. The Japanese people love you and want to be good hosts. Do not blame them."

"Well, thanks!" Johnny exclaimed and scratched his ear. "But ice water is ice water and knowing about it doesn't help much!"

"You think of something." Takaishi patted the tall American's shoulder. "But do not tell anyone that it was I who spoke."

Later that day, Bachrach nearly steamed as he shouted over the telephone in his suite, "Bring up ten buckets of ice! I don't care if you're running short! Get some snow from Fujiyama!" He hung up and started pacing the room. "Eureka! Eldorado! So they think they can beat my boy that way, eh! Well, they've got something coming!" He turned to Johnny, who sat on a couch resting his legs on a low bench, his fingers busily engaged with a piece of string, trying to master a rope trick. "Get undressed!" Bachrach shouted. "We'll just see about who beats whom!" And he disappeared into the bathroom.

"What's this all about?" Johnny leisurely got up and strolled after him. Hovering in the doorway, he saw Bachrach open a faucet, and run cold water into the bathtub.

"I'll give you one guess!" Bachrach growled. Hearing a knock, he went to admit a quintet of bellboys, each carrying two buckets filled with ice and more ice.

"I want you to keep delivering this until I say stop," Bachrach said, and followed the native custom, bowing to the head boy while handing him a tip. Pleased, the head boy relieved himself of his burden and bowed back.

"Me see ice come. Plenty snow on Fujisan."

"There better be! This party is going to last for several days!"

"Ah, so-o! Ice come. No ice — me get snow. No snow — me get ice wate' in lake. Make Bach'l'ach-san happy."

"No ice water in lake," the coach murmured, closing the door after the smiling five, "they've already poured that into the pool!" He picked up two buckets and took them to Johnny who had, meanwhile, undressed. "Start shivering!" Bachrach said, and emptied the ice into the tub. "We've got to get you readjusted!"

While Johnny was literally kept on ice days and part of nights getting acquainted with arctic temperatures, everyone at the hotel thought Bachrach and his boys were having a ball or that someone was suffering from a terrible case of fever. When the day of competition dawned, Johnny was fully prepared, like a penguin, swam faster and with no trouble outraced everyone in the 100-meters, 400-meters, etc. He was hailed as the best swimmer ever to set foot on Honshu Island, and was bestowed with the highest honor any foreigner could receive, a medal presented personally by the Crown Prince of Japan. In addition, Bachrach picked up an armload of trophies on behalf of his protégé.

A newspaperman, Shunjiro Kojima, exchanged autographs with the champion, then wrote glowing reports about his stamina without ever mentioning the odds that had con-

111

fronted him, most probably because of the good reason that he had never been aware of the goings on. Johnny was invited to a round table discussion where he was approached by an official.

"Mr. Weissmuller, you have surpassed my highest expectations," the official said in perfect English. "Your physical acclimatization surprises me beyond words."

Johnny's eyes flashed; he wondered if this particular individual happened to be the powerful person in question who had started the connivance against him. "Most people don't know that I swim much faster in ice water!" He said, with a big good-natured grin that seemed quite sincere.

The Japanese official's mouth also broke into a grin, a narrow one. "Ah, so!" He paused momentarily. "Will you become our head swimming coach?" He continued the surprise proposal with "our swimmers will do everything you say to the letter. Just ask what you want them to do."

With a "back home I've got many to teach," Johnny dismissed the subject. But it was brought up again on the following day when the official had lined up the entire Nipponese swimming team. "Ask them to do anything," he said. "Ask them to cut off their right arm, and they will do it."

"Much good that'll do in swimming," Johnny had to laugh; the statement seemed rather ridiculous to an American.

"Ask them!" the official insisted. "Ask them to get under water and take a deep breath."

"Oh, come on!" Johnny was getting bored, perhaps irritated. "You know very well what happens to a swimmer if . . ."

He did not get further before the official barked a command in his own language and one of the nearby men jumped into the tank before Bachrach managed to shout "Eureka!" Moments later air bubbles appeared on the pool's surface.

"Christ!" Johnny exclaimed, and hit the water. None of the Japanese team stirred a muscle to aid in the rescue. Only after Johnny brought him up did they assist in pumping the water from his lungs. It took considerable time and effort to bring the man to.

"I don't like your style!" Johnny told the official. "And I don't get your whole attitude! You've got fine swimmers. They have plenty of what it takes to compete against anyone in the world on their own! Whatever training they need cannot be given by holding a club next to their skulls!"

What Johnny did not realize in 1928, what few saw hidden behind the outer face including most of the Japanese people themselves was the seed of the Kamikaze that had been implanted in the minds of many. The dragon had begun to test its breath, to show its fangs, slowly injecting venom into the unsuspecting.

Before the participants of the United States athletic team left Tokyo for Osaka and Kobe, Bachrach received an identical offer, to which he replied in a similar fashion. "Strange fellows!" he told Johnny. "I can't understand them."

"Well, some of them," came the reply. "But guys like Takaishi make up for a lot." To which the coach heartily agreed.

Years later, a battle to the death was about to take place on the bottom of Tokyo Bay, between Japanese frogmen and the men of the U.S. Navy underwater demolition teams. The war ended before it materialized. But Johnny remembered his past encounter vividly. . .

After two weeks of successful contests, the Americans sailed for home. Johnny wondered about his relationship to Helen. "Will you write to me when you're in New York and I'm in Chicago?" he asked, and tried to decipher her Mona Lisa-like smile.

She did not answer. He searched her face and, sub-consciously, read her thoughts. With the passage of time, letters would become infrequent. Distance would come between them, blotting out plans and hopes. For a while they would dream of bygone days, faraway places. Then, as they grew farther apart, a twilight would settle on memories, and forgetfulness would follow.

He repeated his question, "Will you write to me?"

"Yes," she replied simply, but when she left him, she signed her photograph, "To Johnny — in Memoriam, Helen."

STRANGE THINGS HAPPEN IN MIAMI

9

THE END of the Twenties rolled closed. Master Frost had once again placed Chicago under a mantle of snow and ice when Johnny left the freezing climate of that wind-battered city, and journeyed south to mix with the elite who, yearly, adopted Florida as a seasonal playground. Various hotels had invited the amateur champion to the Sunshine State for almost as long as he had first joined forces with Bachrach. He performed each Sunday, putting on water shows for the amusement of the wealthy clientele, in return receiving general expenses.

Johnny divided his time between Miami Beach and Coral Gables, which lay some odd ten miles west of Miami. He liked to swim at the latter in quietude, vastly preferring the picturesque surroundings to the crowded hotel pools, but it was at the Roney Plaza at Miami Beach that he first spotted a wide-eyed, puny youngster staring at him as he finished his workout and climbed out of the water. There was something in the sad look of the boy that reminded him of his own youth, a certain pathetic weakness that seemed related to ill-health. The child had grown too fast for his tender age, possibly in limited circumstances, and obviously suffered from a poor physical condition.

Johnny put on his terry cloth bathrobe and strolled over to the boy's side. "Hi, there!" he said, "Aren't you going in for a swim?"

The youngster's anxious eyes beheld him for a moment before he answered. "I don't know how, Mr. Weissmuller. I've never learned."

"Well, now — are you afraid of water?"

"No, sir!" came the quick reply.

"D'you have a pair of swimming trunks?"

"Yes, sir!" The boy's face lit up.

"I'll be swimming again tomorrow," Johnny said. "Come on over and I'll teach you."

"Yes, sir!!!" His dark eyes gleaming with excitement, the boy wheeled around and ran off, leaving Johnny with an amused expression on his face. Poor kid, he thought, and wondered what sort of parents could so completely neglect their son's physical fitness. Maybe they worked too hard and long to spend any time with the child, or perhaps, they belonged to the group that simply did not care. Whatever the case, Johnny wanted to help him.

The following day, the dark-eyed boy was already waiting when Johnny arrived at the pool. "Okay, fellow, get in! You must get wet before you can begin to float."

For several weeks the informal lessons continued at a daily rate with the exception of the Sabbath, when Johnny had to give his shows. After a fortnight, his pupil swam. Yet they kept up the vigorous exercise and, soon, the boy's physique showed considerable improvement, his pale complexion gave way to a healthy tan.

While the rendezvous continued, Johnny's attention had been attracted by a stranger dressed conspicuously in a trench coat, wearing a hat pulled over his eyes that were hidden behind dark glasses. He appeared shortly after the lesson began, seated himself into a vacant canvas chair, and became engrossed in a newspaper, occasionally throwing a quick glance in the direction of the pool. Johnny had never seen him around except at that scheduled hour and once, he happened to spot him while swimming at Coral Gables accompanied by the boy.

"Do you know him?" Johnny asked.

The boy shook his head in a negative reply. "That's funny, I get the feeling he is shadowing you," Johnny observed, but dismissed the subject as absurd.

One day he waited for the boy in vain. At the same time, he noticed that the stranger had also failed to show up. He felt concerned, and began to wonder about some of the peculiarities in the youngster's behavior whenever their conversation had switched from swimming in general to more personal matters. Since Johnny was not given to prying, all he knew was what the child had volunteered to tell, namely that his father's business kept them forever on the move. Even his name had escaped his memory, and he asked himself whether it had ever been mentioned.

Just as he was ready to leave the pool area, he saw his pupil rounding a corner. It seemed to Johnny that the boy had been crying, his eyes were swollen and his voice was still unsteady with emotion as he apologized for being so late.

"What's the matter?" Johnny asked bluntly.

"I've come to say good-bye," the boy said, "I'm leaving Miami in an hour. My Dad said there would not be time to see you, but I wanted to, so he let me and . . ." the boy produced a small box from his pocket, "he asked me to give you this as thanks for all you've done for me." He handed Johnny the cardboard box, 4x5 inches in size, tied with a paper string. Before he left, he turned back again.

"Gee, Mr. Weissmuller, it was fun! I sure hate to go. . ." The sentence trailed off as his eyes became moist.

Johnny had liked the little guy. Thoughtfully, he stared after him, then untied and opened the box. Inside he found a gold buckle studded with stones that flashed in the sunlight like diamonds. "Pretty fancy costume jewelry," he thought, as he casually slipped it into his pocket. He forgot about the gift till weeks later, when he accidentally dropped his bathrobe and the buckle fell out.

"A wrestler's buckle!" a passerby observed, returning it to Johnny. "Looks like the real McCoy! Business must be prosperous in the ring!"

"Tourist!" Johnny thought, "a wrestler, indeed!" and figured that obviously not everyone was familiar with the life of Johnny Weissmuller. But as he eyed the buckle, he got an idea that possibly he could raise a couple of bucks on it. Besides, he hated to be mistaken for a wrestler. Once was enough!

He found a pawnshop and, putting on a casual mien,

he approached the man behind the counter. "What will you give me for this?"

The pawnbroker placed his loupe, a magnifying lense, next to his eye and carefully examined the sparkling stones in the ornamental accessory. He took a long time. Finally, he glanced at Johnny, the lense still hugging his eyeball, enlarging it to a grotesque size. "How much do you want?" he inquired.

"Well, I don't really know," Johnny stammered, stalling for an opening, slightly unsure of himself, "whatever you think."

The pawnbroker's eye loomed ever larger, seeming to look right into Johnny's brain. "Tell you what — I'll give you one twenty-five."

"Is that all?" Johnny exclaimed, disappointed beyond all expectations.

"Okay, one fifty!" the business shark quickly revised. "And that's my final offer!"

"Might as well . . ." Johnny said weakly and thought that at least no one would mistake him for a wrestler again, not that he harbored personal animosity but merely because, after all, he was a swimmer! But in a moment, his jaw dropped open as he stared at the fifteen ten-dollar bills the pawnbroker placed in front of him.

"Sign here, mister! You have six months to redeem this." And as Johnny signed the form in a complete daze, the pawnbroker quickly hid the valuable object behind the steel door of his safe.

Pocketing the cash Johnny left the shop in a trauma. He had never before possessed that much money in his life!

Suddenly, he found himself in the middle of the street between noisy, horn-tooting traffic and screeching brakes. He whirled around and hurried back to the shop.

"Uh-huh! Pardon me again, but could you tell me how much the buckle is worth?"

The pawnbroker suspiciously peeked at him from across the counter. "It is not our policy to give out such information," came the tart reply. "It is yours, isn't it?" He removed the lens from his eye and replaced it with a pair of spectacles. "Aren't you the wrestler who . . ." When he looked up, the doorway was empty.

Pete Desjardins' circle of acquaintances stretched from the Keys to the inland border but none volunteered to pay for a night on the town, so the diver approached Johnny and his newly-acquired wealth.

"I want you to see a girl," he told his pal. "Bobbe Arnst is her name and she sings with Ted Lewis' band. All I can say is — wow!"

"Girls!" Johnny frowned. After Lorelei and the hopeless interlude with the fair Helen, he felt that he should keep as distant from the opposite sex as the north pole from the south. Nevertheless, that particular night saw him at a ringside table.

She was blond and she was fair. Her nose was slightly upturned and terribly cute. Her eyes sparkled with a blue flame as her pink lips formed the lyrics of the song. She had a sweet voice that carried along with it a little girl quality as she warbled, "You do-o-o something to me . . ." and looked from the spotlight into the darkness, her gaze searching, finding, holding on Johnny — or so he thought. Whenever a song was finished, Johnny applauded until she gave an encore. When the show ended, he was introduced to her. When he left the club, they had made a date for the following day.

They went swimming.

He saw her every day. She watched his "ever on Sunday" performances and he spent all his nights listening to her cooing songs. One evening, in the first week of their mutual attraction, he ran into Tommy Loughran, the light heavyweight champion of the world.

"Hi, Johnny! Johnny — you human fish!" The boxer greeted the swimmer. "I've got a terrific idea. Let's place a wager that I can reel you in within ten minutes. D'you know what we could earn for charity! Miami is filled with a betting crowd." Loughran was known as an exceptionally good deep-sea fisherman, and he figured a spectacle of this sort should stir up a lot of publicity.

"Take it easy, pal." Johnny said. "We're amateurs, remember! And this is dealing with money."

"Fiddlesticks!" Loughran dismissed the doubt. "We'll get permission from the A.A.U."

It so happened that a new hotel, the Biltmore at Coral Gables, was to be opened and the entertainment director wanted to promote its spacious pool and facilities. He become enchanted with the plan of putting on something really special and big for charity. "Think of it," he carried on, "The human fish caught by the human kangaroo. Delicious!"

When the A.A.U. came across with their blessing to proceed, Loughran began promoting the show. "I'll pull him

121

in on a rod and reel any day!" he bragged, as Florida's gamblers kept adding to the bets. He did not really possess heavy tackle, not the kind necessary to pull in a 1,000-pound marlin, but he did have one which could haul in a 500-pound sailfish and he aimed to use it on the 180-pound Johnny.

A leather harness was made that looked like a vest, with a hook attached to its back to which a white handkerchief had been attached. The gimmick was that Loughran had to pull in Johnny until this particular piece of cloth hit the tip of the fish pole. The "fish" was permitted to start fifty yards out, and a ten-minute time limit was allowed. The bets were running heavy, divided equally between the angler and his game.

On the morning of the event, the entertainment's promoter consulted Johnny. "Listen, I'm worried," the man said. "This thing has grown above all expectations. I'm afraid it'll cause trouble. In spite of the A.A.U. and their permission, there is some nasty talk going around town that if you win, some of the losers will smear you with the 'pro' title."

Momentarily Johnny was nonplussed. Bachrach was out of town and he knew of no other to whom to turn. "But I've got to win! I know I can! I've always played it straight," he said.

"I know! I know!" the promoter sighed. "That's why we've got to stop the game before it goes too far. Look ---" he pointed to the deck on which Loughran was to stand while throwing out his tackle. "I've had it freshly painted. It's as slippery as treading on eels. If you get close to winning, or losing for that matter, I'll have one of my guys throw a bucket of water onto that surface and Loughran will lose his balance and fall. The match will be called off and all bets cancelled. And the money returned to everyone involved."

"I don't know," Johnny said. "D'you think it really could cause a major upset?"

"Listen, buddy! I've got the 'eyeballs' and 'earlaps' of the world engaged in counting the polls; I know what I'm talking about."

When the time came, Johnny donned his harness and climbed into the pool. "I want to start in shallow water," he announced.

"Suit yourself." Loughran answered most amiably.

Johnny began to porpoise back and forth. The hook held him tight, he felt the pull. He went down and came up with a backstroke. Still, he sensed that his opponent kept a solid grip on the rod. Going underwater again, he pulled at the line, surfaced at once and, using his strong arms, propelled at a fast speed.

"What are you doing?" Loughran screamed. "You pulled my line!"

"I'm a smart fish!" Johnny shouted back and disappeared below the water, bouncing off the bottom in a freakish attempt to gain a comfortable distance from the dangerous pole.

Eight minutes had passed in the struggle. Johnny was still going strong, so was Loughran.

One minute later Tommy Loughran landed on his back. The pail of water had floored him. The people were paid back their contributions. Private bets were off. They had had a good show and free of charge! The hotel paid a nice sum to charity. Everyone was happy and the gag lived on as a conversation piece for some time.

Bobbe helped Johnny remove his harness and both disappeared for the next couple of days. They found shelter in a quiet spot and went swimming.

Two weeks after Johnny had met the singer, he proposed to her. "Will you marry me?" he asked between crawl strokes. In his heart he knew he could be gullible, confused, with his mind clouded with romance and past hurts, but he did not care. He wanted Bobbe's love. He thought he needed it.

They were married at Fort Lauderdale by a Justice of the Peace, two virtual strangers linked in matrimony with no relatives or friends to bear witness to their union. Johnny's only concern was Coach Bachrach, who was expected to arrive from the east any day of the week. Otherwise, he felt carefree and happy, no longer saddled with former doubts.

The newly-weds returned to Miami that same night. Johnny escorted Bobbe to the club. He listened to her soft voice caressing the lyrics, words now meant only for him, the way she sang. The dawn was nearly breaking when he took his bride to the hotel room, a room that was as impersonal as an unsigned, printed card of congratulations, but a room which they, nevertheless, called home the moment they retired.

When Johnny introduced Bachrach to his new bride, the coach gave her a fatherly bear hug and then turned aside. A few days later the coach was standing near the edge of the pool as Johnny climbed out of the water after a practice swim. Bachrach produced a towel for Johnny's hands, a sheet of legal-sized paper and a pen. "Sign here," he ordered. Johnny unhesitatingly put his signature to the document which the coach carefully folded and returned to his coat pocket.

"What did I sign?" asked Johnny.

"My boy," Bachrach's heavy arm went around his shoulder. "You've just become a pro!"

"What!"

"I can't handle you any longer now that you're a married man. You need some income. So you're getting $500 a week from B.V.D. Swim Suits. The contract you just signed is good for five years. You will act as a representative of their product. Go places. Give shows. Talk on the radio. Sign autographs and hand out pictures of the most modern bathing suit on the whole blasted market. You're a made man!"

Johnny went into a light case of shell shock. He remained speechless, unable to digest his new position in life. It had come too suddenly!

He was still experiencing the same sensation by the time Bobbe quit her night club work and returned with him to Chicago where a farewell dinner had been planned in Johnny's honor. The keynote speaker of the evening was C. F. Biggert, president of the Illinois Athletic Club, where the testimonial affair was being held. He called Johnny the greatest "champion of champions" and thanked him and his coach, William Bachrach, for the prestige and glory they had earned for the club, spreading its fame around the world.

The new chairman of the athletic committee, George T. Donoghue, declared he felt he was inheriting a deficit with

Johnny walking out. However, he complimented him and his advisor on their wisdom in taking the step at a time while Johnny was still young, with a chance to carve out a career for himself in business.

Frank W. Blankley, chairman of the bath committee, among other matters, read a resolution from the board of directors, in appreciation of Johnny's services to the club and wishing him the best of good fortune.

W. Gibbons Uffendell, retiring chairman of the athletic committee, said he wished he could trade places with Johnny. He told how Johnny, a gangling, unsophisticated youth, had come to the club more than eight years ago, and pointed out that today he displayed physical development comparable to that of the gods of mythology, and a simple sincerity and personal charm that had won him a host of friends wherever he went. On behalf of the athletic committee, Mr. Uffendell presented Johnny with a handsome, engraved, gold watch.

John Banghart, president of the Otters, eulogized Johnny in glowing terms and handed him, on behalf of the Otters, a substantial check.

Andrew McNally told how Johnny, in spite of the avalanche of flattery that had descended upon him, had remained modest and unspoiled. Many had had their heads turned by an infinitesimal fraction of the adulation that had poured upon him, but Johnny, from the first day to the last, had never "high-hatted" anybody, said McNally. He had always conducted himself as a gentleman, ever the good fellow in the highest meaning of that term. And he complimented Johnny upon his discipline, his strict obedience, even to the most casually expressed advice of his coach.

With that fanfare of praise and best wishes, Johnny left behind him a hall filled with trophies of all shapes and sizes, but he took with him friendship and admiration for his fellow athletes and for the one man who had been responsible for his success, Big Bill Bachrach, whom Johnny held dearer than most, throughout the years to come.

The coach was too overwrought with emotion to say much when they parted. He just hugged his boy, brought out a huge handkerchief and blew his nose. "Darn cold!" he sniffled. "Guess I'm getting old — never had one before."

"You'll find and develop another champion. You always have!" Johnny tried to cheer him up.

For a long moment Bachrach's gaze fixed on Johnny. Then he said quietly, sincerely, and with absolute finality, "For me, there will never be another Weissmuller!" And now, unabashed by mutual sentiment, the pupil and his master embraced each other, and tears ran down their cheeks. A second later, Bachrach pushed his protégé away, "Eureka! Eldorado! Get lost, will you . . ." And Johnny, as ever, obeyed the command.

He made his exit like a sleepwalker, unable to comprehend the immensity, the magnitude of the change, groping his way onto the sidewalk. The night was foggy. The mist, composed of minute globules of water in the air, settled on his face like an invisible net, a film of moisture that freshened his skin as he slowly walked the familiar street.

Suddenly he felt as if a curtain had been drawn from his mind, giving way to thoughts he had never reflected upon before this moment. And he began to ponder about the future, but found that all he knew about life lay in the past.

He remembered so well the anxieties of his boyhood, from the moment frank appraisal of his early environment had set in to the time he had first performed for Bachrach. All he knew was swimming, swimming, swimming . . . and being coached. He was an athletic specialist. He had been trained to better himself in the sport, and pushed onward from victory to victory, like the gladiator of old, who didn't dare think of defeat. His main worry had been to compete successfully in yet another meet . . . and then another. He had had very little time to think of anything else, except perhaps Lorelei and Helen and, then, Bobbe. As a matter of fact, he had practically not thought at all, because Bachrach had always been there to guide him, advise and take care of his needs. Life had been carefree. And now, leaving the Illinois Athletic Club was almost comparable to walking out of a monastery, a sheltered existence, with no knowledge of what awaited him outside the sanctuary. "How many cycles does a life have?" he wondered. Did one always have to start anew from the beginning? What did he know about swim suits, his thoughts continued. He had worn them, ripped them. How many did he wear out, anyway? And how often? What kind of material did they use and why did the seams always fall apart? Now, he would be selling them, if not directly over the counter, at least in advertising and promotion, and what did he know about that?

"I will be a barker in a carnival. I used to perform inside the tent, in the center ring; now I shall remain outside, shouting, peddling my wares."

He had worn his laurels lightly, now he felt their weight on his brow. In the wake of shattered records he left behind, he had always been kept away from the masses. How would he be able to cope with them now? He liked people, but he had had no true contact with them; he had heard their cheers, but a crowd remained faceless. His friends and the select few he had truly known remained behind. "I shall miss my swimming buddies. Whom shall I see from here on but tailors at the B.V.D. factory! But I will be making lots of money . . ."

Money! He remembered when he had yearned for a quarter, when he had vowed to himself that he would get out of the neighborhood he lived in, but he had not really meant to move, just to get away from the gangs and ignorance, the insignificance which had surrounded him. Once he had joined the I.A.C., his prospects had altered. He had become a somebody in a world of nobodies. But he was still Johnny Weissmuller, the champion swimmer! Going into business would never change that!

Yet, where and when would he do his future training? And for what? After his contract with B.V.D. Swim Suits expired, what would happen then? Would he be too far removed from swimming? On the other hand, could he ever settle down to being an executive? He felt a strong doubt about the latter, knowing he was not cut out for such a job. He had spent too much time on the road, he still had sand in his shoes, and water was dearest to his heart. Could the possession of money make the difference? Could he save enough in five years to do afterwards whatever he wanted, or had decided to undertake by then? Possibly he would find a way and a career, he consoled himself quickly. After all, he had made his way against adversity before . . . and had become a champion; surely he had had guidance, but he alone had swum the winning race.

And then he thought of his wife. Bobbe was entering a new life, too. She had been a professional singer. Her career must have meant something to her, and she was giving it up to follow him on the road, to wherever it led. He had to make adjustments, but so did she. Could she depart the footlights without ever regretting her move to become merely a housewife, with its traditional anonymity? Besides, did not Lorelei once object to the identical problems that now faced Bobbe! His new business would still present a lot of traveling. Even if money permitted a home of their own, he would spend most of his time away from it. Had his marriage really been an immature decision? Had his mind truly been clouded, or had it been that he had lacked forethought? Probably! But then ---

The confidence that was part of his nature took over; the optimism that illuminated his entire outlook won out. As quickly as the curtain had lifted, it fell, leaving but a positive feeling that something good would work on his behalf. Time would tell; it would take its toll but he would finish the winner. And then, there was always Bachrach to turn to!

Suddenly he became aware of the lateness of the hour and that the train to Piqua, Ohio, where the B:V.D. factory was located, was scheduled to leave Chicago before dawn. There was still some packing to do, and Bobbe was waiting for him at his Cleveland Avenue home. He charted his course in that direction.

"I baked you some apple strudel for the journey." Mother Elizabeth finished packing a small parcel which she handed to her son. "Lass' es Dir gut schmecken!"

"Your baking always tastes good, Mama!" And Johnny embraced his mother. "We're saying good-bye again. But this time I'll be able to send you money and when we have a home, you and Peter will come and live with us."

"Don't worry about us, Johnny. We are fine. I like my work. I like Chicago. It is my home. I am happy here. Think of yourself, your own life, and your wife. God bless you, my son!"

Johnny took Bobbe's arm and ushered her to the waiting cab. "Bye, Mother! See you soon!" He waved as long as he could see her small figure by the garden gate.

The taxi stopped for a red traffic signal, and Bobbe opened the window and called to a newsboy to bring her a paper. She handed it to Johnny. "Something to read on the train."

He opened it and casually leafed through its pages; suddenly his eyes grew wide and focused on a news photo. He gasped.

"What is it, Johnny?"

Johnny looked at the picture, holding it nearer, then farther, and closer again.

"What's wrong with your eyes?" asked Bobbe, taking the paper and studying the photo. "Why are you concerned with Al Capone's son and his bodyguard?"

The photograph revealed a dark-eyed youngster and a man wearing a trench coat and a hat pulled down over his ears. A pair of dark glasses rested on the bridge of his nose.

Johnny stared at the picture. "Nothing," he answered after a while, "but they sure look familiar! Like a kid . . . I taught to swim in Miami . . . and a creep who always hung around the pool . . ."

"Silly!" Bobbe said, and folded the paper. "How long do you think we'll stay in Piqua?"

Johnny did not answer again. He thought about a gold buckle with many sparkling stones, and wondered — just wondered! As it happened, he never saw it again. The next time he recalled the incident, six months had elapsed and, despite his having the money to redeem it, the pawnbroker refused to part with his prized, and now-legal, possession.

Thus ended Johnny's amateur career as a sprint swimmer. The same year he wrote a book in collaboration with Clarence A. Bush, entitled "Swimming The American Crawl." In it he gave instructions to swim aspirants, dedicating it "To WILLIAM BACHRACH My Coach and to the Members of the Illinois Athletic Club." His final statement on the last page read:

"Anyhow, I've certainly had a great time swimming, and if I had my boyhood days to live over again, I can't imagine anything more interesting to do than just what I've done."

And Johnny, who had never lost a race in the water, entered a new kind of competition, a race through life as lived on land.

PART TWO

AND LEO THE LION ROARED

10

T HE DOORS to Johnny's professional life swung open. He
entered, and saw . . .

The motion picture industry prospered with the talkies.
Radio had woven a pattern of ideas designed to coax an
ever faster-moving population along its daily routes as elec-
tromagnetic waves filled the aether. Society in sundry com-
munities flourished with the times. A cross-section of printed
news items, gossip, fashion, advertisements still further developed or retrograded American morale and mentality. The
world was at peace, and traveling stylish.

Italy tempted tourists with "Variety Is the Spice of Rest."
Hawaii's legends gripped the imagination with the sagas of
the South Seas, aglow with the eerie light of crackling koa
logs, pounding pulses of great gourd drums and ominous
chants of crouching warrior bands. Marking a new climax
in transatlantic nights, public relations employees dreamed
up slogans like "O, the monkeys have no tails in Zamboanga!"
Clothing stores announced the etiquette of riding clothes.
Pink coats, for example, were supposed to be a superstitious
relic of Druid priests and it was as bad form for a woman to
wear white breeches as it was for her to eat with a knife . . .

Aldous Huxley wrote an article that was published in Vanity Fair, titled "Sermons for Cats," in which he found that man and woman are often reflected in the habits of a tomcat and his bride . . . Another writer thought that one of the most beautiful duels in literature was to be found in Balzac's "The Wild-Ass's Skin" . . . A third suggested that to commit murder for insurance money, or for mere pleasure, one had to make it wholesale, and never stop at only one.

That noisy innovation, the airplane, was, at best, a grossly mechanical means of travel — powerful, loud, hurried and smoky. But now, with no artificial power whatsoever, man was invited to soar across mountains and valleys in a glider costing anything between $375 to $1,500. Dr. Mehemed Fehmy Agha was the young Russian whose artistic direction of the Dorland Agency in Europe was responsible, in part at least, for the revolution in modern commercial art. A self-appointed authority on love and marriage problems answered the question whether a girl was necessarily and forever damned because she had taken one false step with a straight "yes!" For doggy razzle-dazzle, someone suggested the Cascade in Berlin, a recent bloom whose spot of a dance floor was pack-jammed and whose band (complete with megaphones) served Yankee and German jazz. A medically inclined detective concerned himself with the congealing of the post-anterior muscles in the axillary fold of the vivarium and that it was very typical . . . In bridge, a series demonstrated the greater opportunities for errors in bidding against those in play . . . A trial lawyer showed that a woman could murder whom she chose if she followed certain wise procedures . . . And someone received a telegram that read, "Out of the question, dear. So sorry you must stall."

Readers wrote and harassed magazine editors to the point of frustration with questions like: "I should also like to know whether it is more correct to have this opening laced as closely as possible, forming a parallel line, or whether it is considered de plus rigueur to have a considerable open space at the top, forming a V-effect down the front of the shoe!" To which part of the answer suggested that perhaps, in such a dilemma, it was safest to use a zipper! The dernier cri, and pictures of HER (who?) appeared in nearly every issue . . . HE (who?) left his post because of the greater urge of the movies and . . . But of late years HE (who?) had forsaken his peaceful and meditative occupation and devoted himself solely to books about strange crimes . . . HER (who?) legs were too beautiful, she told them, and casting directors would not look at her face . . . And someone wrote, "I like sports, and I like to read about them, but the sports writers of today are dreary creatures at best!" . . . A woman objected to a very offensive article — "Marriage for Profit!" Pro and con arguments arose as to why it was discreditable, under the age of thirty, not to be shy? And congratulations went to New Jersey for bringing in the largest flock of cuckoos that had been their good fortune to gather together in years . . . Whereas, for the past many months one had lived a good deal in Europe, one naturally swore that everybody, for instance, knew that Maillol and Despiau were sculptors of the very first order! A car traveled faster because of the Ethyl anti-knock compound it contained . . . And B.V.D. Swim Suits ran their stripes in a daring opposite direction, not in the conventional horizontal, but in vertical lines. All this, with a hearty laugh, a passionate fondness for tennis and Americana, formed the outer crust of civilization during the era when Johnny ventured forth to challenge the business world.

One of Johnny's first assignments took him from Piqua to New York City where, boosting sales with his personal appearances, he accidentally ran into John Harkrider, a former costume consultant and designer for Florenz Ziegfeld. Harkrider told him about a movie that was being made by Paramount called "Glorifying the American Girl" and starring Mary Eaton. The motion picture happened to include a colossal production number, a cavalcade of great lovers through the ages starting with Adam and Eve, which he, Harkrider, would put on as the grand finale.

"You are my Adam!" he enthusiastically exclaimed, and practically guaranteed the job. "What do you have to lose?"

"Just the fig leaf!" Johnny remarked drily, with a smirk in his eye.

And he almost did! Holding Eve in his strong arms, he stood atop an elevated man-made globe, as a tremor suddenly shook its stable, anchored foundation, and the Garden of Eden began to rock, dangerously. No one ever discovered the cause for this upset; moreover, it happened on the east and not the west coast, where an earthquake might have been responsible. And, in those days, no jets broke through sound barriers. Be that as it may — Johnny's feet hugged the very platform he was stationed on; at the same time, he valiantly supported a nervous Eve crushed against his broad chest despite her frantic efforts to place her kicking feet onto safer ground. Alas! Her restless feet . . . But the leaf withstood all and survived.

However, more was to follow. Johnny's first encounter with the silver screen seemed totally jinxed when B.V.D. executives learned about their contractee's brush with filmland. How could Johnny's portrayal of Adam benefit their swim suits, they asked, when all nature lovers would henceforward drop decent bathing attire in favor of a shame-inspired fig leaf at most. They threatened legal intervention and the issue became such a nuisance to the studio that the scene was almost dropped on the cutting room floor. Most likely in the end, it remained in the film even though Johnny never saw the picture and never verified the fact. Nonetheless, his name was erased from the credits and a long shot revealed little of his charms.

His second appearance on the screen occurred with the blessing of B.V.D., in a sports short which Grantland Rice produced in slow motion, then a novelty medium. He swam, giving a dutiful display of his sponsor's product, showing water lovers that without the daring vertical stripes of the B.V.D., no human fish could exhibit true elegance.

The stock market crash passed Johnny by with little effect upon his life. His company sent him on a prolonged trek across country. Everywhere he visited department stores, gave swimming lessons to prospective customers' children, signed autographs on stills in which he was pictured wearing the mentionable unmentionables. The store accounts soon transferred him to the West Coast, Los Angeles, and business at the Broadway and May Companies. He and Bobbe checked into the La Leyenda Apartment

Hotel on Whitley Street between Highland and Vine. Thrifty with Johnny's earnings, they chose a single room with an in-a-door bed and a small kitchen.

Auld Lang Syne had been sung in the land, and the Thirties saw many a future name staying at the La Leyenda. Bing Crosby and Bill Frawley, among others. Johnny's urge to swim led him to the Hollywood Athletic Club on Sunset Boulevard in search of a proper training pool. This club catered to the physical fitness of celebrities who went there to lose that little bit of extra poundage that looked unpalatable when enlarged a ten-fold on the magic screen. Moreover, the celluloid stereotype image of wide shoulders and narrow hips, flat bellies and mammoth chests had set an example of glamour to millions of moviegoers throughout the world.

Usually, Johnny took Bobbe with him to the athletic club. She liked what swimming had done for her legs, and claimed that her gams had vastly improved since she had become a devotee of the sport, and serious about its master. "Swimming has stretched my muscles, made them pliable. I've become a long-legged gal. Beautiful!" she beamed.

The way to the pool took them through the gym where they walked past many narrow-shouldered, broad-hipped, dumbbell-lifting individuals who were hardly the heartthrobs of movieland, yet who filled some specific capacity within the giant industry itself. Naturally, Johnny's trained, fit-looking body fell subject to envious glances, much to the amusement of the young couple. Sometimes, Johnny went forth alone while Bobbe preferred to go shopping. This was one of these days.

Cyril Hume worked out at the club. Enjoying a station among the highest paid writers in Hollywood, he had been assigned the first screenplay about Edgar Rice Burroughs' hero of the jungle, the script of "Tarzan, the Ape Man." Sol Lesser, who owned the rights to the Tarzan movies, had given MGM permission to go into production, this for a considerable return. When Hume saw Johnny sauntering past, he was immediately thrown by his wrestling instructor. Lying flat on his back, he groaned, "Who's that?"

"Weissmuller, the world's champion. He comes to swim here." The tutor grabbed the writer in a hammer lock. The latter winced. "Stop it! I must meet him — ouch!"

"Okay — Okay!"

Minutes later Cyril Hume confronted Johnny at the pool. "How would you like to test for Metro?" He asked.

"Test for what? My swimming days are over; I've become a pro."

Hume explained. A role. A movie role, that of Tarzan the ape man. Johnny glared at him in disbelief.

"Me? — Tarzan?" The famous words were born.

Hume told him how they had tested close to a hundred. He invited Johnny to have lunch with him at the studio's commissary, where he could meet some of the stars.

"That's for me," Johnny said. "Will Jean Harlow be around?"

She was. So was Joan Crawford, Norma Shearer, Gable, Wallace Beery, Marie Dressler, Jackie Cooper, and Garbo! He saw them all and said "Hello!" After lunch was over, Cyril Hume told Johnny he wanted to introduce him to Bernard Hyman, the producer of the film, and Director "Woody"

139

Van Dyke of "Trader Horn" fame. He ushered him to one of the executive bungalows.

Mr. Hyman sat behind an impressive over-sized desk cluttered with absolutely nothing except a Daily Variety and the Hollywood Reporter, which his secretary had earlier marked, circling certain items in red. Hyman yawned.

Motion picture producers belonged to a long line of inquisitive, hard-working, soft-living, disarming, and some-times charming "Mr. Know-Alls" who kept their livers intact because they preserved them in alcohol, their hearts because they had children, and their minds because they always found someone to blame for sundry personal mistakes. Of course they had ulcers! Perhaps because God, at times, in-terfered. Or the head of the studio?

"Are you bowlegged?" Hyman asked Johnny, and swal-lowed a pill, an answer to Alka-Seltzer in the thirties.

"No!" Johnny answered, perplexed.

"Take off your shirt."

"What do you mean?"

"Van Dyke — tell the guy what I mean."

Van Dyke turned to Johnny. He explained in so many words that he had to strip for the simple reason that this was a make-believe industry, muscles that showed through material often were phony, broad shoulders padded, and even a person's skin could reveal an ailing body, especially when it belonged to someone who was, unfortunately, a Hollywood nobody. He then leaned closer and whispered that he knew this was not Johnny's case history, for Hume had told him what a perfect specimen he confronted. How-ever, it seemed best under the circumstances to yield respect

140

Tarzan fights the horrible Zumangani for his life in the Pit of Death. (Johnny Weissmuller in TARZAN, THE APE MAN.)

Jungle Lovers. (MGM photo by Hurrell)

Alike the Garden of Eden. (MGM photo)

The safari party (Benita Hume, William Henry, Herbert Mundin, John Buckler, Darby Jones and others) watch Tarzan swing off into the trees as Jane (Maureen O'Sullivan) smiles consent. (MGM photo)

Emma, the elevator operator. (MGM photo)   *Tarzan and Boy. (MGM photo)*

"Ungawa, Jackie!" (MGM photo by Clarence S. Bull)

"White men with guns no good — Tarzan take guns away, break them." (Philip Dorn, Tom Conway and the Jungle Trio) (MGM photo)

family portrait (Johnny, ureen O'Sullivan, John effield and Cheetah.) GM photo)

No freeways in the sky. (MGM photo)

Johnny gives lessons in physical fitness to (l. to r.) John Sheffield, Cordell Hickman and Gouley Green. (MGM photo)

Hollywood chartered his course.

On the Allure.

Johnny and Lupe returning from Europe after an encounter with a Queen.

"Spanky," pet of OUR GANG, meets Johnny. (MGM photo)

Tennis Lessons . . . Harvey Snodgrass (right) gives Johnny and Jackie Cooper some pointers. (MGM photo by Wm. Grimes)

The race is on for Wallace Beery, Joe E. Brown, Johnny and Mickey Rooney.

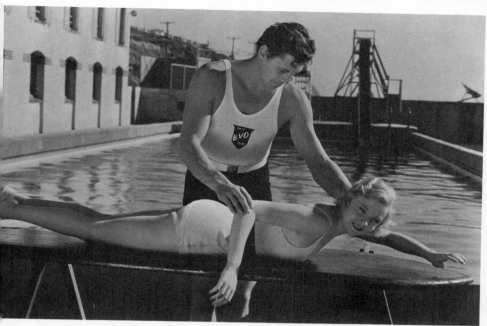

Measuring a surfboard on Una Merkel, Johnny displays his B.V.D.'s. (Photo by Clarence Sinclair Bull)

Johnny receives his badge as a lifeguard at Santa Monica beach, Calif., and is congratulated by Captain George Watkins of the lifeguard force, and Chief of Police Clarence Webb.

Renewing acquaintance, Marie Dressler meets Johnny again after their paths crossed in Amsterdam. With her is director Clarence Brown. (MGM Photo.)

Tarzan and Jane menaced by savage Gabonis in a thrilling moment of TARZAN ESCAPES. (MGM photo)

Grand Army of the Republic. (MGM photo)

" Tarzan love Jane!" (Maureen O'Sullivan) (MGM photo)

"Tarzan love Jane!" (Brenda Joyce) — Copyright, 1950, RKO Radio Pictures, Inc. — Courtesy of Sol Lesser.)

Johnny, the dramatic actor . . . (MGM photo)

Mother Elizabeth approves of Johnny's playmate. (MGM photo)

and display understanding. Cyril Hume, meanwhile, had seated himself into a spacious leather chair and had lit a cigarette. The writer had long since conducted his wrestling from behind a typewriter or within his instructor's powerful grip. Both, he calculated, in relative safety.

Johnny stripped to the waist and bared his muscular upper half to critical appraisal. A silence fell that lasted for several long moments.

"What's your name, son?" Hyman finally asked.

Johnny wondered how quickly "the guy" had gained the title of "son," but he uttered the syllables of his name with clarity, a most articulate manner as taught him at Saint Michael's School by several distinguished brethren.

"Wait a minute—" Hyman swallowed another alkalizer. "Come again?!"

"John-ny Weiss-mul-ler."

"Terrible!" The voice behind the desk announced. "Much too long for a marquee. Find a short, exotic name."

Now Van Dyke spoke up. "Mr. Hyman, do you know who this is?"

"A hunk of flesh with a fine torso!"

"Barney, good God, Weissmuller's the world's swimming champ; he's won laurels everywhere including the Olympics."

"He hasn't been written up in Variety! Really, 'Woody,' you know I never look at sports pages."

"Pity," — Van Dyke thought and forgot at once. Cyril Hume had found his cue. "Will you agree to test him?" he inquired politely, getting to his feet.

"Well . . ." Bernard Hyman considered, eying the threesome. "Go ahead." The authorization was tempered with gall, "one more or less doesn't really matter." He buried his face in his hands, and became engrossed in an open trade paper, a sign meaning dismissal to his subjects.

Rumors, the forerunners of success or failure, spread across the studio lot where Leo, the lion, roared. That swimmer, what's-his-name? was going to win the part coveted by everyone. Why? No one apparently knew, except that he had never lost a race in whatever(?)sport. The gossip filtered far from Culver City to the heart of Hollywood, the La Leyenda Apartments, and into the ears of Bobbe. The words carried an ominous message, a forewarning of doom to their young marriage. Metro-Goldwyn-Mayer had never made a habit of blessing a matrimony which bridled one of its future stars with permanent love. Once the leading forces within its complex core had picked a newcomer for grooming as a potential moneymaker, the system that existed within the hallowed walls of sound stages managed to freeze affairs of the heart to an extent where they wound up at the bottom of a cooler, well-pitted in ice. Blissfulness such as came with children, the fruit of normal living, was denied a select few who were acceptable as white mice to be placed onto the ever spinning wheel of fame and fortune. A most formidable objection considering the values involved, gained, yet burned at a common stake which bound naive believers with ignoble mercenaries, and where they unwittingly shared an identical fate at the instant the pole was driven into the ground by an amusement-lusty public.

Bobbe did not want to stand in the way of Johnny's career. Yet she did not want a divorce. She hurried to a

142

spokesman of the inquisition and begged him to intervene.

"Help me!" she pleaded. "Let him fail this test. Let him escape Hollywood. Give him back to me. Please!"

The executive looked at the blond girl with the blue eyes, but whatever his decision his thoughts remained well-hidden behind his smiling, mystic mask. He sent her away with regrets and a pat on the cheek. His conscience was pure. He knew that his voice carried little value in present production procedures.

Johnny passed the screen test. He was offered a seven-year optional contract with a starting salary of $175 per week. In the same breath in which he expressed his amazement, he refused to accept the bargain. MGM's lion roared so loudly that Culver City trembled and shook. Johnny immediately became a challenge to the higher echelon.

"Why? Why? Why?" They implored, argued, reasoned.

"Simple. B.V.D. pays me $500 without six-month option periods, and for more than four years to come. Supposing I'll make this picture and the public will throw some rotten eggs at the screen . . . I'll be washed up! Maybe I'd better play it safe and turn this down."

"Get Weissmuller!" The word went out. "Get him!" All of a sudden he had become a prize property. The cork had blown off bottled-up emotions. Leg-men were sent to wear out their shoes. They even remembered his kilometers-long name. Finally they met his price. Johnny liked the idea of becoming a movie star just as long as the money was good. He approached B.V.D. Swim Suits.

Their answer was a plain "No!"

Metro-Goldwyn-Mayer's lawyers tackled B.V.D. . .

Their answer was "No!"

The lion roared louder, and in desperation. They negotiated again. And wrote again . . .

The deal was closed! In return for Johnny's freedom, Metro permitted all the contract players of said studio to pose, and be photographed, in said B.V.D. swim suits, including stars like Garbo, Crawford, Harlow, even Dressler! Johnny received his release to mix his blood with the lion's; his signature was affixed on a piece of printed paper that tied him down for seven years for a salary that began with $500, with raises upping it to $2,000 and more within the given period. At the same time, he stood to lose everything if his contract was not picked up after one or any option expired, because this clause was a security the studio never omitted to include at the expense of their players' security. But Johnny stood to lose more ---

"Get rid of your wife!" the studio said. Leo had gone to sleep now, once his prey had been captured and was being held. He was a well-fed lion and hardly suffering from hunger pangs. He could wait.

"I love her." Johnny fought the edict.

"Do you want to stand in the way of his career?" the studio asked her, as Leo snored on.

"I love him!" Bobbe struggled against the verdict.

"Get rid of her!" they repeated to him.

"Give him a chance!" they told her again.

After much poignant suffering, many quarrels that sprung from a thousand needles stuck into the doll-lovers by the star-making machine, Bobbe quietly packed her bags.

"I'll go back and visit mother. I've still got a voice,

Johnny. I guess we both have careers; sooner or later they'll get the best of us. Besides," she said, and smiled ruefully, "Metro gave me $10,000 — it is a lot of money!"

"Yeah!" Johnny said, carried her bags from the little room at the La Leyenda to the waiting taxi, walked to the corner of Hollywood Boulevard, and watched her cab disappear among the bright lights in the direction of Downtown, Union Station, divorce and oblivion.

OF VINES AND CHEETAHS

11

"**I** WAS RIGHT!" Douglas Fairbanks Sr. said, "Remember the conversation I once had with Sol Lesser? I told him Tarzan should be played by a newcomer and suggested you."

"You turned out a good prophet!" Johnny's white teeth flashed in a smile. His hair hung over his ears in straggly waves, he leaned against a tree trunk, his bared, bronze-skinned body clad in a mere loincloth that tied below his waist. His hand rested on the hilt of a Bowie-type knife, its blade hidden within a leather sheath. He looked the very image of his role.

The new Tarzan and his visitor stood in a wilderness of hanging vines, tropical plants entwined with exotic blooms framed against a backdrop of a sunless canvas sky. The enormous arc lights were turned off, the cameras left idle, the sound equipment silent. The crew had not yet returned from their lunch break. Moments later, as if a magic wand had passed over the scenery, the set came alive with activity. People began filing in through the two entrances of the sound stage: mixers, grips, assistant cameramen, boom operators, cable and propmen, the second assistant director, a wrangler.

146

"Time to check your make-up, Mr. Weissmuller."

The old-time acquaintances shook hands and Douglas departed but not before he extended his usual invitation, "Pickfair is always open, Johnny; drop in any time." Pickfair! Guarded by gates that seldom opened except to admit the few. "Tarzan" made his way to his portable dressing room where the beauticians of the trade went to work on his hair, body and face make-up, and a shapely first-aid attendant renewed a small bandage on his hand, a scratch he had received swinging through the trees and which, after the operation was completed, was rendered invisible to the camera's eye with more dark liquid make-up.

Johnny did not mind all the fuss and stir that went hand in hand with his brand new career. On the contrary, he rather enjoyed it. Except for his hair! He had never forgotten how he lost his first preliminary tryout on account of long tresses and, whereas he still shortened it in front, it managed to blot out his vision when submerged in underwater stunts within the studio's glass-windowed tank. MGM had insisted, and stipulated in the contract, that his hair had to be grown past ear length, and had to remain uncut as long as he was employed by the studio.

On the set the arc lights were turned on and a stand-in was going through the motions of the first set-up, tracing his steps in the identical route Johnny would later take during the shot. Prolonged exposure to these lights could impair one's vision, resulting in klieg eyes, also Johnny's skin too frequently suffered from extensive burns. In later years these beams of high actinic power were replaced as the science of electronics advanced.

He thought about his next scene where he had to run through the jungle, followed by Cheetah, and jump onto the elephant's back. He liked the contact with beasts. All his life he had been fond of domestic animals. He had learned how to ride bareback at the old Armory in Chicago, where he had volunteered to exercise the horses. He had loved Hans, his Dachshund, although Hans hardly embodied the call of the wild. Back in Chicago, too, he had visited the zoo and stood in front of the cages for hours, fascinated, staring at lions, tigers, bears, panthers, and laughing at pranks the monkeys played. He had especially been enthralled with the big cats, with their easy relaxation as they prowled about, each muscle rippling and visible beneath their silken hides. Whenever possible he had awaited their feeding time, listened to their growling as they watched the trainer prepare the food. When it was handed in to them, he saw it devoured in a few short seconds. Sometimes the trainer had let himself into the cage to pet a lion or bear; Johnny had wished to be in his shoes.

A golden-maned lion named Jackie was brought to work in the Tarzan film. Jackie was one of the biggest, most powerful beasts Johnny had ever encountered in captivity, with large, strong, polished white teeth that certified no need for a dentist's chair. Johnny observed the trainer closely as he led Jackie onto the set, holding him on a leash attached to a regular dog collar strapped around his neck.

An athlete develops a sixth sense in many ways, but Johnny in addition understood animals. Unafraid of the lion's mighty looks he walked to his side and placed his hand on the beast's skull. Jackie's head tilted, his impressive mane brushed against Johnny as his nostrils drew in the human's smell.

"Be careful!" The trainer warned. "He isn't used to you yet."

Johnny petted the lion. "Hello, there, Jackie!" he said. "Don't lose your nerve with Tarzan."

The cat's rasp tongue began licking the man's arm, it seemed to like the taste of liquid make-up. From that moment on he slobbered his affection constantly all over Johnny, heading to his side the first thing in the morning and greeting him with a "schmaltzig" lick. Finally, Johnny had to push the lion away; his skin was beginning to suffer from too much sandpaper-tongue love.

When he met Emma, the elephant, he had fed her peanuts and an occasional apple. By now, he knew her so well he could instantaneously pick her from an entire herd. He played with her, taught her all sorts of tricks, even to lift him up with her trunk.

Of course, Cheetah the chimpanzee remained the undeniable star of the animal thesps, and knew it! He also presented the most difficult problem during filming. Parading up and down the stage making a monkey out of himself in the truest sense of the word, Cheetah became bored with rehearsals, lights, and the entire caboodle; so he began scratching himself, shifting his fanny from one foot to the other until, suddenly, he soared up into the rafters, scaring the workers atop the scaffolds half out of their wits and, hanging onto the highest beam, swinging and voicing "uh! uh! uh!", he began throwing whatever happened to be in reach at the screaming assistant directors below.

"Get that ape down!"

"The chimp's gone berserk!"

"Cheetah! Pretty boy, come down to dad-da! Come down you son of a --------- gorilla!"

Bang! — exploded a light bulb next to the trainer's feet. Crash! — went a screen crowning an innocent by-stander. Rip! — tore the sky backdrop.

"Uh! uh! uh! uh! uh!" sounded the triumphant cry of Cheetah, the star of hairy apes.

"Shoot him down! Shoot him down!" hollered the distraught director.

"You can't! The chimp's worth a mint!" pleaded the distressed trainer.

Someone produced a B-B gun, took aim and fired it in rapid succession. "Uh-uh-uh-uh-uh-uh!" came the wail from above. A surprised, deeply remorseful Cheetah descended from the upper spheres to pick B-B's out of his lower ones until the sky had been patched up, the lights replaced, and "action!" called. For a while now Cheetah behaved, dutifully climbed trees, jumped onto Emma's back, kissed Tarzan's cheek, and performed all the stunts his ancestors had once upon a time taught his distant relatives, who had just made a sporting target out of his tender regions. But only just long enough till all was forgiven and forgotten; the moment he felt secure he went on another rampage!

What Johnny learned about chimps was that these little rascals were more dangerous than the most ferocious of jungle dwellers. They grew rapidly, and some exceeded a small human's height. Young ones were cute and relatively harmless, but the older they grew the more vicious they became. Their long arms were strong enough to break a man's limb in one powerful grip. And their teeth itched to bite anyone who happened to attract them unfavorably. Animal trainers generally worked with several look-alikes, never keeping the apes professional for more than five or six years. By that time they became increasingly hard to handle and greatly perilous toward people. During Johnny's picture career he worked with some eight different chimps.

When Johnny first met Cheetah I, the ape bared his teeth, his sly eyes searching for a sign of weakness or fear in the man. Johnny took his hunting knife from its holster, held it close to the chimp's nose so that he recognized the object, then knocked it hard against the ape's skull. After replacing the weapon, he offered Cheetah his hand.

Momentarily, Cheetah glared at him in anger, then the inscrutable grin returned to his versatile puss and he puckered his lips, grabbed Johnny's outstretched fingers in a hearty shake. From this instant on a lasting friendship was born between the original Cheetah and "Tarzan" Johnny. Whenever the ape henceforth decided to play it rough, he always checked Johnny with a glance to see if the latter was watching, for if he was, he needed only to place his hand on the knife and Cheetah quickly withdrew into a corner, covering his eyes with both arms and showing a sheepish expression of shame. In the early Sixties, Cheetah I died in the Griffith Park Zoo in Los Angeles, an old, old pro whom Johnny visited almost monthly, receiving always a warm welcome from his jungle pal.

The script obviously presented no difficulties to Johnny who considered himself lucky in comparison with other actors who had, after a hard day's work at the studio, to go home to study their lines for tomorrow. "Ungawa!" — "Me Tarzan, you Jane — (or) — You Jane, me Tarzan!" — "Tarzan hungry, go home, eat!" — "Tarzan swim now." — "White man with guns no good!" (directions read: Tarzan takes guns away, breaks them across knee). — "Cheetah come!" . . . These were as plentiful monosyllables as he ever used with slight variations. "Too much talk twists Tarzan's tongue."

But it was THE YELL that meant Tarzan! The yell summoned elephants and scared unfriendly natives, sending a sensation down the spines of the rest of civilization. Director Van Dyke accidentally learned about this famous sound that escaped his star's throat during an early rehearsal when Johnny, swinging on a vine across the sound stage, let go the yodel he had developed and trained at his grandparents' farm. Seconds later the whole studio lot was buzzing with excitement. The call of the jungle had been born. After it had been safely recorded and stored away, Johnny did not have to strain his vocal cords to exhaustion but merely mouth the battle cry. Nevertheless, Johnny felt little strain and happily carried on regardlessly.

Van Dyke was a "he-man" director and knew how to handle actors and action (despite Cheetah!) and Johnny liked the solid, guiding touch of his authority. Bachrach had taught him the value of discipline and rules; he never failed to co-operate fully in everything required of him in his work and status. Whether the company spent a day shooting on the sound stage, at MGM's back lot jungle, or on location at Sherwood Lake and/or Forrest (the name given after Douglas Fairbanks Sr. filmed his version of "Robin Hood" at this particular spot), Johnny was ever punctual, easy to get along with, and kind. He was happy now! In a simple, unsophisticated fashion he had found in his screen career a place for himself that linked the present with his past. He swam as much as he liked, performed gymnastics, wrestled, ran; in his spare time he played tennis and golf; in short, he was able and had the time to follow all the sports that pleased him, giving him fun. His first movie would not reach the market for a long while, but fans everywhere already familiarized themselves with the fact that their idol had made good in Hollywood; moreover, his own identity, that of a swimmer, became synonymous with the character he portrayed. Edgar Rice Burroughs spoke kindly to him and said he vastly preferred Johnny as his hero, despite his own son's ambitions, who had tested for the part and lost. He took Johnny under his wing, invited him to his home in Tarzana, in the San Fernando Valley, which had received its name through his writings, first published in 1914, and he told Johnny how he had once made a mistake in one of his stories, placing a tiger in Africa, instead of the natural habitat in Asia! Burroughs had never journeyed to the Dark Continent, making up his sagas from research and figments of his widespread imagination, similar to the tales of a popular German writer, Karl May, who had never left his homeland yet described the American West, as well as the chasms of the Balkans, with the utmost vision and authoritative reference.

Johnny's financial matters gave him no worry; he spent his money freely on friends, sending monthly allowances to his mother, who still preferred to remain in Chicago, at the Turn-Verein. Metro kept their human property further occupied by sending him, in his free time, to study singing and elocution with Mr. Morando, a famed voice coach who also supervised the vocal sounds of another great name, Nelson Eddy. Mr. Morando improved the quality of Johnny's voice by teaching him the proper use of the diaphragm, eventually lowering his voice. In running through the scales his natural gift of song ripened, his tenor voice acquired richness in modulation and, subconsciously, he dreamed about following a course that would lead him closer to the pleasures opera had given him in his youth. Just one single shadow occasionally fell on his happy-go-lucky disposition: when he woke at night, to find his bed empty of love and companionship. But he was too easy-going, too sunny-natured a fellow to begin a psychological search through his innermost being, or to clutter up his mind with imaginary ink blots or to sulk about the state of his romantic affairs.

The meaning of time as such had vanished from his agenda, had become nebulous. He lived from day to day, unconcerned about tomorrows, swinging on the vines that strung him to his career, in a city that knew no hourglass or rules of behaviour except to measure success versus failure or, worse, insignificance. All things beautiful blended into an illusionary Fata Morgana; only when the traveler grew weary, reaching out for the cool invitation of the oasis, did he find it a total mirage.

"Tarzan, the Ape Man" was the first speaking version of the series of movies which had started in the silents back in 1918, with "Tarzan of the Apes," in which Elmo Lincoln appeared. Lincoln pursued his Tarzan through two more encores, the last in 1920. The same year saw Kamuela Searles as the son of Tarzan, and Gene Polar as yet another copy. Frank Merrill fitted into two more. James H. Pierce made one picture called "Tarzan and the Golden Lion" (sans Jackie!). Then came Johnny Weissmuller! In between his films one read that various actors challenged his sovereignty, like Buster Crabbe, Herman Brix, Glenn Morris and later, Lex Barker; Gordon Scott and Jock Mahoney followed; but somehow critics the world over agreed that none ever matched Johnny in the role to which he brought his own brand of truth. Perhaps it was on account of this sincerety that he remained THE jungle prince, holding his throne time and weatherproof.

The story of Tarzan and Jane is as well known as the story of Adam and Eve, and not too far removed in its entirety. For, without seeming blasphemous, the first human couple lived in a garden which harbored a vast selection of animal species resembling the wilderness where Tarzan made his home. All the living creatures lived in spiritual accord with nature and each other, like children, pure, healthy and free of prejudice. But Eve succumbed to the forked tongue of the snake; and Jane listened to greedy strangers. Both temptations resulted in near disaster, more so for the biblical pair! However, the end of Tarzan and Jane was never really concluded by their creator. True, Tarzan's offspring remained only Boy, and single. Whereas Adam's sons founded a dynasty. But while Boy only killed for food and in self-defense, Cain murdered his brother, Abel! And there fiction got separated from life . . .

Petite, dark-haired Maureen O'Sullivan fitted into Johnny's arms to perfection the moment Tarzan rescued Jane from her first jungle hazard. And the millions of Edgar Rice Burroughs' fans accepted her at once. Everyone agreed they made perfect mates, and the co-stars received the studio's blessing for their on-screen bond of matrimony. In reality, Maureen was deeply in love with John Villiers Farrow, motion picture director and author, whom she married, bearing him seven children. Johnny admired Maureen's poise and ladylike manners, but never felt romantically inclined toward his leading lady; however, he considered her a wonderful trouper and a great sport.

When the feature was finally canned, it was previewed at a local cinema. Johnny became an overnight sensation. He traveled to New York for the grand première, where he checked into a hotel near Central Park which was owned by Marion Davies, and patronized by all Metro-Goldwyn-Mayer celebrities who stayed in town. As he registered at the desk, a vivacious little brunette caught a glimpse of him on her way to her suite. Before she entered the elevator, her Latin eyes once again flashed in his direction, measuring his broad back.

LUPE VELEZ

12

JOHNNY HAD finished unpacking his suitcase when the telephone rang. He lifted up the receiver.

"This is Lupe Velez," a soft, accented voice said. "I am on the floor below you, will you come down and have a drink with me?"

Johnny thought it was a gag. "So I'm the king of England!" he informed and hung up. A moment later it rang again. Over the wire came a torrent of Spanish. Then the phone went dead.

Johnny scratched his ear. He dialed the desk. "Is Lupe Velez staying at the hotel?" he inquired, and, receiving an affirmative reply, he asked to be connected with her suite. He felt rather sheepish when he heard her voice answer. "I'm sorry," he apologized. "You know how it is, someone is always pulling one's leg. Is the invitation still open?"

It was, and half an hour later found him in Lupe's presence. She served him pink champagne, and it was a new sensation. Johnny's drinking habits were as yet unimpaired, his only experience an occasional glass of light wine. The bubbles went into his nose and tickled his throat; he sneezed and his eyes began to water.

"Why are you crying?" Lupe wanted to know.

"I'm n-n-n-not c-c-c-crying!" Johnny managed to stammer between sneezes. "It's this bug juice you gave me to drink!"

"But Johnee — it's pink champagne. $20 a bottle!"

"Maybe that's reason for crying . . . I've never tasted it . . . hub-tshu!"

Lupe became convulsed with laughter, she laughed until she cried. Johnny cried too because of the champagne. They looked at each other's running eyes and burst into another fit of laughter. She threw herself on his lap, shrieking, "Johnee, you are the funniest man I have ever seen! You are a child!"

Hollywood's fiery little pepper pot, its snapping little fire cracker, its exploding little tamale Lupe (pronounced Loopie) Velez, nicknamed Whoopee Lupe, Mexican Wildcat, The Queen of Hot-Cha, The Mad Velez, was in actuality born Guadalupe Villalobos Velez, in San Luis Potosí, Mexico, on July 18, 1910. Her father was a colonel in the Mexican army, her mother an opera singer. She was educated in a Mexico City convent and later in San Antonio, Texas. Her convent schooling was designed by her parents to temper her Latin liveliness and calm her flaring hot disposition. But Lupe decided she had had enough of sheltered living and, at 15, got a job dancing in a musical stage revue in Mexico City. She was engaged because of her display of spirit and verve, more so than through her dancing ability, which was about average. Her parents forcefully removed her from there and sent her packing to San Antonio, where she lived at the convent and learned to speak English. Somehow, Lupe managed to keep in touch with the outer world and was strongly recommended to Richard Bennet for a role in "The Dove". She arrived in the film capital with high hopes that turned into a crushing disappointment the moment Bennett looked at her and found her too young and inexperienced. However, Lupe, once in Hollywood, was not going to quit that easily. She got herself a job at The Music Box Revue, and producers began to pay attention to the little Mexican spitfire. She made a series of comedies for Hal Roach at his studio in Culver City. Then came the big break through Douglas Fairbanks, Sr., who selected her from among countless other aspirants to portray the part of a wild mountain girl in his production of "The Gaucho." Stardom quickly followed.

Lupe stood five feet short, and weighed a cuddlesome 109 pounds, by no means considered skinny. Her hobbies included roller skating, bicycle riding, and she was a very handy boxer as well! In fact, everything she did was con mucho gusto! She was always accompanied by her two Chihuahua pets, Mr. Kelly and Mrs. Murphy as she called them, and even took them along on the bicycle to which she had attached a special little cage to hold her two dogs. She was constantly full of fun, mischief, keeping her production companies on the qui vive? level of awareness. Extremely popular with co-players, she was loved by the work crew.

Recently a shadow had fallen on the gay and happy little bombshell. Her much publicized romance with the tall cowboy, Gary Cooper, had come to an end and Lupe was left

159

heart-broken. Cooper's studio had seen disaster in their relationship and, with typical hardness against lovers, sent Gary caravaning to the plains of Africa and on an extended tour of Europe, where his name soon became linked with that of a countess, Dorothy Taylor di Frasso. L'affaire Velez-Cooper was fini! Lupe vowed she wanted to fall in love again, but only with a man of Gary's type. "He ees my type of man! I weel only love hees kind!" she tearfully promised through the press.

Then she saw the tall, dark-haired young man in her hotel lobby. Something struck that certain note within her strange, lovelorn heart. The moment she reached her suite she dialed Johnny Weissmuller.

Deep down in Johnny's heart he knew that Lupe carried a torch for Gary. He knew that he reminded her of Coop and that she had picked on him for that reason. He understood her loss . . . he also had suffered through his studio breaking up his marriage in similar fashion. Rather than stay at the hotel, he took Lupe out and together they explored the familiar and unknown regions of the big city. Pretty soon Lupe started to get serious, so did Johnny.

Lupe vehemently denied rumors of an existing romance. "I loved Gary", she said, "I am a woman who tells of her love for a man to the whole world. Johnee and I are friends; that ees all." They returned to California and pictures, and still gossip pursued their constant outings. "He comes to swim in my pool. I am always surrounded by my family when he is around. Sometimes he just walks past me and says, 'Hi, Lupe!', and jumps in the pool. I never see him because I must go somewhere else."

And Lupe did go somewhere else, she went to see Errol Flynn. Yet she always came back to Johnny. They made a stunning couple, this little five-foot brunette who fitted under the six-foot-four Johnny's armpit. Wherever they went their popularity followed them. As the days passed, Lupe's denials about romance grew more mellow and less evasive. "I like beeg guys!" she cooed. "And Johnee, my Popee, ees a beeg guy!"

Johnny told the press that he liked Lupe too. "She is so alive. We have lots of fun together."

When some patron at Ciro's night club in Hollywood tried to pick a fight with Johnny because of his long hair and partly on account of his lady-friend who had made eyes at the actor, it was Lupe who got to her feet, clenched her little fist and, without much ado, punched the troublemaker right smack on the nose. "Holy mackerel!" the stupefied victim exclaimed. "Tarzan has to hire some girl to do his fighting!" Lupe's tiny fist waved once again under his nose. "You beeg ape! You leave my man alone! Eef he ever pick on you, there will not be enough for minced pie!" Johnny hated to get into brawls; nonetheless, he inquired politely if the heckler cared to step outside and settle the issue. "No thanks!" the man quickly retorted, "I've had plenty from one of the family." He took his girl's arm and left in a hurry.

"Popee!" Lupe threw her arms around Johnny's neck. "He called us a family!"

Lupe's house in Beverly Hills was located on 732 N. Rodeo Drive, a two-story Spanish-style mansion, surrounded by picturesque landscaping. Entering the hall, a staircase led to the upper floor where her bedroom overlooked the garden with the swimming pool. At night, the moonlight shone through her window and the sickle of the moon found its reflection in the silver rim framing her round black bed where she rested until early afternoon hours, sleeping the sunlight away so she could enjoy all of Mme. Luna's soft moonbeams. Like a rare, tropical flower, Lupe unfolded her petals at night and, instead of morning coffee, dewdrops freshened her lips. Before she went to sleep, she knelt in front of her little shrine of the Holy Virgin, and begged forgiveness for anything she might have done wrong the day before. Then she retired, her mind at peace with God and the world. And in her dreams, the image of a tall man changed profiles from Cooper's to Johnny's and both melted together until she no longer could divide their blurred images. She called each by the other's name, smiling, turning over in her sleep. As the two merged in her subconscious mind, her feeling for love too became blended until she no longer doubted that it was Johnny she truly loved.

She sighed with contentment and, without knowing it, she had chosen her "beeg" husband.

ABOUT PROFILES

13

A WOODEN CRATE, twice the size of a large coffin, was delivered onto the "Tarzan and His Mate" set. The transportation team set it down and, after demanding a signature, departed. The brief exchange of business tickled Cheetah's curiosity. Tied to his trainer's chair, the ape gingerly opened the sailor's knot, and quietly, after stealing a look at Johnny's dressing room, hobbled in the direction of the mysterious arrival.

Cheetah pressed his ear against the wooden object and listened. All remained silent. The lid had been tightly secured and tied down. The chimp leaned closer and knocked on it. Suddenly, there came a hissing sound from its enclosure. Cheetah took a fast leap backwards, but in a moment approached the box again. On his second try, Cheetah knew how to handle the situation; the instant he knocked he jumped back and waited. The funny noise repeated itself again. Cheetah became excited. Forgetting caution he began to sound off and jump around, scratching himself.

A clean-shaven Johnny stood in the doorway of his dressing room, naked except for a turkish towel wrapped about his hips, and demanded decent covering. He could not get ready for the next take; someone had pinched his loincloth! A search brought others but none that fitted. While a great production marked time, the G-string was finally discovered in a locker amid chamois-skin window-cloth rags. A hopeful janitor had removed it as a souvenir for his teen-age daughter!

"What's the matter with Cheetah?" Johnny asked, when he appeared on the set. "I've never before seen him act that way." He soon discovered the box and learned of its content. He laughed. "Is it time yet?" He was informed that it was not. "Well, let's take a look anyway!"

With the help of a workman, Johnny untied the straps and unscrewed the top. Cheetah's nose being in the way, he finally managed to lift the lid.

A crocodile opened its teeth-laden jaws and emitted a sound such as comes only from crocodiles, period!

Cheetah forgot to call "uh-uh"; he jumped over Johnny's head, did a somersault in mid-air, and headed in the opposite direction as fast as his legs could carry him. Johnny burst into loud laughter. "Hey, Cheetah! Come back here, you yellow-bellied ape!" But the chimp took care not to return or knock on any sizeable crate from there onward. Whenever Cheetah had to perform in a scene with crocs it took twelve to fifteen takes anyhow, but he was certainly not going to place himself in jeopardy without cameras. Besides, were not chimps part of the natural prey of a jungle croc?

Crocodiles used in the Tarzan films were brought from an alligator farm on Los Angeles' outskirts. Some of these reptiles measured more than 15 feet. They were transported in crates holding three feet of water, and could hardly be described as amiable creatures, especially after such a trip. Nevertheless, Johnny wrestled the best of them. Such combats were dangerous in spite of all the safety measures taken by trainers and the studio's employees, and Johnny often walked away with a raw skin or wounds caused by the fierce underwater struggles. Naturally, no crocodile was ever killed in the stunts, for knife blades used in fight sequences slip back into handles, releasing a dozage of dark liquid which discolors the water like blood. They were well protected by the Humane Society, whereas Tarzan had to take care of his own protection, as well befits an ape man.

When Johnny encountered his first rhinoceros, he felt slightly uneasy until he rode one and found that when a rhino charges, it goes straight ahead. Rhinoceroses are near-sighted animals and slow in turns. As long as a man took care not to get in front, or side-stepped a moment before, the beast would harmlessly plunge along its merry, even way. Mounting was easy, but the sandpaper texture of the rhino's back caused skin irritations.

The strangest ride Johnny ever took in his entire life was atop an ostrich. And that one was truly for the birds! But coming back to alligators, Johnny remembered Bachrach's description of the San Blas Indians and how they supposedly outraced crocs. "I guess," he thought, "I've finally gotten into their league!"

Johnny always wore a brown terry cloth bathrobe when he visited the commissary for lunch; the color had been chosen to hide make-up stains. It has been accounted that he used a total of 50 gallons of liquid cosmetics plus 15 pounds of body grease in the swimming scenes, during his first film.

All eyes turned in his direction the moment Johnny entered the spacious dining area where the hostess quickly offered him priority and he was ushered to a window table at the far side of the room. Even actresses like Norma Shearer and Jean Harlow said that he was as sensational a hunk of man as they had ever seen. Sometimes, for publicity reasons, he took Cheetah along. Naturally he was constantly beseeched by autograph hounds despite MGM's strict rules not to admit outsiders. Studio tours were arranged daily with some getting special permission to eat in the commissary with the stars.

He owned a car now and in the mornings, when he drove onto the lot, his fans stopped him at the gate, begging for his signature. The same happened at night.

What had become routine was interrupted on one occasion when Johnny found that Jackie, the lion, had been left unattended on the empty stage at night. It was a Friday, and Johnny looked for Jackie's trainer, but without result. The man had probably taken a quick ride to the bar around the corner . . . and never made it back. Johnny tired of waiting, took Jackie by his leash and ushered him into the front seat of his automobile. Quite content with the novelty outing, the lion obliged, settled back and enjoyed the ride. But the fans! Of course, they loved seeing their fearless hero in such company; nevertheless, some fled and none ventured to risk coming forth for an autograph.

The first red light signal in Culver City stopped their car. Johnny looked at the lion, and yawned. The lion looked at Johnny, and yawned back. It was the end of the week and both felt lazy, overworked, and content with each other. Johnny promised Jackie a huge steak the moment they reached home, sweet home.

Then, a car pulled up, stopped for the red signal, and a drunk leaned out of the window, next to Jackie.

"Hey, Buddy — Hic! Which way to Venice?"

Before Johnny could lean forward and reply, the lush's eyes grew wide in horror and disbelief. He stared at the lion, stepped on the gas, went through the red light, and in the distance a bottle smashed into thousands of pieces on the asphalt road. A pity, Johnny never learned if the cure were permanent.

Johnny had moved into a small house, where his only visitor at week-ends was Lupe. And that evening she crossed the threshold and was greeted by Jackie licking his chops, at the door. "Oh, hello! How are you, amigo?" she said, took off her gloves and looked for Johnny. When she found him, she kissed him, then removed her shoes. "Why do you entertain lions, and tell me nothing?" she asked. "I will not share you, Johnee!" And she settled in a chair, making herself at home.

A few weeks later Lupe was called away on location, to Nevada. Johnny flew up to see her, sans Jackie of course! It had not been planned, but on the spur of the moment, they found a justice of the peace to marry them. Johnny returned to Hollywood on Monday, and went straight to the studio and a spectacular scene in an elephants' graveyard, leaving Lupe in the arms of her leading man on the sun-parched desert of the Sierra Nevada.

167

"Tarzan, the Ape Man" and "Tarzan and His Mate" were among the biggest moneymakers MGM studio had put out, and naturally the top brass was anxious to repeat the performance. Johnny's fame had spread all over the world. Even Ethiopian Emperor Haile Selassie had sent for a print of his second picture, claiming that the terrain resembled that of his own country and lent itself for study in defense strategy. Rumors, however, belied this and stated that Selassie had become a hopeless fan of Tarzan and wished to view his films whenever possible, as the Italian high command was also doubtless doing.

The third thriller changed names from "Capture of Tarzan" to "Tarzan Escapes," which sounded more daring to producer Sam Zimbalist, who had been given his first screen assignment as associate. Richard Thorpe directed and Cyril Hume, once again, wrote the screen play. Maureen O'Sullivan still acted as "Jane", but censorship slapped more clothing on her pretty back which had kept the Hayes Office in a cold sweat during some past semi-nude underwater sequences. The new film, too, saw Jackie taking a plunge in the lagoon, and completely au naturel . . .

A marked change in this latest effort to chronicle the wild and fantastic adventures of the jungle-dwelling couple was the tree-house that MGM had rigged for them. The set designers had gone way out to lend comfort and cozy intimacy to this home that included everything from a good baking oven to something that looked like an electric fan but which was run by Cheetah. The bed on which Tarzan whispered beautiful monosyllabic love to his spouse was made up of bamboo and tropical leaves topped by luxurious furred skins any lady in civilization would yearn to wear, provided she did not drool over the ape man instead. And admittance was gained by means of an elevator operated by the pet elephant, Emma.

While everything ran smoothly in Tarzan's film household, rumors were beginning to spread that not all was quiet and peaceful on his home-front. And the papers slyly remarked that Cheetah in fact understood Johnny much better than Lupe did. There was trouble brewing in Paradise but it had not yet reached its peak of fermentation.

Soon after their nuptial day Johnny discovered that he had married a night-time gal whereas he was strictly a day-time boy. Lupe's Latin temperament agreed with being on a constant merry-go-round of parties, people, places, going out or inviting in, and this almost nightly. When Johnny came home tired and worn out after a long day at the studio, wishing for rest and relaxation, Lupe was already dressed, waiting for him to clean up and join her night life. She knew that he had to get up at five or six in the morning, arrive at the studio and be in make-up by seven to begin work at eight, yet she would not listen to his arguments or pleas for compassion.

Johnny disliked the crowd Lupe mingled with and, unaccustomed to alcohol, he felt bored in a company that passed from one binge into another. At first, wanting to please her, he tagged along, playing her game, but refusing the drinks everyone tried to pour down his throat. Lupe taught him what the boys at the I.A.C. had omitted, table manners and etiquette, how to behave with ladies and how to handle a knife and fork in proper fashion. In short, she taught him how to be a gentleman.

Between pictures they traveled to New York and stopped off at the Central Park Casino where Eddie Duchin played. There he also met George Gershwin, and became entranced with his music. The great occasion was to be one of those elaborate charity affairs, and Johnny bought his first white tie and tails. He admitted to having looked rather comical with his long hair and evening garb, and sought the quiet corners. But Lupe always insisted on making an entrance! Even at the fights, Lupe would never enter until the lights had been turned off and then, as they walked down the center isle to applause and loud cheers, "Tarzan and Lupe are coming!" the lights went on again. The boxers stopped their punches in mid-air, and everyone saluted the couple with Lupe taking bows to left and right in grand dame fashion. After the lights once again had been subdued, and the commotion had died down, Lupe seated herself in front row center and, as the fight progressed, her Mexican spitfire disposition gave way to shouts, "Geev eet to heem!" And all ladylike composure completely deserted the little woman with her rooting presence, as if it had never truly existed at all.

Lupe suffered from an incurable fear of prowlers. She had all her windows secured with iron bars that Johnny disliked immensely. He felt caged, like the big cats he remembered seeing in Chicago's zoo, but he loved his keeper and submitted to her whims. Next, Lupe's phobia prompted that a tear gas container be installed in their car. One night she pressed the wrong button! And Johnny got his lesson in playing cops and robbers . . .

He bought a 34-foot schooner and changed its name from Chula to Santa Guadalupe in honor of his bride. Their first voyage was to take them to Catalina Island, a little more than 20 miles away. In L.A. Harbor, Lupe admired her sleek namesake and, soon, they sailed merrily past the lighthouse. Outside the breakwater, however, the sea turned rough, and waves tossed the boat about. And Santa Guadalupe made Lupe sick! To Johnny's disappointment, he had to turn the schooner about and go back. The following year he sold the little schooner and bought another, larger and heavier. This time he listened to the superstition that forbade the re-christening of seafaring crafts because that supposedly brings bad luck, and he kept the original name of Allure. Even Lupe decided she liked the 50-foot sailing vessel much better and, in the future, the Allure introduced moments of tranquillity into their stormy lives.

Fame was beginning to take its toll on Johnny's reputation. After his second Tarzan film, some reporter in Chicago visited the Turn-Verein where his mother still worked as head cook. He learned about the existing relationship, and wrote, the moment he reached his typewriter, a venomous bit of smear calling Johnny the Man-Monkey who had forsaken all his duties while pursuing his pleasure in the manner of an anthropoid ape and, who, by refusing to support her, was forcing his own mother to continue her menial work at the Turn-Verein.

The reporter's story hurt Johnny deeply. He had constantly insisted that his mother come and live in California, but the old lady had begged not to be taken away from her Chicago home, her friends and the environment she knew and loved. Now she had to follow her son because of the harm implied by her absence but she cried, feeling miserable, displaced, and totally at a loss. "California will kill me," she said, "It will rob me of my remaining vigor in late years. I don't want to be just a burden, I want to be active! All my life I have enjoyed independence. If this is the price of fame — maybe, you should not have become so famous."

The studio issued a news release to that effect, labeling the insinuations of the reporter as baseless, as lies and slander, all in very small print hidden in some corner of the daily papers distributed at large. Most of Johnny's fans remained loyal, but there were some who wrote spiteful letters to the star, threatening him with everything including total damnation of his soul.

Time, like any river, went on. Grass grew over the issue. Mother Elizabeth came to live in Los Angeles where Johnny installed her in a house with Peter, his brother. But the old lady mourned her lost haven for many, many years. All of a sudden she felt old and useless to society. And Johnny, whose press had always treated him with respect and kindness during his athletic years, now learned the bitter lesson that once a larger-than-life screen image has been projected and has taken over, every detail of his self and those closest to him assumes monstrous proportions such as only science fiction could design.

Returning to work after another one of Lupe's nocturnal flings, Johnny felt worn and tired. It promised to be a hard day; they had scheduled the stunt where he, while locked in a steel cage, was to be thrown off a cliff by the villains.

During rehearsals, the cage was placed next to the studio tank and Johnny climbed in to test it for size. He closed the lock behind him, not realizing that the escape hatch had not as yet been adjusted. An elephant (not Emma!) paraded up and down the stage. Under the mammal's weight the dirt gave way and suddenly, the steel cage toppled and fell into the water. Director Richard Thorpe, cameraman Clyde de Vinna, George Emerson, the animal trainer, and several others leaped into the tank and heaved in frantic desperation at the cage. It took more than a few minutes to get it back onto the bank. Johnny was found unharmed. He had held his breath - - - well, just about! When he was released, the first thing he recalled was his experience in water polo. "This is nothing," he said, "in comparison with the three minutes I once stayed under. But —" he added with a smirk, "I felt a bit more uncomfortable this time, maybe because I wasn't sure my absence had been missed by the other players!" Quite an irony it would have been . . . if something drastic had come of the incident . . . in five feet of water!

That evening, on the verge of exhaustion, he drove home without bothering to change from his brown bathrobe to proper clothing. As he opened the front door, he was greeted by a grating voice calling "Hi, Garry! Hi, Garry! Pretty boy . . ." Lupe's parrot, a gift from Cooper, paraded on his bar and continued the monotone conversation with a torrent of Spanish. One of these days, Johnny thought, I'll tape this bird's "Schnabel!" Before he reached the stairs, he was confronted by his wife and a bunch of strangers all dressed in evening wear. "Johnee, you are late!" Lupe scolded. "Look at you! Quickly, go and change, Jack ees throwing a partee tonight and everyone, but everyone, ees invited!"

Johnny looked at his wife and, wordlessly, continued upstairs. Without taking a shower, he threw himself upon the bed and closed his eyes. He had had fun with her . . . he loved her . . . but he knew it had to end! That same night, after an awful row that kept most of the neighborhood awake until the early hours of dawn, Johnny took his first drink in self-defense. Before he left for the studio, they had made up. Lupe accompanied him to the car and swore in the name of the Holy Virgin that she would alter her ways and become a good "Hausfrau" — no more fights, no more night clubs, no more separations! A few days later she was off to New York to participate in a radio broadcast. As ever, the press beseeched her to give an interview, and tell them about the tempest in her household.

"Fight? We all do! Johnee and I may fight, but no more than the rest of Hollywood. They call each other dear and darleeng een public, and then go home and smack each other een private. When Johnee and I get sore, we get sore no matter where we are! I am broken-hearted Johnee could not come with me to New York. Our careers keep us too much apart. But nobody understands! People are trying their best to break my marriage. But they are not going to do eet!"

One reporter asked her about the publicized speculations of an eventual divorce. "What divorce? Maybe we sometimes want to sue — eet ees human! But we never get them!" She interrupted her train of thought by producing and reading a part of a letter which Johnny had sent her.

174

"My dearest darling," it read, "I still love you more than ever. I will never leave you again."

The vivacious Mexican actress swallowed a sip from her cherry flip and ordered a round for everyone present at her hotel suite. Then she said: "The first year ees the hardest. Johnee and I have been married a year and seven months — from now on eet ees going to be all right!"

She returned to Hollywood and went into complete seclusion at their residence, with only Johnny around whenever he drove home from his daily job. She stuck it out for several weeks, playing the part of a housewife with a vengeance. The couple planned a vacation in South America, an extended, much-belated honeymoon. A re-write job on part of the Tarzan script upset the breakable crystal chalice filled with elfin spirits of expectations. Lupe became restless. She became herself! Pffft, went harmony . . .

John Barrymore was fond of wine, women, song, Shakespeare, betting, and Tarzan and his ape! He bet Johnny $50 that the chimp would bite someone during a scene with the British actors, whose clipped accents had already provoked a discord in Cheetah's eardrums. Johnny accepted the proposition with some reservations, for the simple reason that he had to watch his jungle comedy relief constantly, if only for the sake of the other actors' welfare, and therefore had to win the bet.

"Actors, my dear fellow, come a dime a dozen!" said the incomparable Barrymore, and blew his nose. "They all lack profile, with one classic exception!"

"I wish you would reverse your bet; at least I'd know

175

you won't be jilted," Johnny reasoned. "Cheetah's got a lot of scruples. And I must keep him in order."

"Well, me lad! I'll reverse it and I'll bet you he won't bite anyone. I've a full afternoon available and I've brought my survival kit! Sooner or later you will have to turn your manly back, and that glorious caricature of our forefathers will still perform the inevitable spectacle of bloody mayhem. Win or lose, it's worth a try! My sense of smell is most profound."

Johnny kept a constant eye on the chimp. The bet meant little to him, but he hated to see a co-player hurt. He had learned that Cheetah's hair stood up in a bristle like a cat's just before he readied himself for attack. If that happened, he was ready to nip him with the handle of his knife. But the chimp behaved like a perfect gentleman.

"Why do you have to be so goddamn pious!" Barrymore mused. "Let him go! I want to see how it happens!"

"But you'll lose your fifty!"

"Sportsmanship, old boy! All for the sake of sportsmanship!" Barrymore rolled his eyes, and soon was seen placing side-bets as to whom the chimp would attack, if he did . . .

——"The moving finger writes, and having writ"——The inevitable had to happen! Johnny was called into his dressing room by some publicist. Before he retired from the set, he left specific instructions with the trainer to keep an alert eye on Cheetah, who seemed extremely well-behaved this afternoon. Moments later, he was summoned by loud wails, curses, shrieks. He rushed back to the scene and found utter chaos. Cheetah had bitten one Englishman and a guy from Brooklyn in the same stride! The trainer was hitting the ape over

176

the head with a rubber hose. First-aid helpers assisted in bandaging the chimp's victims. Blood was flowing, seemingly enough to fill buckets. A woman had fainted, and someone tried to fan her back to normal.

And Barrymore laughed!

"That sonofabitch did it! It cost me fifty bucks, but he did it! It was worth every penny! I've never had a better time in all the years I've wasted in this dreary place!"

Barrymore did not know it then, but the producer henceforth barred him from the set as a troublemaker. However, Johnny often visited the great actor in his own environment on stage number so-and-so, and, completely enthralled, listened to the flawless delivery of his dialogue.

"How do you do it?" he asked. "How can you memorize all these lines?"

Barrymore's heavy lids half-closed over his eyes. He gave Johnny a bleak glare. "You must be joking! Or have you spent too much time in the jungle?" And Barrymore took Johnny on a tour of the sound stage. Everywhere, but everywhere! he saw objects fully covered with written words, Barrymore's speeches. The black shields cutting reflection on both sides of the camera had them. The hidden parts of select furniture had them. The wall opposite the photography angle had them. In fact, Barrymore started the idiot sheets of today's television!

"How can you perform if you have to search for your lines?" Johnny wondered in awe.

"Dear boy!" Barrymore drew himself erect. "I give it the eyebrow and the twitching of the nose. I roll my eyes until I come across the next lyrics. How can I act if my mind is cluttered with abortions some nincompoop put on a roll of toilet paper. If they want Barrymore in films, they better cater to his divine madness." And the famous brows lifted twice; the expressive eyes rolled upward to heaven; the fine nostrils widened; his classic profile turned, giving a vague gaze in the general direction of an assistant director who had just approached and whispered that everything was ready on stage; and with an elegantly arrogant sweep of his mantle, the actor's actor departed to give posterity something to talk about!

"Paris Film Job to Take Lupe From Tarzan!" the head-lines screamed, and continued in smaller print that the lovers' reunion had been brief, for the peppery Latin actress was leaving Hollywood again on December 4th, for a film engage-ment in France. With characteristic independence Lupe said that over there they paid more, twice her Hollywood salary, that she would be foolish not to accept such an offer. Be-sides, the separation would only last for seven weeks! She never worried about spending the Christmas holidays and New Year's away from her spouse, who, the papers quoted, had to remain because the studio wanted him to study voice culture. No sooner had Lupe left . . . than she returned with tears and remorse. The guarantee of $50,000 had not been deposited in the bank by the Parisian Cinema Company, and Lupe never risked working for nothing. The deal was off and Santa Claus, after all, visited the Weissmullers, bringing Johnny a pair of boxing gloves with a note that read, "Dar-ling, so you can punch me if I leave you again!"

Johnny, meanwhile had found his way back to his past

and its quiet happiness. He often swam off the beach at Santa Monica and made friends with the lifeguards on duty. He was named "Honorary Member of the Santa Monica Life Guards" and, daily, waited for his turn to save lives like the rest of them, bringing forth a considerable quota, especially when winds caused a rip tide.

These lifeguards were Johnny's kind of people. They talked his language and he talked theirs. He brought them some publicity in telling MGM about the worthy cause they were serving, without getting any kind of glory in return. So the studio ordered Maureen O'Sullivan to go along and, in a photographic layout, she posed as the victim of poor swimming habits whom Johnny and the boys rescued from a watery grave. They demonstrated in many photographs every phase of artificial respiration and first-aid. As a result of this noble exploit, and attendant display, Santa Monica beach became a hangout for the lovelorn maidens of Greater Los Angeles, and many a handsome lifeguard had to save his own neck from being hitched in the rescue melee. However, none held it against Johnny; for every one of the men deep down in his heart desired to perform an act of mercy, especially if, at the same time, he was considered the Don Juan or Casanova of the Southland.

The Tarzan set was open to visitors, particularly the studio's stars. One day, a tall honey-colored blonde, hiding behind dark glasses, let herself through the two heavy doors leading onto the stage. Her perfect bone-structure betrayed her. Garbo had come to watch Tarzan perform.

"Your Tarzan films make me forget everything," she told

Johnny. "I always ask the studio to give me a private show-ing. Oh, they are so good! I always feel as if I had slept for hours!"

"Is that an insult, Greta?" Johnny asked.

"No!" She was horrified at the thought. "No, please un-derstand! They freshen my soul, they relax me! When I am alone in the projection room, and see you surrounded by all these dumb, godly creatures on the screen, heaven smiles at me. I feel like an unborn child free of worldly affairs. I feel I want to go to Africa!" Garbo sighed, and her dreamy eyes with the long lashes closed. "The unknown adventure always remains distant!" Then suddenly she stiffened, the half-smile disappeared from her sensuous lips and, like a scared deer, she turned and fled from the man-made jungle into which she had brought her luminous presence.

Hereafter, Garbo reciprocated by declaring her own tightly closed set open to Johnny at all times.

She was replaced by yet another royal visitor, the Prince of Siam, who insisted on a grand tour of the tree-house, and a picture with Tarzan and Jane.

AI, CHIHUAHUA!

14

LIFE AT the Weissmullers began to border on the ridiculous as the battles on the home front continued. It seemed as if the fuse to set off a time bomb were constantly lit, and no extra effort was needed to detonate one around the clock at any given hour of the day or night. Similar to the occasion when Johnny, finally, decided he had to have moral support in a household with three yapping little Mexicans, his wife and her two Chihuahuas, not to mention the prodigious bird, and determined to add a dog of his own to the family. He found one he liked in a pound and Otto, standing on his hind legs as tall as Johnny, happily sniffed his way across the threshold of his new home.

Lupe caught one glimpse of the shaggy mongrel, and the neighbors, getting a whiff of the approaching cyclone, barred all windows and took off to the cellars. "He'll kill my leetle dogs, that great beeg brute!" she screamed. "He'll kill my leetle Chihuahuas!"

Five minutes later the worst was over. Things were calming down considerably to a mere first-class squabble when Lupe happened to glance over at the huge, bearskin rug . . . and there lay Otto the Horrible, the menacing brute, with one little dog sleeping on his back . . . the other biting his tail. Mr. Kelly and Mrs. Murphy, the two Chihuahuas, had completely stolen Otto's heart which for so long had lacked affection in the dreary surroundings of a dog pound whence Johnny had rescued him, just in time before his execution. And the big brute had promised himself to keep good watch over everyone and all who were responsible for his break in life, as well as to honor, obey his master, and to do him no wrong!

Lupe was stopped cold the moment she layed eyes on this tranquil sketch of perfect canine harmony. As quickly as her temper had flared it subsided and tears of remorse filled her eyes. "Popee! We fight about nothing! Darleeng, this ees too silly!" She sat on the floor and cried bitterly. "Johnee, we must save our marriage. We'll live like Claudette Colbert and Norman Foster. You live een your house and I live een mine!"

Johnny did not go for the idea. For a while they reasoned. Johnny won out. Lupe kissed him. "I will not lose my beeg husband for a leetle fight."

Some of the neighbors wondered about that "leetle" fight, which had made the Civil War seem like a bean-shooting contest.

The next day Johnny went out and rented an apartment. He had had enough! His clothes were all moved over to his new abode by a puzzled muttering butler who had, on many occasions, gone through the motions of packing and unpacking but never thought he would see the day the stuff would actually leave the house.

Lupe spent all day away from home. When she returned that evening, entering the front door, there was a strange stillness about the place. Her glance fell on the hall cabinet which she had ordered specially made to store Johnny's swimming medals, that shone through the glass, reflecting the dull glimmer of the hall light. She climbed the stairs and opened the bedroom door. There stood her round, empty bed. Its silver rim reminded her of the moon lost between black clouds. She moved to the window and opened it. As she peered out, she saw the shadowy form of Otto, hovering about the empty swimming pool. The dog emitted a low wailing sound that tore at her heart. An overpowering loneliness seized her and with a sob she flung herself onto the bed and wept bitterly. The candle that always burned before the little shrine cast weird flickering shadows against the walls. Lupe suddenly came to her feet and, running all the way, she hurried to her car where, pressing the accelerator, she zoomed off in the direction of Johnny's place. Minutes later, her small flying feet carried her across his doorstep . . . and into his arms.

A blissful period of peace descended on the neighborhood and all week long only cooing sounds enveloped the North Rodeo Drive house.

Lupe told the press that she was just a "yes" woman to Johnny. Every day she would say but "yes, darleeng!" Only Sundays she reserved for a small spat that, she maintained, kept her in training and physically fit, as otherwise bottled up emotions might cause an ulcer.

"Tarzan Escapes", meanwhile, had undergone further changes. The prop department had master-minded some huge, wired bats that, in the action, descended from caves and suddenly made off with unsuspecting victims. It was all terribly scary and exciting, but much too much so because the children in the preview audience shrieked with fright, hiding their little faces in the folds of mothers' protective clothing. There was nothing left but for MGM to withdraw the film. The studio ordered all gruesome scenes cut and replaced with re-takes, for which the actors were summoned. After many months of hard work, director Thorpe had achieved a complete change in overall effect. The film was turned into a motion picture which appealed to young and old alike. The epic was almost two years in the making. However, fortunately, movies in the thirties were designed for profit and produced on a carefully planned budget which allowed for unexpected hazards and expenses, unlike calamities of later years wherein a single spectacular could place an entire studio onto the verge of bankruptcy.

Between films Johnny spent much of his time on his schooner, the Allure. Metro kept their star idle, paying his salary but refusing to loan him out for other feature assignments, fearing his Tarzan image would be destroyed through different roles. They permitted him to give swimming exhibitions and to perform in aquacades, but pictures were out, period. The studio also took a dim view of his sailing hobby, and the fact that Johnny loved to skin dive. Nevertheless, Johnny always managed to slip away with his boat for the coves of Catalina. "If Metro asks," he would say, "tell them I'm a thousand fathoms under the sea and to call me up sometime!"

The Allure was a sleek two-masted craft that slept six

people, and its captain's quarters sported the luxury of a wide double bunk that folded into the ship's hull during the day. His prize possession aboard was a chronometer, a ship's clock presented to him by his studio crew members. Their names were engraved in the shiny brass circular frame with small, projecting handles, a miniature ship's wheel. "To Tarzan" it read "from James McKay - J. Marchant - Len Smith - Art Smith - Willard Vogel - Al Scheving - Chet Davis - Hank Forester - George Lee." Every half hour added another bell until four hours had elapsed, then eight bells sounded, and the new watch began. Years later, when Johnny had been forced to sell his beloved schooner, he kept the clock, had it repaired, and thoughtfully listened to the hours tick away, marking time. And he remembered the people and their friendship that still meant a great deal to him.

Johnny had engaged a regular skipper to take care of the Allure and, often, when the schooner remained anchored at Catalina, he took a speedboat to the Isthmus from the mainland, making it in an hour and a half. On these occasions, he went forth alone because Lupe had not yet learned to be a hearty sailor, and cared little for the big, blue sharks that haunted the crossing. Johnny never thought of taking along a life preserver despite warnings by the Coast Guard of rough seas in Windy Lane, as the yachtsmen call the channel. But then, Johnny had never learned to fear water.

The anchored Allure became a famous tourist attraction, and word spread the moment her owner arrived on board. Rubberneck observers strained their eyes to catch a glimpse of the swimmer when he dived off the pier at the Isthmus and swam out to the schooner. One day they saw him enter the water but never come up. Word was carried back to the island that Weissmuller had met his fate below the sea, had been eaten by one of the sharks that occasionally visit the coves. Catalina was in an uproar and, sending out search parties who found no trace of Johnny, finally retired for the night while messages were flashed back to the mainland. MGM, alas, practically had baby chimps for the next few hours! No one had bothered to look in the most logical spot, namely in the schooner cabin where Johnny slept in safety and with pleasant dreams until the sun came up out of Laguna, across the bay. What had happened was that Johnny had dived from the pier, "cruised" deep along the bottom and had come up on the other side of the boat, which he climbed, heading straight for bed. "Gee," a rubberneck said, "but we looked under the pier and you weren't there. It's as if you had come up in Pomona!"

To keep their star out of mischief, the studio decided to send Johnny back east. He sidetracked to Chicago where he visited Coach Bachrach. "How are they treating you, Johnny?" Bachrach wanted to know. "I hope all this adulation hasn't changed your style as a human being!"

Johnny considered. He knew that basically Hollywood had not interfered with his character but yet, somewhere along the line, it had left its mark. Lupe had briefed him about all the back-door slander and gossip that somehow goes hand in hand with the lives of celebrities, pursuing them across continents. Most of it was enlarged a thousand-fold by a willing news-thirsty press, like a small skin blemish magnified larger than life until it reaches the ugly proportions of a cancerous growth. Some, however, was true and Johnny, who had always rinsed his feet in clear water, now found that earth had a habit of leaving dirt clinging to his shoes. Yet he knew that he could always remove the shoes, leaving his feet clean. He had learned about "ambi-sextrous" relationships which hardly measured up to any code of morale, but lay piled in a heap of dung over which large painted flies buzzed, to give life to the homunculus. He had seen nocturnal Bacchanalia rape decency herself to assuage carnal appetite. He himself had remained pure by distance but the knowledge he had gained had basened his outlook on human values. Or had it? The thoughts became too deep. Characteristically, he dismissed them.

"I have missed you, Bach!" He said. "I guess, there's no one in Hollywood on whom I could ever rely as much as I used to rely on you."

Bachrach patted his shoulder, his fatherly face lighting up, one eye closing in a wink. "D'you remember what I told you when you swam? I said, 'Keep going! I'm not a bit tired!' Well, boy; just keep reminding yourself, and you'll be all right!"

Later that same week Johnny had more opportunity to think about their short encounter. He, accompanied by a Mr. J. McKinley Bryan and his wife, visited the Stork Club in New York, where his longish screen haircut and the dark glasses he wore got him into trouble with a lieutenant of the U. S. Navy. It seemed that an argument followed, concerning his strange appearance. The dispute involved the flicking of a cigarette from someone's hand and . . . a black eye. The next morning the papers had a field day with "Tarzan of Films Plays Role in Fisticuffs at New York Night Club." As it turned out, Johnny had had nothing to do with the entire unsavory affair, except only to stand his own ground. Someone else had done the punching and, immediately, the celebrity's name had been dragged into headlines. After the news had run its full gamut, a retraction was issued, and the star exonerated. But the man who had always lived for honor and clean sportsmanship, who knew well that millions of American teen-agers modeled their behaviour after his, had once again encountered degradation within his own spirit.

Lupe was away in London at the time and, worried, Johnny wired her his explanations. He had to return to California by train, however, to square things with the studio. But before he departed New York, he had to stop by The Times offices for photographs. Cheetah, too, had been brought there for the occasion, since the idea behind the publicity was "Tarzan of Cinema Meets Prototype of Comic Strips", with the photos showing Johnny and the ape admiring their cartoon counterparts. Tarzan and his chimp were also given the grand tour of the Times Building, in which the various functions vital to the production of the daily papers, from the linotype machines to the proofroom, were shown and explained to him. Someone there brought up the subject of the recent blatant articles, and apologized for the manner in which the news had been reported to the public. Johnny held no grudge: it was not in his nature; still, he wondered how such nice guys could in the same sweet breath spill such swill into print.

On this occasion, the publicity had no ill-effect on his career; on the contrary, he even received a most unusual request from a fan club in Illinois: Would he, they asked, send them his shorn locks? They wanted to divide the hair and place it into lockets for all the girl members. If his tresses did not manage to go around, they would arrange a drawing. A postscript read that less hair caused less trouble, so why not remove the temptation from hecklers, and make the ladies of the club happy!

Johnny's popularity brought along a never-ending collection of newspaper comic strips, devoted to his swimming feats, his Tarzan portrayal and personal life. A series of vacation cartoons once showed Johnny, looking famished and drawn, recuperating at a milk farm, with a caption that read, "He thinks about Lupe. Fine age we live in, when a woman can drive a man to milk!" In the same layout Garbo and Stokowski were seen driving off into the wild blue yonder, and Eddie Cantor, Boris Karloff, Howard Hughes, Edgar Bergen with Charlie McCarthy were pictured searching for some unlikely spot en route to no-man's-land. Even "The Katzenjammer Kids" once managed to drown Johnny when supposedly he was giving them swimming instructions. His life story was incorporated into sundry comic books which sold like hot cakes. And with his name attached, even race horses got into the swim.

Before starting his next picture, Johnny joined Lupe in London for another reconciliation. Lupe had taken a dim view of the Stork Club incident, but the moment he arrived, was back in the arms of her "Johnee - Popee!" That night, blissfully, Johnny retired and, picking up a book, relaxed from too-much loving affection his little wife had bestowed upon him, and he thought about the nicer things in life. Suddenly a shoe whirled across the bedroom and hit him on the forehead. In a torrent of Mexican and American Lupe began to accuse him of night-clubbing alone in New York while she was crying her eyes out for him in London Town. Johnny jumped from his resting place and started chasing her about the room, ducking as other objects near-missed her target. Johnny's sleeping habits included the wearing of pajama tops only, and Lupe, screaming "help! murder!" ran out of the suite to find refuge in the spacious veranda-type hallway of the hotel.

London's Claridges was, and has remained, the most exclusive hotel accommodation in England's capital, a place for royal visitors, where mere commoners had to belong to a very special elite, admitted only after meeting certain high recommendation standards. Lupe had accomplished the impossible securing residency in these esteemed quarters despite the fact that her well-known temperament had left the management in a constant, cold sweat. Personally, Johnny thought that Tarzan had gained them entry, for had he not been the offspring of Lord and Lady Greystoke and, therefore, qualified by rights of noble birth?

No sooner had she opened the door and escaped than lights on the third floor were turned on in every window, and messages flashed to the distraught, hand-wringing hotel personnel that a major Donnybrook was going on up there. On the second round down the hall, the entrance to a suite was slightly pushed ajar, and an elderly lady in long sleeping attire and frilly night cap peeked through the doorway.

"Go a little faster, Johnny!" the lady called out, as Johnny began the third lap, passing by with his pajama top filled with air like a sail during a hurricane. "You'll catch her the next time around!"

He managed to shout a quick "thanks", took her advice, and caught up with his fiery bride on the windward beat. The rest of the night was spent in relative peace, except for Claridges' highly proper employees whose tradition-bound nerves rattled on through morning until a note, delivered by a red-eyed manager, reached the Weissmullers. It spelled out its message in no uncertain terms — eviction from the premises after an allowance of time for packing.

Half an hour later, the same manager — the red in his eyes now suffusing his cheeks — delivered a second notice, this one apologizing for the first, canceling its text, and asking the couple to please remain guests at the hotel. Bewildered, Johnny later queried a butler about this change of heart.

"It's the Queen's order, Sir!" the servant said.

"What Queen?" Johnny wondered.

"It seems, Sir, that last night you passed the chambers of the Queen of Denmark — or — was it Holland? And Her Royal Highness, learning about your dilemma this morning, flatly stated that if you are evicted, she would move out as well. A very powerful sponsor to have, indeed, Sir!"

Goodness! Johnny pondered. Could it have been Queen Wilhelmina, who, at the Olympics, had handed him the medals in 1928? Could she be the one who had turned into his guardian angel? He remembered so well her motherly, affectionate face at the Amsterdam Olympiad!

"Go a little faster, Johnny! You'll catch her the next time around!" — The words rang in his ears with an all too familiar clearness. "Eureka! Eldorado!" he thought, "I hope she doesn't think I am neglecting my training!" But he quickly consoled himself, "She must have known that it would not have taken me a full three rounds in the water!"

Johnny began working on "Tarzan Finds a Son", the self-explanatory title adding young Johnny Sheffield as Boy to the cast. Henceforth, the jungle duo became a trio and, when the picture found its release, it was considered a brilliant inspiration, an A-plus to the filmed movie series. Boy Sheffield was only five years old, a husky fellow with a natural flair for athletics, as Johnny soon found out when he taught him how to swim. In a relatively short period of time, the child performed like any old trouper, doing underwater stunts like an adult pro. Tarzan Jr. let his hair grow long after his film-father's fashion, looked his miniature image, almost as if he had truly been born his flesh and blood.

This motion picture was shot entirely on location at Silver Springs, Florida, chosen because the river and lakes of the vicinity have the clearest water in America, a "must" for underwater photography.

A "diving camera" was introduced which recaptured the swimming sequences in their entirety. It worked something like this: The cameras were mounted on a counter-weight apparatus that descended toward the water at the same speed as the falling divers, thus registering their movements in the air close up as they straightened out their dives.

One camera worked at normal speed, the others in slow motion. The diving episode, surface swimming and swimming under the water employed not only the above-mentioned, but also a submarine camera and periscope.

Like all movie actors, Boy Sheffield had a young double for some of his stunts, a youngster by the name of "Gooley" Green, who looked astonishingly like him but surpassed him in height and age.

Johnny's ears were beginning to give him trouble, perhaps attributable to his many years of swimming and stunt diving. He had developed a chronic infection and his doctor advised him of serious possibilities. Johnny discovered that by pouring distilled alcohol into them the moment he left the water the spirits dried his inner ear and checked any remaining dampness, the possible source of the trouble. Nevertheless, he often experienced earaches at night and, consequently, suffered from insomnia.

Lupe in turn did little to help throughout the seemingly endless nights he tossed about without finding rest. She had returned from Europe, but their careers kept them apart most of the time. Johnny wanted children, and he had thought that she felt the same. Yet their marriage remained fruitless. Lupe had become forever more independent, and even their stormy fights had cooled somewhat into a temporary armistice. Her name had been linked in the newspapers with other men, but Johnny refused to believe in the common truth that smoke often betrays a fire. Whenever they got together, he noticed new bits of jewelry, expensive baubles she liked to wear around her arms and neck, but he was quite familiar with her passion for diamonds and, believing her story that she had bought them from her earnings, never gave the trinkets a second thought.

But further conjecture in the press and hints that Lupe and Johnny were headed in separate directions though remaining under the same roof did not help marital problems. Then came Lupe's statement to the press: "There will be no divorce. Johnee and I are still fine friends, but we go our separate ways. What ees wrong with that? He does what he wants. I do what I want!"

Johnny found plenty wrong with that! He had not realized that all that remained of their marriage was being friends. He still cared for Lupe, and he had no apparent reason to doubt her feelings toward him, except, perhaps, that mutual friends had reported seeing his wife in the company of screen newcomer Jon Hall at the boxing matches. However, all rumors proved false and unfounded in this particular name association.

During the filming of "Tarzan Finds a Son", Cheetah once again started a rumble with the supporting cast, composed of such fine names as Henry Stephenson, Ian Hunter, Frieda Inescort, Henry Wilcoxon, Laraine Day and Morton Lowry. The chimp's known hatred for accents, because he could not understand the words these people spoke, had increased with his age. Constantly, Cheetah picked on anyone who sounded the strangest; usually, he jumped across the table and poked him or her in the nose. Unfortunately, Johnny could not always keep watch and, selecting Stephenson, the grand old actor got a real whopping from Cheetah just when he leaned forward to indulge in some delicious fruit tidbits of the jungle's offering.

"I say," the fabulous trouper remarked, nonchalantly rubbing his smelling organ, "nothing like this ever happened in Shakespeare!"

The original version of the movie was written to end Maureen O'Sullivan's career as Jane. Maureen had married her Farrow man, and intended to retire after the birth of her first child. The screen play was supposed to kill her in the last scenes with Tarzan and Boy remaining behind to console each other. But as the picture progressed, and praises of its daily rushes reached Florida, Maureen decided to remain for more of the same and so . . . the death scene was cut and she, miraculously, recovered from her mortal wound in Tarzan's arms, begging his forgiveness for her mistake in having wanted to return Boy to his inheritance in England.

However, Johnny's mate in real life was less submissive. As more and more rumors caught up with him, he got permission to return to Hollywood for a few days and, unannounced, surprised Lupe. He found her admiring another diamond tiara worth a small fortune. He knew that her income could not possibly permit such luxury, and openly accused her of infidelity. Lupe laughed in his face and denied everything! The argument left him heated yet unwilling to fight. He took off to the golf course instead, but not before he had told Otto, the loving mongrel, to watch his wife during his absence and keep her out of mischief. Otto took his master's casual remark literally. When Johnny returned hours later, he found a frightened, half-hysterical Lupe sitting in a corner with Otto stalking her, growling whenever she tried to move. The dog had relentlessly followed his master's orders and kept Lupe safe, but lonesome and scared.

Some weeks later Johnny received word on his Florida location that Otto had perished through poisoning. Johnny had lost a faithful friend. Lupe informed him that an unknown stranger had performed the dark deed, but Johnny had his own suspicions about the killer.

Gossip has a way with people. It has an evil tongue that destroys love, trust and honor, because its ugly shell often hides a small corn of harmful truth.

The day came when Johnny packed his bags for the last time and moved out, never to return to the Rodeo Drive house, while Lupe issued a statement to the reporters: Three little words that said, "Marriage - - - eet steenks!"

Mr. Kelly and Mrs. Murphy had gained a free field for themselves.

A RAKE, A SHOVEL AND A BASEBALL BAT

15

A WRITER ONCE interviewed James Dunn, hoping to collect enough material for a biography. But all that Dunn talked about was a mysterious nonentity, a man answering to the initials of J.M., golfer, muscle man, vagrant, humorist, gambler. He shunned publicity, never permitting his picture to be taken, but he knew all the red-blooded males on Hollywood's roster of famous names, and in return enjoyed an infamous reputation in their midst.

This man frequented the homes of stars with his dubious presence; living off their generosity, he stayed with one or another for weeks. If stranded between invitations, he was known to rig up a tent at Lakeside's golf links, the playground of celebrities, whence the stories of his incredible golfing exploits spread through the locker rooms across Southern California.

Johnny belonged to the Lakeside membership, and often met with other golf enthusiasts for a game on the 18-hole course. On a particular morning he joined Bob Hope and Bing Crosby, but lacking a fourth player, he happened to notice J. M. taking a practice swing with a baseball bat instead of using his wood. He brought this to the attention of his friends. The trio cornered J. M.

"Who needs clubs!" J. M. bragged. "I can play using nothing but a bat, a shovel, and a rake."

"That I've got to see!" exclaimed Crosby.

"What'll you bet?" J. M. showed interest.

"Well, I'll wager $500 for every hole you make one under par or better."

"How about you?" J. M. asked the others.

Johnny shook his head. "Count me out," he said. "Me, too," replied Hope, "betting is more in Bing's line."

J. M. nodded agreement, took another ball, placed it on a tee, picked up his baseball bat, stepped back and - - - the ball whizzed through the air like a bullet, landing in a sand trap in front of the green, an estimated distance of 300 yards away.

For a moment, Crosby looked stunned. "Lucky break!" he murmured but added confidently, "let's see you get out of the next one."

J. M. packed a shovel lying nearby, found a rake, and the foursome headed in the direction of the ball. They discovered it firmly imbedded in the sand. Crosby let go a hearty laugh. Hope stood back; folding his arms he observed the distance to the green. Johnny took out his sand wedge and went into practicing motions. Without a change of expression, J. M. relieved himself of the rake, placed the shovel into position and hit.

The ball flew up dropping onto the green.

Crosby's smile froze on his face. Johnny submitted a low whistle. Hope silently nodded, unfolded his arms and marched to the round, white object, six feet from the hole. J. M. turned his rake, holding the stick like a billiard cue. "Just like pool!" he exclaimed.

"It'll be quite a putt!" Hope remarked.

"Enough to call the elephants!" Johnny agreed.

"He'll never make it!" Crosby denied, but his voice sounded less sure.

J. M. readied himself for attack, armed with his up-turned rake. He paid no attention to the threesome's vocal calculations, his eyes focused on the ball. For several seconds he remained motionless, then, striking the ball, it rolled, and rolled, and - - - "Birdie!" J. M. shouted, throwing his unique putter away he began to dance around like a madman, screaming with laughter.

Crosby stood as if a bucket of cold water had landed on him. Hope shook his head in disbelief. Johnny broke into a yell which might have summoned the elephants providing Lakeside had not been a private club and, therefore, safe from trespassing.

"Give me my money! Give me my money! The next one'll be an eagle!" J. M. continued his raucity. Wordlessly, Crosby opened his wallet and produced the stake.

"Take it," he said, after a pause, "I'm through betting today!"

J. M.'s other peculiarly effective forces lay in his stupendous strength. He stood only 5′ 10″, but his sturdy build seemed a concentrated unit of physical power. He once bet Oliver Hardy, the fleshy partner of the Laurel and Hardy comedy team, that he could lift him up single-handedly.

Hardy accepted, and without much ado, J. M. came up with one arm and sat the heavy comedian onto a public bar.

On another occasion, J. M. became annoyed with a stranger who picked a fight with him in a parking lot. The man, seated in his Buick, shouted insults at J.M., who happened to block his immediate passage. J. M.'s hot temper flared. He made a charge like an angry bull, and lifting the front end of the car high, he let it drop back onto the asphalt with a crunch. As soon as the stranger managed to get over his initial petrifaction, he beat a retreat heedless of traffic regulations.

Jack Oakie, too, suffered because he misjudged J. M.'s boiling point. Coming from a formal dinner engagement, he stopped by at the clubhouse, where he began to needle the strong man. J.M. listened quietly, swallowing a number of cocktails, then, getting to his feet, he backed Oakie into a corner and, tearing his full dress suit in half with one solid rip, he calmly left him shivering in his underwear.

Johnny's time almost arrived when he tried to prevent J. M. from throwing an opponent atop a burning oven! In a drunken stupor J. M. mistook Johnny as his foe, grabbed hold of his arm, twisting it almost to the breaking point! Then, recognition suddenly set in . . . and he let go. However, the same night saw J. M. getting even with a vengeance. Without Johnny's protection the real enemy suddenly found himself face to face with J. M., who heaved him upside down into a gym locker, closing and locking the door. By chance, a possible mayhem was avoided because others noticed the incident and released the man before true harm came of the affair.

But despite all of his crazy stunts, J. M.'s popularity was never blackened, possibly because his manners whenever in the company of the weaker sex always were beyond reproach. No lady ever heard him use a single swear word, or saw him fall out of line. On the contrary, he set himself up as a shining knight to shield the fair, mostly wives of his celebrity friends, when their husbands were barred by threats of unfavorable publicity from actively participating in a Donnybrook. Once he even protected a future bride of Johnny's by hitting a four-letter-word-user underneath the table. After the deed was done he looked up apologetically and commented, "Let's get out of here, Johnny. I'm afraid that guy's bleeding all over me!"

Between pictures, life had a habit of turning dull even in Hollywood and actors amused themselves with giving parties. Often minds were made up on the spur of a moment, much too late for formal arrangements, invitations, or the like. Then someone came up with a brain wave! He telephoned a used-car lot, hiring several salesmen to deliver a number of automobiles to the front of his mansion. Within a short period the word had spread through the neighborhood that so-and-so was giving a party, and in no time another dozen cars were added to the original camouflage. When enough guests had been gathered in this manner, the host informed the suppliers to remove the bait.

Johnny seldom partook of such gaieties. Only if a special friend telephoned a personal invitation did he turn up. With the exception of his golfing pals he remained distant to Hollywood's select circle, preferring his lifeguard buddies at Santa Monica, or, paddling along on his surfboard a quarter-mile from the pier.

Skimming along over the glassy surface of Santa Monica Bay on a surfboard was a moment of ecstasy known in those days to but few men. The board was heavy by modern standards; it was hollow and formed of plywood, and leaked, thus contributing to the weight as it became waterlogged. Today's surfer boards are balsa wrapped in fiberglas or plastic, and are as light as the breeze, sometimes sailing high, when they get away from a surfer after a spill in bouncing waves.

But Johnny, crouched on his knees and pushing the board forward like a torpedo with great driving oar-like thrusts of his arms, was quite happy with his mount . . . and far from bored . . . as he might be at a Hollywood party.

As the board knifed toward the late afternoon sun setting off Point Dume, Johnny turned slightly to port, shook the salt-wet locks from his face and looked off to Catalina Island, dimly outlined in the blue haze hanging over the hills of Palos Verdes.

Gulls wheeled and soared as the late sun lighted their plumage. The great Pacific glistened and rippled, rising and falling in a slow surge against the horizon. The cool spray kicked up by his board felt good.

During these moments Johnny was content. This was His world!

Then, he picked up a wave, shoreward bound. As the board gathered speed, Johnny rose, Hawaiian style, and danced along the board until it hit "the soup"!

After a day of surfing Johnny made a habit of jumping the fence at Norma Shearer's house, near the beach, where he spent the rest of the afternoon teaching the two Thalberg children to swim while Norma, described by Johnny as a very kind, genteel lady, prepared sandwiches, and served tea for all.

While Metro jealously guarded Johnny's Tarzan image, keeping his career remote from customary loan-outs, the studio, nevertheless, disliked the fact that their star received his weekly salary at times for nothing but loafing around. An enterprising, promotion-hungry idea man soon came up with a remedy. He reminded the executives that Johnny attended diction classes at Mr. Morando's and, possibly, had developed a true sense of drama, a talent hitherto overlooked by casting scouts.

"We'll put elegant clothes on his back. We'll give him a drawing room setting with the latest finesse in decor. We'll use a beautiful actress with golden hair, creamy skin, and ruby lips to portray his demure, loving wife. We'll hire a couple of brats (pardon me!), little angels, from central casting as the children. Finally, behold! We see his photograph . . . handsome, debonair, a prince of a man. And then, we'll undermine it all the moment we see a red-eyed, drunken, disorderly ogre stagger across the threshold of the sweet home. Alas, as he manhandles the family, it becomes evident that he, indeed, is the husband whose addiction to alcoholism or worse, narcotics, has taken a gory hold of his faculties. What horrendous shock! But . . . as we introduce Johnny 'Tarzan' Weissmuller's new dimensions to the world, proving beyond the slightest doubt that he is the greatest living tragedian since the actor who played a similar character in the odes of . . . of . . . well, you know, that Greek fellow's epistles."

Johnny learned about the screen test a week before it took place. He prepared himself for the role in all seriousness. Studying his lines in front of a mirror, he tried developing a technique of his own but was unsure of just how to go about it. He remembered what Jack Barrymore had told him about the twitching of the nose. Thus Johnny began lifting his brows, rolling his eyes and mimicking the twitch. He even added another self-invented scene stealer, he wiggled his ears!

On the fateful morning, he nonchalantly sauntered onto the sound stage, dressed in a sports coat complete with ascot, feeling ready for the big test. He was greeted by a crew member, "Hiyah, Johnny! I didn't recognize you with your clothes on."

But the assigned director had a different comment as he walked a circle around his star. "Excellent! You look the part."

Johnny reciprocated with a courteous bow. "Thank you!" he said, threw his head back and looked blasé.

The director escorted him to the set where he introduced him to his leading lady. "Charmed!" Johnny said, and kissed the girl's hand.

"Yes! Yes!" The director became ecstatic. "This was the man before he succumbed to the wiles of liquor. Now you must recapture his fall! Remember, we're testing you for dramatic impact! When you arrive home, you're gassed, half out of your mind. You see your wife but don't recognize her. You light a cigarette. She comes to you, tries to make you lie down. But you start beating her. The children hear the commotion, run down the stairs and, seeing you hitting their mother, begin to wail pitifully. Hearing their little voices swelling in a crescendo of misery, something rings a bell within your mind. You drop your bruised beloved to the floor and cry out, 'Oh, Heaven, have mercy on me! What have I done?!' Then you stumble out of the house and into the night, a broken man." The director wiped his brow, overcome by emotion. "Get it?"

"Have no fear," said Johnny, straightening his ascot. "I'll do it!"

"Good!" The director beamed. "Much depends on this test. If all goes well, Metro has offered me a feature." He took a turn back to the arena, and Johnny followed him in the manner of a victorious gladiator.

Places! Camera! Action!

The door opened. Johnny, alias the gentleman turned ogre, entered. He made a straight dash to the table, where he found a cigarette and matches. He began to ignite the tobacco, puffed and puffed, but the cigarette remained unlit.

"Cut!" The director called, and walked to his star's side. "You must look stagnant like a puddle of foul water. Remember, you're stoned! Emaciated through overindulgence! Please try it again."

This time a big smoke cloud arose, settling around Johnny's face. He started to cough violently.

"Cut!" The director shouted, and joined Johnny for further consultations. "We'll get you another brand of cigarettes," the director promised. "These must be stale." He commanded, "Props!" before leaning closer to Johnny and, striking a familiar note, he whispered, "Just think — you've had a real binge. The world is going round and round. Your

205

mind is pitch black but you see pink elephants floating in the air . . ."

"No kidding!" Johnny interrupted, "I thought all elephants are gray . . ."

After a double take, the director dropped the subject. "Action!" sounded for the third, and last, time.

Johnny sprinted through the door, a wild glare in his eyes. He lit the cigarette. The children cried on cue as their make-believe mother screamed the oxygen out of her lungs. Johnny twitched his nose, but it began to itch so he picked it. His ears failed to waggle, he scratched them instead. He forgot his lines, because rolling his eyes he inevitably remembered to search for hidden dialogue cues.

"Cut! Cut! Cut!" The director screamed. "The hell with it! He can't light a cigarette! He can't act drunk! He doesn't know his lines! He only fiddles with his hands . . . If this is supposed to be dramatic acting, the Keystone Kops played tragedy!"

Johnny glanced about, absolutely bewildered. "But I've never smoked in my life!" he said. "I've never drunk anything but 'bug juice' which makes me sneeze, and once I had some brandy!"

The exhausted director packed his briefcase. "Forget it, Johnny. Do me a favor and return to your vines!" he muttered, making a hasty exit. He disappeared from the lot, was never seen or heard of again until A.T. (after television), when the lighted tube discovered his latent ability, which had been treated to such a frustrating blow the moment he became involved with histrionics . . . jungle style.

After screening Johnny's acting, MGM relaxed its

reins, allowed him time for solitaire, but stipulated that he must keep his weight down between films. Ever since the end of his active swimming career, he had had trouble keeping slim. This weight problem sent him to a clinic at La Jolla, where losing 25 pounds seemed like a breeze for a reasonable fee of $500 covering a five-week stay. The strict rules of the establishment agreed with him, reminded him of his training under Bachrach. He consumed 1,800 calories in 24 hours and, soon, surpassed his hopes with the scales registering a loss of 30 lbs. He retired early each evening, reading himself to sleep. However, his literary pursuits never included Freudian theories, the sophistication of diplomacy nor the doctrine of moderation in all things of Plato. Thus it happened in the fourth week of his diet that Johnny learned an unread lesson, the immediate result of his intrinsic honesty, his basic straightforwardness.

He received a wedding invitation from one of his best friends, a high-ranking action star. The two had been like brothers for years and Johnny, naturally, threw his strict regimen to the winds, attended the nuptials.

Champagne flowed to fill buckets. Choice tidbits preceded a richly laden dinner table, but Johnny's unaccustomed stomach hiccuped against this substantial nourishment, surrendered completely to the sparkling wine. Soon he felt dizzy; still, once the first sensation of intoxication had passed, he carried on with gusto. The "bug juice" awakened memories! Long since forgotten talk rang in his ears! The past suddenly became all muddled up with the present. And . . . en vino veritas! Thoughts about his estranged wife entered his mind as he glared at the bride, drawing a parallel line.

He wanted to warn his friend, tell him about the hurts that clouded his own mind at the sound of wedding bells . . . but all he did was make an asinine remark, one that touched upon the chastity of womanhood. Other members of the party tried to limit his insults but he, no longer capable of controlling himself, got to his feet and shouted clear across the room, "Why did you have to marry her, you fool! It would've been cheaper to buy her!"

Whether this outburst was caused by true concern, overheard gossip or his personal bitterness is known only by Bacchus. Johnny remembered nothing the next morning when he was aroused to find himself evicted from the health oasis for returning late and causing a terrible commotion. All he knew of the incident came from acquaintances who enlightened him with different versions. All agreed on one point, however: that the groom sprang on him like a wounded animal defending his mate. And all that Johnny could think about was "My God! I've lost a friend in a blackout. Why?!" How ironical that just prior to this he had failed his screen test, unable to portray the emotions of drunkenness in a convincing manner.

Johnny was becoming painfully aware that people in love are in a world apart and no one, but no one at all, should interfere in their mutual sanctuary, regardless of relationship or law. But, strangely, whereas a friendship between men is often lasting, strong, genuinely lacking prejudice except but for an honest desire to speak the mind; women are seldom friends, neither among themselves nor with the men they marry, despite their efforts to seem different. There are, of course, exceptions! And the highest link between

208

two individuals is a good, solid marriage. Nevertheless, divorces are rather common, and frequently leave a row of misunderstood emotional connections behind; moreover, they usually involve outspoken friends, who later regret their contribution.

Though this particular marriage ended in court, still Johnny had lost out for good. It had all happened accidentally anyway, because Johnny never had claimed to be an expert on love's triangular shape composed of man, woman, and ego. How could he have? with his own affairs running a gamut of changes. Lupe had received a cash settlement for his folly . . . whoever, then, could call "the little women" the losers?

When Johnny next played golf with J. M., he sadly confided in him. "I've gotten another lesson like the one you gave not so long ago. Only this one was for real! I was raked out of dramatic parts. Shoveled out of money. And my best friend feels like breaking a baseball bat over my head."

"That's living!" J. M. remarked philosophically, and shot two birdies at once — one on the green, the other atop a power line that paralleled the golf course.

BILLY ROSE'S AQUACADE

16

T HE EMPIRE STATE had decided to add a Marine Amphitheatre to the amusement area of the New York World's
Fair of 1939. It was to house the greatest aquatic spectacle
ever presented anywhere under the sun, and its accomplishment was entrusted to one of America's brilliant showmen,
Billy Rose.

Popularly referred to as the Aquacade, this mammoth
outdoor theatre contributed substantially to the architecture
of the Fair with its vast proportions, dimensions required to
accommodate the genius of Rose's fertile mind. It boasted
the largest seating capacity of any structure there. The huge
stage, set out on the water, had a depth of 200 feet and a
width of 311 feet, and enjoyed an overall perimeter of 500
feet to welcome the dancing toes of the Aquagals. When
the 275-foot pool was filled it weighed 3,500,000 lbs. Three-
hundred-thousand pounds of steel was used in its construction and 200 piles were driven to support it. At each end of
the stage rose the two 75-foot diving towers. The intricate
lighting system housed more than 500 lamps ranging from
2,000 to 4,000 watts, including 150-ampere arc lights that
were employed for even more colorful effects. Twenty elec-

tricians were constantly stationed in the recesses of the Amphitheatre and the stage. Despite the vastness and complexity of this electrical maze of operations, all signals functioned to perfection as, on any starlit night, the first giant lamps on the roof stabbed through the darkness with their columns of light, while the sides of the stage were flooded with softer illumination. When finally the arc lights glared, giving each detail a minute sharpness, the entire scene became silhouetted against the background of a nocturnal sky, forming a bewitching sight.

Prior to the opening of the Aquacade, one newswriter had queried Rose, tongue in cheek, "Do you think this show will come up to your standards of the colossal?"

"Well, judge for yourself," Rose answered offhandedly as he pointed over the water to the distant shoreline. "We're using Long Island as a backdrop!" To the reporter this reply sounded typical of the showman whose scope of activity had probably even appalled Ziegfeld and Barnum, and he enjoyed his display of quick wit. However, little did he realize that Rose, who had long since learned not to leave anything to mere chance including the image of his own dynamic personality, was simply repeating the line which had served him well once before, at the construction of the Aquacade at the Great Lakes Exposition on Cleveland's lakefront. Asked a similar question, he had answered, changing the description of the backdrop to, "the Dominion of Canada!"

Billy Rose had engaged scores of pretty girls as his aquafemmes, aquagals, and aquabelles. Hired handsome aquadudes, aquabeaux, as well as the Fred Waring Glee

Club. For his two top stars, he chose Johnny Weissmuller and Eleanor Holm.

A host of other names such as Gertrude Ederle, the first female to conquer the English Channel, and Pete Desjardins, Johnny's friend and Olympic double-crown diving champion, had also been chosen to fill the entertainment bill, that included Everett Marshall, whose forte was grand opera.

MGM had loaned Johnny to Rose for a weekly salary of $5,000, but while Metro collected the bounty, Johnny still received his regular studio pay check which, at that time, was reported as exactly half the above fee. The difference was pocketed by the studio, a customary procedure based on contract stipulations. And since his pay was picked up by his business manager, his actual allowance depended on the latter's generosity.

Working for Rose and his chief aide-de-camp, John Murray Anderson, presented no novelty to Johnny. He had coupled with Eleanor Holm before at the Cleveland Exposition. He had been signed to do four shows a day, seven days a week. In each performance he appeared twice and again in the grand finale. His fans saw Tarzan sans his customary loincloth; instead he modeled a variety of stunning, glamorous swim trunks including a pair of golden ones. As it happened, only B.V.D. swim suits were worn in this Aquacade of 1939, and Johnny was reminded of his past association with the company whose trademark sported a tiny sea horse holding onto a pair of monocles. Yet somehow, his B.V.D. days seemed now so very, very distant.

The high spot of the spectacle was a swimming waltz to the orchestral accompaniment conducted by Vincent Travers in which the talents of Johnny and Eleanor made swimming a true art form. While she swam the backstroke, he used his crawl stroke. As they gracefully skimmed through the waters, it often seemed to the audience that Eleanor Holm swam as fast as Johnny himself, but actually her feet were stably planted on his hips. He was the propelling force. Nevertheless, Eleanor Holm was much more than just a pretty mermaid, she was an Olympic champion in her own right, having acquired the backstroke title in 1932, at Los Angeles. National magazines had called her the ablest and most photogenic swimmer on the U.S. Olympic team. Ziegfeld had implored her, at 16, to join his Follies, but she had refused and he continued to camp on her trail from one amateur victory to another. She had briefly retired in 1934, and spent one year singing and in the movies, which also included a Tarzan film, but opposite Glenn Morris. When she returned, she captured the outdoor title for the 100-yard event the following year. Scandal had marred her next Olympic trip to Berlin. She was suspended for "roistering at the bar", a charge which was never substantiated to the satisfaction of the newspapermen making the journey. But she was left out of the race. The same year saw Hitler refuse to shake hands with the incomparable Jesse Owens.

Billy Rose, sensing Miss Holm's drawing power because of the wave of indignation that swept the country as a result of her suspension, immediately prevailed upon her to turn professional. She took his advice and her career began to glitter in the firmament of water shows.

During an early rehearsal Johnny watched Rose audition performers, among them a stubby, jovial-faced comedy diver who did a full gainer, switching the customary entry, to hit the water flat on his stomach. He wore a canvas suit to his ankles which at impact caused a loud splash. Rose turned to his assistant. "Get rid of him. We don't want him around," he said. Johnny happened to overhear this remark and intervened. He told Rose that, in his opinion, the diver's stunt seemed like a very funny, extremely daring novelty. "That's just it," Rose said after listening. "It's too daring! He'll kill himself on the first night. He'll never last through four shows. Sorry!"

The assistant informed the dripping, happy-faced guy with the deep dimples in his cheeks and chin of Rose's decision. Johnny observed how the latter's face grew sad; a forlorn expression showed in his eyes a moment before he glanced down at his hands which still clutched his tattered bathing cap. Johnny went to console him. "I think you did a great dive, but Rose is right; it seems awfully dangerous."

"It's okay . . ." The stranger flushed as he managed to simulate a smile. "Guess I'll just keep on trying!"

"You'll succeed!" Johnny promised.

"Yeah!" The rotund face lifted as he winked at Johnny with a tear still shining in his eye. "I'll set my own style! One of these days, they can't afford to turn me down. Why, I might even quit this water bit and go legit."

"That's the spirit!" Johnny said, shook the man's hand, then asked, "What's your name?"

"Jackie Gleason!"

And the stubby fellow waved a brief salute before he departed. In later years, at banquets and on golf courses, both men often recalled the incident.

Johnny's dressing room was forever surrounded by girl performers, a fact observed even by Dorothy Kilgallen, the Voice of Broadway. In a dialogue just before dawn, someone called Eleanor conducted the following cross-examination on the night life of the town. (Quote:)

E.: Good morning. Where have you been?

D.K.: Oh, everywhere. From the World's Fair to La Conga, from Dave's Blue Room to El Morocco, from the Cotton Club to the Kit Kat.

E.: What were you doing at the World's Fair?

D.K.: Looking at Johnny Weissmuller.

E.: Oh, you mean the Aquacade. How was it?

D.K.: Simply super. It bowles me over. And if it amazes us city folks, imagine the effect of all that color and beauty and talent upon the country people who've never seen an ordinary Broadway night club show. Imagine water ballets, gorgeous showgirls, a Morton Downey chorus, Eleanor Holm in a rhinestone bathing suit and an American flag finish, all for the price of one admission!

E.: And Johnny Weissmuller's shoulders.

D.K.: Yes, all the chorus girls out there have developed crushes on Johnny. When he walks by backstage, there is sighing like the rustling of leaves.

E.: You even sound like you might be doing a little sighing yourself! (End quote.)

Johnny spent his time between performances sightseeing the rest of the Fair. But he was mobbed by enthusiastic fans and, soon, had to relinquish these outings. However, there remained one attraction which kept on luring him back again and again: a hot dog stand where they also served sauerkraut, both his favorite delicacies. He discovered that by sneaking through the basement he found an exit to Midget Village, whence he could make a straight dash to the "Wienerwurst" hut. His only problem was hiding among the midgets! Thus he used his jungle technique, crawling on all fours pressed against the ground. Nevertheless, his secret-way was soon detected by the water-chorus lovelies and, pronto, the word went out!

But his most ardent admirer was none other than the incomparable Tallulah Bankhead, who displayed no qualms about revealing her feelings. "Dahling! You are the kind of a man a woman like me must shanghai, and keep under lock and key until both of us are entirely spent. Prepare a leave for ten days!" When Tallulah breathed, even the Alps felt her warm exhalation and blamed it on a descending Foehn. When Tallulah spoke, the earth trembled, even in Hemingway's Spain. When Tallulah commanded it took herculean strength to resist.

However ---

Johnny still fervently pursued his desire to open people's eyes toward physical fitness, which he considered his bible. The two Aquacade stars were approached by leading newspapers and given space to write a series of articles covering basic swimming lessons. His entry into the printed news world gave Johnny an opportunity to voice his thoughts, and he did so clearly, simply, emphatically. Every child should know at least enough swimming to reach and hang onto a canoe, or to sprint a hundred yards to shore and safety. He was a firm believer that these instructions should be included in every school's compulsory physical education program, maintaining that in the olden days Egyptians and Romans had kept the doctor away by constant, vigorous bathing. Swimming presented a feasible exercise even for older people, whereas other sports, with the possible exception of golf, were too rough on those past middle-age.

His love for youngsters whose optimistic viewpoints he enjoyed had remained steadfast; he vastly preferred their endless enthusiasm for outdoor living to, for instance, the mundane crowd Lupe had brought into his life. He ran into her accidentally on one of his infrequent visits to a restaurant, Toots Shor's, which at lunch resembled an Olympic meet between the four-year intervals.

Dempsey sat in a corner with Jesse Owens giving ear. Bill Tilden conversed as Pete de Paolo and a sportsman of the movies, John Wayne, listened in. Grantland Rice and Paul Gallico were engrossed in talk. And Max Baer had found Del Webb and Dan Topping to discuss the future of the Yankees.

When Johnny made his way to his table, he shook hands with Ed Sullivan, who had always been a part of the world of sports and the people who immortalized it. As they reminisced about the times when teen-age had bound their friendship, many memories came alive . . . the happy and the sad that spelled out their past adolescence — like the untimely passing of Sybil Bauer . . .

Lupe interrupted their talk. She approached Johnny amiably. "Johnee, I read in the papers you have met a nice society girl. You will marry her, no?"

"I will marry her, yes!" Johnny answered, and mentally

compared his bride-to-be with his ex-wife. Ne'er a more different twain!

"But she ees not an actress!" Lupe quipped. "She will be no fun for you, Popee!"

"I've had fun!" Johnny said. "I want peace!"

Lupe shrugged, returning to her escort. "Poor Johnee, you do not know that peace only comes in the grave." He did not know then that she had uttered the first subconscious thoughts of her ultimate, fateful decision that was to purify her fiery little soul in purgatory before death placed a calming hand onto her troubled brow.

Johnny had met Beryel Scott at Pebble Beach during a golf tournament. He became attracted to her quiet, unassuming disposition, her modest charm, poised urbanity — neither forward nor shy. He had pursued her from the moment they met, disregarding an introduction someone offered. He simply took her hand and, seating himself beside her, kept everyone at a distance. When she failed to meet him on the following day, he telephoned everyone in town, leaving little messages in coffee shops, hotels, cocktail lounges, with friends and relatives. Beryel had never met such a man; her young heart, too, succumbed to his looks and fascinating influence.

The more Johnny got to know the twenty-one year old brunette, the more he liked her refinement, education, gentleness in manner and, after all the tornadoes that had crossed his path with Lupe, Beryel seemed to possess all the qualities desirable in a woman, all rolled into one delicate, engaging package of femininity.

Beryel's father, an authority on Oriental carpets, dealt in the rug business. Beryel was known as a San Francisco socialite, but she had been born in Toronto, Canada, on Walker Avenue.

But mostly, Johnny yearned for children denied him in his former marriages. His youthful looks belied his age, and even though he tried to hide it from Beryel, he had reached his 35th birthday. Bachelorhood held no attraction for him; he felt a deep need for something more permanent in life, and Beryel Scott seemed heaven sent to fulfill his expectations. He began to see in her the woman whom he could picture as the mother of his children, as his companion now and for as long as the future lasted.

Before leaving California, he had purchased a corner lot in Brentwood, just next door to Joan Crawford's lovely mansion on Bristol. Beryel went with him to approve the architect's plans. Both had talked about possible additional construction; nurseries, playrooms, where little Weissmullers would grow into teen-agers. Their home would be a peaceful haven for children and a proper setting for Beryel, the woman fit to help creation produce the natural.

Johnny expected Beryel in New York within days, and while they had not yet set a date for their wedding, both had agreed it should take place soon. He hoped that she would consent to marry him at once. Meantime, he waited, performed, and played golf, at intervals.

He showed possibilities of golf greatness when he found time to play at Wheatley Hills, as in the pro-amateur tournament which Ray Kilthau and Stewart Boyle won with 67. Kilthau had teamed with Johnny before, and after this particular match, he told the "Brooklyn Eagle" that Johnny was really a prospect for the big-name tournaments. Firstly, because he had a good command of both the beginning and end of golf: he could drive and he could putt, and, secondly, he had a much-better-than-average iron game. He did not overswing, followed through well and had strong wrist action.

"A good 75 golfer," Kilthau said. "Considering that he's still doing four swimming shows a day, I think his golf is amazing."

However, when Johnny was queried by reporters on his preference in games of relaxation, he replied that golf was okay but that he would rather swim at the beach. This peculiar answer was meant very much in earnest. "There's quite a difference," Johnny told the reporters, "between swimming in a show and swimming for the fun of it. At the beach you can relax, mentally and physically, but when you're swimming for exhibition, you have to be alert all the time and that's a definite strain."

In all the years that had passed since Johnny had left his amateur standing behind, he had waited for some up-and-coming young athlete to shatter his records — but none appeared. "And I'm sore at them too," he laughed, "for not doing it before this."

He had traveled to New York and the Aquacade for a proposed stay of six months, but the strenuous schedule which kept him in the water most of the time brought on renewed ear trouble. When his own cure of drying the inner ear with pure alcohol failed to remedy the constant aching, he consulted a specialist. The doctor advised him to stop swimming for a while until the chronic ailment was brought under control, fearing that complications could easily cause deafness. Johnny wired Metro. But the studio stalled, not realizing the seriousness of the matter; they hesitated, not caring to break their contract with Rose.

Johnny kept on performing.

One night, just before the last show, a familiar face was seen backstage.

Prompted by an idea Chris Dumphy had put into his mind, Bing Crosby had come to participate in his friend's metier. The crooner looked at the many clown suits hanging in a dressing room, picked out one, then informed his pal, Johnny, that he had accepted Dumphy's bet to do a dive, replacing the regular comedy performer. Johnny tried unsuccessfully to talk him out of it. High diving is extremely dangerous, even when one is at the peak of physical condition.

Bing was determined to make good the wager. He donned the funny suit, his pipe still between his teeth, and sauntered to the tower.

"Ladies and gentlemen! The next comedy dive will be performed by none other than Bing Crosby in person!"

Everyone thought it was a gag. Only Johnny felt panicky as he watched Crosby mount the 20-foot platform, his pipe still in his mouth. "If he dives head first he'll break all his teeth!" Johnny called to fellow swimmers, then alerted some to stand by in case of emergency. "When he gets to the edge of the board, shove him in. That way he'll land on his rear. It's safest!" "Der Bingle," meantime, took bows to the applause of an amused public. He stepped forward, smiling, then glanced down! Below him the water seemed dark, and far away. The lights glared around him. He stepped back half-way; the board vibrated beneath his feet;

suddenly he began to feel dizzy. He sat down. Johnny's rescue team approached him, but before they reached his side, Crosby got to his feet, strayed to the very end of the platform where he started jumping up and down.

"If he dives with that pipe, he'll jab it right through his throat!" Johnny worried. "Come on, boys, this is the moment!" At that instant, Bing was propelled into space with a push on the derrière. Feet first he fell, frozen smile and all, his pipe still firmly clenched between his teeth, landing on his posterior. He was dragged to safety by three of Johnny's handy men. As he climbed out of the water, his first concern was to collect the $100 bet from Dumphy.

"You call that a dive?" Dumphy argued. "You were shoved! Your seat got splashed! That's only worth $50 in my book. So take it or leave it!"

"Okay, you chiseler, I'll take your $50, but remind me to put our next bet into writing," Bing said, but not unhappily. He changed into his own clothes, and took Dumphy out for a drink. And this remained Crosby's cheapest personal appearance forevermore.

The following morning, Billy Rose called Johnny to his office. "You almost ruined me last night!" he scolded, pacing the floor. "If Crosby had been hurt, for Christ's sake, he'd have sued me for a million!"

"You mean," Johnny said innocently, "that instead of five, you'd have only made four million dollars profit?"

"Oh, get out of here! And tell Bing if he ever comes up with any more of his great ideas about high diving to use them in someone else's production. Better still — tell him to jump in the ocean!"

Johnny felt like soaking his own nerves. But with the Pacific too far removed, and the Atlantic too cold, he chose the steam room at the New York Athletic Club where, again, he ran into Ed Sullivan.

"Let's have a workout!" he suggested when the mercury climbed the ceiling. "How does 20 laps sound to you?"

"Just fine!" said Ed.

And as Johnny went "up and down" the pool . . . Ed went "up and down" the shower . . . Both quitting come curtain time.

On August 20, Johnny took Beryel Scott to Garfield, New Jersey, where Mayor John M. Gabriel married them in the Town Hall. Sherman Billingsley, a New York night-club operator, was best man. Later in the day Johnny got back to the Aquacade in time for his four customary performances, with five on week-ends. As ever, the honeymoon had to await a more opportune time and place.

Shortly afterwards, Johnny sent another cable to MGM, it read, "If you want me to continue as Tarzan, you must get me out of the Aquacade. Doctor informs I'll lose my hearing if I go on giving daily shows." This time the studio came through with an immediate release. They were not likely to jeopardize their money-making star, not under these circumstances. Buster Crabbe was chosen to replace him in the Aquacade. However, Johnny's association with Billy Rose continued the following year, when he starred at the San Francisco Fair on Treasure Island.

War clouds had gathered and burst over Europe. Hitler's armies marched into Poland. Great Britain and France declared war. Russia sealed a non-aggression pact with Germany. Italy's entry came in June, 1940. The conflict threatened to spread into a world-wide combat. As yet, the United States had kept out of the battle, but many had already volunteered, crossing the Atlantic to join the Anglo-French forces.

Beryel was pregnant with her first child, and Hollywood had never seen a more excited, expectant father than Johnny. Since the very first day he had heard the news, he planned how to teach his son to swim. Of course, if it happened to be a girl, she would be equally welcome, the odds being what they are. There have been many great femme athletes throughout the years. The stork had promised to deliver the C.O.D. package in September, during the new Aquacade; so Johnny took his bride to San Francisco, securing the Stanford Hospital for the delivery of his first-born. While Beryel remained in the care of her parents who lived there, Johnny checked in for rehearsals, joining Billy Rose in a search for a new West Coast swimming partner, since Eleanor Holm had stayed in New York.

Among those auditioned for the big break was a most-attractive, shapely girl who answered to the name of Esther Williams. She nimbly passed through the screening process which narrowed the margin of a hundred contestants down to ten starry-eyed hopefuls. After Rose selected the final five, Johnny was called in. He took one look at the tall brownette, and made his decision. Esther stepped into Eleanor's shoes.

As Johnny taught her all the routines, he found that he had picked a versatile athlete for a co-star. He often discussed her potentials with his friend, a comedy diver named Bill Lewin, who had replaced his former partner. "You know, Bill," Johnny said, "this girl has the makings of a star. Not only in the water! I think I'll invite some MGM bigwigs to come up and take a look at her movie potentials." He did, and Esther Williams became ESTHER WILLIAMS, but only after the sweet, genuinely unaffected young lady had declined several times, for personal reasons . . . like getting married, and hoping to raise a family. As it turned out, her fiancé changed his mind and faded from her life. She became a movie star. However, years later, when Johnny happened to run into her accidentally on the studio lot, her disposition had changed entirely. She coolly acknowledged his greeting with, "Aren't you gaining a bit of weight?" "Thanks!" Johnny replied in passing, doubting he had ever heard this word from her lips, regardless of his current inflection.

The Fair on Treasure Island opened and, of course, followed the Rose tried-and-true pattern of success. After all, he was using San Francisco's Golden Gate as a backdrop! But as one cynical reporter remarked, "I guess he goofed for once, because he couldn't keep Alcatraz from spoiling the view!"

On September, the 23rd, baby John Scott Weissmuller was born. His anxious father escaped the hospital room where his wife was bedded at the first sign of her labor pains. He frantically screamed for a nurse, alerted all the orderlies on duty, and kidnapped a doctor, not an obstetrician but a psychiatrist, from the side of his confused patient.

His mission completed, Johnny fled to the nearest bar to await news of the blessed event.

> *And he who gives a child a treat*
> *Makes joy-bells ring in Heaven's street,*
> *And he who gives a child a home*
> *Builds palaces in Kingdom come,*
> *And she who gives a baby birth*
> *Brings Saviour Christ again to Earth.* *

Bill Lewin brought the word. Johnny rushed to the maternity ward and layed eyes on his newborn son, tears of happiness welling up inside him as deep gratitude filled his being. He felt a loving devotion toward his wife, at peace with God and the universe. At long last he had everything his heart desired, a son, love, a home, money, success. He stood on top of the world, at the end of a rainbow, and he saw its multi-colored spectrum reflected with the sun's luminous light. A lucky man!

* The Everlasting Mercy — John Masefield, 1878—

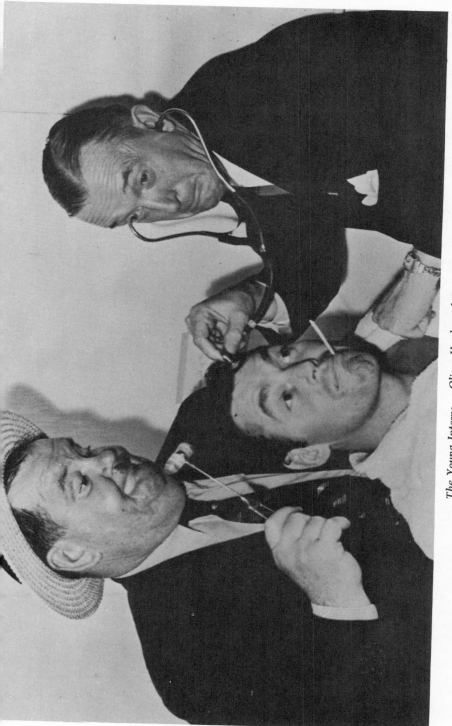

The Young Interns — Oliver Hardy and Stan Laurel
(alias Dr. Catsey and Dr. Killdart) working over "patient" Johnny.

Groucho Marx approve of a pretty athlete's foo (Photo by Elmer F. Ec hardt)

At San Francisco's Fair on Treasure Island, Johnny and Morton Downey greet a visiting dignitary accompanied by Errol Flynn. (Photo by Elmer F. Eckhardt)

Johnny and Esther Williams crawling in three-quarter time. (Photo by Elmer F. Eckhardt)

Contributing a $5,000 yell to the war effort. (MGM Photo)

Busy King Johnny and his royal brood.

"Queen Beryel and the two princesses."

Johnny teaching John Scott to dog paddle.

No swimming on the Pyramids! "That's why I brought my camel . . ."

"I am calling you — Pharaoh who? Sphinx-a-loo!"

Forever blowing bubbles

Proud fishermen! (Johnny, Allene and friend at Acapulco.)

FACTS AND FAIRY TALES

17

THE PITTER-PATTER of little feet in the Weissmuller household soon multiplied with the birth of two baby girls, Wendy, born June 1, 1942, and Heidi, a year later on July 20th, both in Los Angeles. Thus, as fairy stories go, the royal couple moved their little prince and his sisters into a larger castle on Rockingham, overlooking Mandeville Canyon.

The Spanish-Mediterranean mansion surrounded by tall, shady avocado trees, with its badminton court, swimming pool and small guest house down a slope, where once upon a time Charles Laughton had studied in privacy, had originally been built by Helen Twelvetrees. In this stately residence, Queen Beryel reigned freely, holding court during the absence of her husband, busy King Johnny, who daily ventured forth to fight wild beasts, villainous knights or dangerous Hottentots in Culver City's backlot. Returning with his weekly bounty, a loot condensed into a wide strip of paper people called a check, he bought all the comforts, necessities, toys, for his illustrious family. The famous father's conquered trophies filled the interior of the house, serving as support for little Wendy, pulling herself up on her tiny legs. Throughout the living room, discarded playthings waylaid occasional visitors. And in the kitchen, a fresh supply of pablum was always on hand.

As the children grew, hard-working Johnny spent his weekends close to the pool, playing porpoise with the two eldest, while infant Heidi peacefully slumbered in Queen Beryel's arms. Their pets, Dinny and Shep, both terriers, chased each other around the spacious grounds, barking, joining in with the happy sounds of laughter and baby talk that echoed through the principality.

Thus they lived in their secluded realm, protected on all sides by the greatest land in the world. Only a single concern interrupted the tranquillity of the absolute monarchy within the Republic.

Far distant tyrants in the land of the rising sun had sent flights of fire-spitting dragons to attack Pearl Harbor, and a real-life war had called upon all Americans to come forward to destroy the unjust might of a Hitler, a Mussolini, and a Tojo. Johnny's age and children had kept him out of active fighting, but he had joined the film industry in playing a vital part in keeping up the morale of the braves on furlough from Guadalcanal, Europe, or wherever the long arm of the allied powers was stretching to rescue the enslaved. As time piled up, he spent less and less of it at home. His family was left to their own devices, with long, dragging hours of loneliness.

Ever since the great conflict had spread to include the United States, Johnny had done his share in assisting the defense by raising funds for the war effort. Together with Bing, Bob, and Maurie Luxford, "Mr. Golf of America," he journeyed to tournaments, raising millions of dollars in the attempt. As he traveled the country far and wide, he stirred up the emotions of the good people of Uncle Sam's land to drop dollars, and/or aluminum into the purse of their government. In Texas, a generous oil tycoon bid $5,000 for hearing the Tarzan yell from his vocal cords but once! At Camp Pendleton recruits were being trained to dive off a 30-foot platform. Some of these boys were reluctant, had never before been near the water! After Johnny got through entertaining them with his aquatic comedy diving routine from that same platform, most no longer found it tough to follow suit. "If Tarzan can jump into a tank of cold water, then so can a marine!" the slogan went out. The same patriotic motives made him visit hospitals, cheer up disabled veterans, put on shows in armed-forces bases. United he stood with other entertainers circling the Hollywood "Round Table," taking part wherever possible in his country's struggle to help mankind survive, doing what he could do . . . as did so many stars of stage and screen.

The Hollywood Canteen was opened in October, 1942, admitting some twenty-five hundred men each night to the redwood planked building on Cahuenga Boulevard just off Sunset that resembled a double barn on the outside, but left a kaleidoscopic impression with any newcomer on the inside. Tables, chairs, a dance floor which seemed much larger than it actually was, a stage, a snack bar running the length of the room and a great crowd of uniformed G.I.'s milling among a hundred pretty junior hostesses under a Gargantuan beamed-trellis ceiling from which hung wagon wheel chandeliers, with pendant kerosene lanterns converted to electricity. Opened Mondays through Saturdays between 7 p.m.

and midnight, and Sundays from 2 till 8 p.m., the men of the armed forces patiently queued up in front, under a sign that read "For Service Men." They awaited their turn to pass into the Gay Ninetyish scene with a touch of the old frontier, sprinkled with Hollywood's special brand of glamour, the stars . . . in person . . . alive . . . and talking. Starting with Bette Davis, the Canteen's prexy, all of filmdom's royalty showed there, entertaining, serving, signing autographs, posing for snapshots, and lending a sympathetic ear where listening helped most. Fire regulations permitted only 500 at a time, but those who entered eagerly departed just as willingly to give a fellow soldier an equal chance for memories. Of the 6,000 workers who helped in the operation of the establishment, only nine were paid; all others volunteered. It took $3,000 weekly to run the canteen, but this sum never presented any problems, especially after Warner Brothers bought the motion picture rights of the story, paying out $250,000 toward the upkeep. No one worried again about soliciting funds.

As Beryel was left with the diapers, Johnny washed dishes at the Hollywood Canteen. He talked to the men, shared coffee and doughnuts with them. And there he ran into his former neighbor, la belle Crawford, and noticed, surprised, how the reserved Joan managed to captivate her already captive audience. Johnny had always considered her more mysterious, more silent than even Garbo! Even after having lived next door to her for almost two years, and, after selling the house to Robert Preston, after meeting her many times on the studio lot, he had seldom passed the conventional greeting stage. Now he saw her with the service men, informal, at ease, relaxed, her wit sparkling, her conversation flowing freely as if coming from a running brook.

Buster Keaton, too, came to entertain the military with his sad, dour expression. Johnny remembered how Buster had always broken up when he had taken Cheetah onto his set. Naturally such film footage was edited to maintain the comedian's serious-faced image, but Buster had added several juicy profanities to his dialogue which a soundman's earphones missed picking up. Only later, when the sound track was spliced with the film did the harassed cutter demand an audition with the director. Johnny decided that a repeat performance could easily prove hilarious and, one day, smuggled Cheetah in. To his great surprise, Buster continued his act without so much as flinching an eyelid.

Such then was the general feeling of the Hollywood Canteen, an outgoing affection for the common cause, that personalities either restrained their private follies, or gave themselves wholly in contrast to their natural reserve.

There was the grim side, too, and Johnny had a part of it.

The routine looked easy — but! For almost two years, without benefit of publicity ballyhoo, Johnny had also been risking his neck twice a month at the Long Beach Naval Base showing trainees how to swim out from under water covered with flaming oil or gasoline. Just to illustrate what could be done, he even dived into the flames from a 15-foot platform.

Beryel knew about these stunts, worrying constantly despite her husband's assurances that it was really nothing, just singeing the eyebrows a little.

However, the film parade took him back to work. He completed "Tarzan's Secret Treasure" and "Tarzan's New York Adventure." The latter ended his contract with Metro-Goldwyn-Mayer. His option was dropped because of the foreign-market losses inflicted upon the studio by World War II. It also broke up the team of Weissmuller and O'Sullivan. Maureen temporarily retired from the screen to have a family. Yet more was to be said about these two epics. Veteran movie critics who had seen all the Tarzan films rated Weissmuller and O'Sullivan as the best screen combination, and said that the finest Tarzan pictures were turned out by MGM back in the days of Irving Thalberg. Thalberg had always insisted on lavish productions, grandiose spectacles. The first two films had cost a million dollars each; the third, "Tarzan Escapes," doubled the price. When Thalberg died, however, MGM decided to economize on these adventure stories. Henceforth, locations suffered severe losses from bad weather, causing miscellaneous difficulties all around. Nevertheless, MGM's policy of using only high class actors right down the line continued. In "Tarzan's Secret Treasure" the featured cast included Barry Fitzgerald, Reginald Owen, Tom Conway, and last, but not least, Philip Dorn, of "I Remember Mama" fame.

This actor Dorn had appeared in a number of leading roles on the American screen, but few recognized in him a top European star, who, under the name of Frits van Dongen, had captivated ladies' hearts in pre-war German "Tobis" films. The list of his credits included such spectacles as the legendary love story of a maharajah, filmed in two parts, the first entitled "Der Tieger von Eshnapur," followed by "Das

Indische Grabmal"; as well as others like "Verwehte Spuren" and "Die Reise nach Tilsit" in which, both times, he starred with a controversial but talented Swedish actress, Kristina Soederbaum, whose husband, producer Veit Harlan, later achieved notoriety with his anti-Semitic movie "Jud Suess," in which he cast his wife as the title-role portrayer's rape victim.

Philip Dorn or Frits van Dongen, was a Dutchman by birth. He escaped the Nazis in time to appear in U. S. propaganda films against the Third Reich, but in spite of his charm, ability, and co-stars like Joan Crawford, Irene Dunne, etc., his career never quite got off the ground in Hollywood. He eventually retired from acting, and settled down in West Los Angeles with his wife, who had shared all his tribulations and glory.

In "Tarzan's New York Adventure," the scene where Tarzan climbed the Brooklyn Bridge to dive off into the East River, Johnny, as always, perfomed his own stunts. He ascended the large suspension bridge on his hands and feet. Only when it came to the actual plunge, which no man could have taken without killing himself, did Metro decide to use a dummy. Tarzan's likeness, thrown into the great stream that united the boroughs of Manhattan and Brooklyn, was soon lost from sight.

However, such was not the fate of the affable Johnny nor Burroughs' ape man. No sooner had he parted company with Leo the MGM lion than Sol Lesser picked up his contract, signing him for more of the same. Future Tarzan movies were to be filmed at the RKO-Radio Studios in the heart of Hollywood itself, and the switch merely brought along a slight inconvenience caused by the longer drive to work. "Tarzan Triumphs" found its release in 1943, followed yearly by other features, "Tarzan's Desert Mystery," "Tarzan and the Amazons," "Tarzan and the Huntress," "Tarzan and the Leopard Women" and finally, "Tarzan and the Mermaids." Judging from these titles, Tarzan's jungle yell might easily have turned into a wolf call!

The producer surrounded his masculine specimen with harems of gorgeous, untamed femininity, all curved amply in the right places, all approving battles till final conquest or death. He also found him a new screen mate in Brenda Joyce. Maureen's replacement, tall and blond, had played her first important role in the Tyrone Power-Myrna Loy film "The Rains Came," in which she wooed George Brent away from the path of evil. She was married, had two children and was proud to be cast in a sarong role. She seemed a good choice, unafraid of working with animals, swam fairly well and her only fault, according to Johnny, was that she scared him out of his wits driving an automobile. Due to the gas rationing, each took turns motoring to location. Said Johnny, "but I'd feel safer riding an elephant or a camel!" Another thing bothered him somewhat. "I don't know what those kids are going to think when they see me with a blond Jane. Kind of looks like Tarzan's been playing the jungle a bit."

This impression was shared by a few others, including columnist Sidney Skolsky who visited the set, and was told to search for Johnny behind some bushes. Well! He walked through the jungle, saw Johnny, in his loincloth, sitting on a bench and — playing gin rummy with a chimpanzee!

"How's everything?" Skolsky inquired after his initial shock. "Terrible," answered Johnny. "I'm out about $200, I've just been blitzed. This new chimp is making a monkey out of me." For Cheetah had been replaced with a younger look-alike, passing as a twin, with but one major difference, though hard to spot. This ape vastly preferred to be addressed as "her," bringing along all the scruples of her sex, with the usual misbehavings.

Emma, too, had resigned and Tantor took over the role of elephant. Otherwise all had remained uniform and calm with "Boy" Sheffield continuing in the part. There was a moment of excitement when Johnny had to beat an alligator to shore when the 'gator broke the protective tape around his jaw and almost made a meal out of the swimmer.

At home, Beryel was getting restless. The big house was becoming a burden with the shortage of domestic help. She saw little of her husband, felt lonesome, depressed and neglected. As much as she tried to understand the reasons for Johnny's many absences, she still found it hard to co-ordinate her life, to center it only around the children. She had borne her babies, one after the other, and, still so young, lacked companionship and fun which she had hoped to find in her marriage. She took to brooding, finally resolving that she, too, had a right to find some enjoyment in life. Thus, she joined exclusive club memberships, arranged bridge parties at her home, and often invited groups of intellectual friends over to discuss art and poetry.

Johnny, in turn, found little in common with Beryel's friends. He had spent most of his life in the company of athletes, on the golf course, or at work. Whenever he returned from a schedule of personal appearances or from the studio, he felt like a quiet evening at home with his wife and the children, or like going to the movies. His inner self had never felt the need to psychologize, craving no deeper learning than such as he had accumulated through the years, mixing with people of all professions, traveling the face of the earth.

Johnny expected Beryel to understand his busy schedules, his increased popularity which placed certain demands onto his shoulders, but now found an unhappy wife greeting him with tears in her eyes the moment he deemed to return home.

Johnny was experiencing moments of jealousy too, noticing Beryel's attachment to strangers, friendships that had sprung from a meeting of minds. On the other hand, he forgot to notice in his active whirl that Beryel truly suffered from neglect. The fairy tale that had begun so full of promise seemed to have fallen under a wicked spell. When Beryel decided it was best to sell the oversized mansion and buy Uplifters Ranch #2, on Latimer Road, close to Will Rogers Polo Club, a slight but definite rift became evident in their relationship.

The new house had no pool, and Johnny often did not bother to stop by at home before crossing the street to swim at the clubhouse, where he occassionally took one drink too many before nightfall. Beryel resented that kind of behaviour; her youth handicapped any understanding of her husband's motives. After a while Johnny's soirées became more frequent, lasted longer. He went to visit his mother. Sitting close to her, silent for hours, he brought his untold thoughts to Mother Elizabeth whose watchful eyes noticed a poignant suffering in her son's face; yet she never asked anything about his domestic life.

And Beryel went home to her parents also. They, too, recognized in her demeanor the sad tale of a love turning sour. But, equally discreet, neither pried into their daughter's affairs.

The emotional connection between the two further suffered through the intervention of Johnny's business manager, Bö Roos, who resented Beryel's taking an active interest in their finances. After she discovered certain discrepancies among Johnny's payable accounts, Roos told his client that Beryel was too extravagant in her expenditures. Johnny, who thought of Roos as his friend, and who knew nothing about his monies except what Roos cared to let him know about, immediately took his concern out on his wife. From then on the fissure widened; the couple spoke but little to each other. Had they communicated, talked about their difficulties, misunderstandings, a solution might have been found but, inevitably, Beryel sued for divorce in December, 1943, charging grievous mental suffering which made it no longer possible for them to remain living as husband and wife.

Despite their troubles, Johnny had not anticipated this turn of events. Shocked, and deeply grieved he pleaded with her to reverse her decision. She finally consented because of the children. John Scott was now 3, Wendy 18 months, and little Heidi Elizabeth five months old. For a while it seemed that at least their offspring would live happily ever after, united with both their parents.

A Paramount unit, Pine-Thomas Productions, offered Johnny a contract for three pictures. They had heard about his desire to mingle with civilized, fully dressed men and women on the screen, unbounded by monosyllabic sounds, the jungle and swinging vines. Basically, Johnny had nothing against Tarzan, but he felt entitled to try a different approach to the public.

"Swimming gave me my start, but my pal Tarzan did the real work. He set me up nicely," he said, but added, "I feel I'm now in the position to risk a change. With clothes on, I may not even have to starve myself all the time. I've nothing against the loincloth, but this constant diet is murdering me."

The proposed film fare included roles of an army flyer, a combat correspondent, and a cowboy in a western with music. "I've no fixed idea about shedding my jungle role entirely," Johnny said, when queried by reporters. "I've still got a contract with Lesser. But I'd like to move into the Douglas Fairbanks type of action pictures. I'm no great actor, but my fans like me, so why shouldn't I give it a whirl? I've been wearing animal skin scanties too long. My chest is calloused from beating it, and I've climbed more trees than a lumberjack! My lines have read like a backward two-year-old talking to his nurse. I remember once I was supposed to point somewhere and say, 'you go.' I must've been feeling talkative that day, because I pointed and said, 'you go quick.' 'Cut!' the director yelled. 'What's the matter, Johnny? We don't want to load this scene up with any long speeches.' You see what I mean!!! And with this war on, it's good to get into an uniform, even if it isn't for real!"

Lesser granted Johnny his leave of absence between pictures, to follow his urge. His first stop was at the barber's, where, taking a shearing for art's sake, he received his first straight cut in years, his lost locks plentiful enough to stuff a pillow. As he walked out of the shop, he saw two small boys in a nearby tree playing Tarzan. He thought he would give them a little drama and let out the jungle yell. The kids stopped, slid down the bark, and cornered Johnny.

"Who do you think you are, Tarzan?" One freckle-faced rascal guffawed.

The other sneered. "These jerks who think they're for real! If you're Tarzan, where's your hair?"

Argument fini — a fait accompli!

A few months later both of the pictures with the war-time settings were called off. Feeling World War II's end close at hand, Pine-Thomas decided not to risk a film of this type at present. The agreement with Johnny still stood, but had to await a proper script. The screenplay for the western had previously been rejected by the duo, also.

Johnny trimmed 35 pounds off his waistline and returned to climbing trees.

The present and ex Mrs. Weissmullers often met at the beauty parlor. The two women felt friendly toward each other as they talked about Beryel's children and their father, without gossiping about his virtues or faults. Beryel had always admired Lupe's looks even without a trace of make-up, while Lupe liked the other's even temperament.

Lupe's name had lately been linked with that of Harold Ramond (Maresch), an Austrian actor who was being groomed for stardom, but whose reputation was that of a roué. Before disappearing under the dryer, Lupe told Beryel she had to talk to her in private, but the opportunity failed to present itself on that occasion.

Soon, thereafter, Lupe invited the Weissmullers to a cocktail party. Again she approached Beryel, and it seemed to the latter that there was something she was trying to confide to her. However, the house was over-crowded with guests, and Lupe only managed to inquire about the children, and to ask her to please drop by the following day. Beryel detected a note of utmost urgency in her voice. It sounded almost like a plea.

On the next day, Beryel arrived late in Beverly Hills. She noticed several strange cars parked outside the house and, considering a moment, she decided against going in. Not knowing who was present, she feared her visit might be misinterpreted, and she did not want to be exposed to rumors. Thus, she turned her car around and drove home.

Two days later the headlines screamed:
"LUPE VELEZ TAKES OWN LIFE"

Frantic fans surrounded the house on Rodeo Drive, broke through fences, shattered windows, forced their way inside before Mrs. Beulah Kinder, Lupe's secretary and friend, managed to alert the police. The fanatic followers snatched only photographs, leaving other items of value alone. Among those removed was one written in Spanish from Gary Cooper. Another signed "Venida," given to Lupe at the time of her marriage to Johnny, that read, "May you both walk together through life with a song in your heart and a smile on your face." Her portraits, snapshots with

Johnny, and one inscribed, "Lupe, dear, may you always laugh and be happy, Tony." The fans, or fanatics, fled before the law arrived to restore order. Mrs. Kinder burst into tears.

Lupe's body had been discovered earlier, peacefully bedded in her upstairs room, an eternal slumber closing her sparkling eyes forever. Next to her an empty bottle of Seconal, a powerful sedative, had been found, with her last will, and farewell notes to Mrs. Kinder and Harold Ramond, her lover. In this second letter she blamed him for her suicide, her's and her unborn child's! "You did not want us, now we will never be disgraced!" the damning truth read. A medical examination revealed that Lupe had, indeed, been pregnant. Her testament left $125,000 in holdings, plus $50,000 in cash, jewelry, personal effects and two cars, to be distributed between her mother, relatives, and Mrs. Kinder. The text of her note to the latter was never revealed in any press, but many presumed that it held the true key to her anguish. She had asked to be buried in her homeland. And, after all inevitable legal matters had been straightened out, her mortal remains were shipped to Mexico. Meantime, she was taken to a funeral parlor, where she lay in state, dressed in a full-length ermine coat, looking more beautiful in death than ever before in life, a strange peace visible on her finely-chiseled features.

When Johnny saw her, with Beryel on his arm, he could not believe that she had really taken her own life. "Not Lupe!" he thought, over and over again. "Not Lupe! Not her! She had been so alive, so active, in love with life! She could not have killed herself because of a man!" He never

241

told anyone how deeply her death touched his being. He had loved her and, in a sense, had never truly stopped. He brooded about his little Latin ex-wife, forgetting about Beryel, who, in turn, thought her own disturbing thoughts.

Lupe had come to her in desperation, she suddenly realized, wanting to ask for advice. Had she not constantly mentioned the children? It was natural that she would have turned to her, because she, Beryel, had carried Johnny's children, weaving an invisible bond between Lupe and herself. If she had only known! Perhaps the tragedy could have been prevented? Perhaps — no one would ever know!

And Johnny's thoughts continued. Lupe could not have been pregnant, he argued in his mind, she never was with him. Maybe she looked into a mirror some morning, and did not like what she saw . . . He knew how much she had dreaded growing old! But then, her being with child was, after all, verified by a physician. Yet, he remembered a case where the medical profession had mistaken a malignant growth for a baby. He would never find out!

A sordid trial got underway. Harold Ramond stood accused by Lupe's family. At the same time, the actress' relatives removed the ermine coat from Lupe's cold shoulders, fighting about its possession on this side of the grave. Ramond, eventually, disappeared from sight. He was no longer welcome in Hollywood where all studios closed their doors to the man who had driven their colorful little spitfire into suicide. His single film to date was cut beyond recognition, all his scenes dropped, leaving but a longshot of three men in the finale, without a clue to the mysterious third.

Guadalupe Villalobos Velez Weissmuller, however, was

buried on December 27, 1944, in Mexico City, thirteen days after she had resolved to violate her life and religion. All through the night thousands passed her bier, among them Dolores del Rio, her former rival in films, whose superior dramatic talent had constantly infuriated Lupe, and added fuel to her jealousy. Even Mexico's most popular comedian Mario Moreno (Cantiflas) remained at the funeral home until 4 a.m. Then, a Catholic responsory service was said, and Lupe found her last resting place at the Dolores Cemetery.

Dies irae — Deus vobiscum!

After Germany's surrender, the United States Treasury Department issued Johnny a scroll which read: "In recognition of distinguished and patriotic service to the Cause of Freedom, rendered in behalf of the War Finance Program of the United States Government, this citation is awarded to Johnny Weissmuller. Given under my hand and seal on July 4, 1945. (Signed:) Henry Morgenthau, Jr., Secretary of the Treasury."

World War II ended in August, 1945, with Japan's unconditional surrender. The same month Beryel's attorney filed another divorce suit, but it was not brought to trial pending a property settlement.

In the age of the atom, even fairy tales had become obsolete.

18

T HE IMPACT of the loss of his family through the legal separation left Johnny in a state of misery so profound that the very ground seemed pulled from beneath his feet. In his wretchedness he thought about self-destruction, found himself on the brink of it and, once, as he swam he contemplated darkly how easy it would be to go under and never again see the surface of the cool water that reflected the blue of the sky. His friends tried to pull him together and back into the daily routine of work but to no avail. As he hit the bottle in his most unhappy moments, he felt like a man who had received the death sentence in some medieval hall of justice. Picturing himself a prisoner at the bar, people everywhere began to look to him like judges whose stern wooden expressions showed neither friendliness nor hatred, just cold, hard, impersonal, objective tools of law. The book of rules lay open and the finger of the supreme justiciary pointed to "Guilty or Not Guilty"—the words trapping their victim without giving him a chance to escape the unspoken sound that crept up the high walls, whispered from each corner of their perfect symmetry as it clung to the arched gothic windows, floating back again with the last glimmer of the vanishing sunlight he no longer saw in his obscure mind.

Guilty . . . ?

Or not guilty?

Was he guilty? What then was his guilt? No man was perfect; but for the price he had to pay in life. Only astute suffering washed clean, but how many tears later did peace once more take possession of the heart? when all worth living for had suddenly been splintered into matches that burned to a crisp.

His children were too young to miss their father. Only the boy asked questions at first. He soon forgot, however, because he had not seen him often enough to feel deprived of his company for long. The little girls played on with their dogs, while their mother, nursing her own disillusion, carried on her chores. But Beryel's youth helped her forget more readily that which she could not forgive, whereas Johnny felt completely lost and, once time had eased his hurt, deeply embittered.

Another complication arose which hardly helped matters along. The California Cabaña (Deauville) Club in Santa Monica harbored unique luxuries and included several bars, an indoor as well as outdoor pool, complete with cabañas, steam rooms, shower rooms, a barber shop, with its interior decorations amounting to $45,000 alone; a mere trifle in comparison to the grand total of expenditures of $466,000 quoted as of August 15, 1946, not to mention the original purchase price. The orchestras that played there were always the name bands of the season, and a list of the famous co-owners registered names like John Wayne, Joan Crawford,

Merle Oberon, Robert Walker, George Seaton, Harriet Parsons, Frank Borzage, Red Skelton and Johnny, among others. These stars often performed in the evening's entertainment line-up, with Johnny and Skelton doubling up in a comedy-dive routine. But regardless of the big-time talent, nobody could save the club from going financially down the drain. Everyone lost money. It became quite evident that, once the novelty had worn off, Santa Monica with the rest of the Southland preferred to remain fond of back-yard barbeques, or dining along the Strip. Thus Red took Johnny's arm and both shrugged off their losses. As long as their incomes flourished, neither felt like crying bitter tears. Both realized, of course, that the club's purchase had been ill-advised by their business manager, Bö Roos, also a stockholder as well as secretary-treasurer, but they also figured that he was definitely a nice guy and entitled to one mistake. And, listening anew when some choice property became available at a reasonable cost, Johnny again went into partnership with most of the original stockholders, investing in a joint purchase of the California Country Club's golf course. At about the same time, he was talked into buying a unit of the Los Flamingos at Acapulco. Roos handled both deals.

His mind on other matters, he relied one-hundred percent on his management to take care of his finances. The well-oiled pipe line continued a transfer of his funds.

Work ultimately provided the solution to all problems as Johnny joined Pine and Thomas under the Paramount banner.

The producers had chosen "Swamp Fire" as a starring

vehicle for him, offering a record salary of $75,000. However, Johnny who had worried about a quarter in his childhood now looked on the almighty dollar as just more grass growing on an already lush meadow. Thus, not the money but the work itself became the standard of value, the basic attraction.

The screen story of "Swamp Fire" was set in Louisiana's bayou country, with its hero a man who had lost a ship in the U.S. Coast Guard but who regained his confidence when he was reinstated as a Mississippi channel pilot guiding boats along the great river. Virginia Grey and Carol Thurston were chosen as the riverside romancers and Buster Crabbe, at one time Johnny's foremost rival, was picked to play the role of a native trapper. The relationship between the two swimmers dated back to early amateur competition in the water, with Johnny taking away the honors from Buster's silver platter. He had defeated him in swimming meets and overshadowed his efforts to break into the Tarzan character; in short, strained feelings prevailed, caused by Crabbe's playing second fiddle to Weissmuller. In the new movie both stood a chance to fight out the biggest underwater tussle recorded on film. The producers willfully hoped for a sizzler, but discovered to their disappointment that the men conducted themselves according to the rules of the cinema, with a professional attitude which left no room for personal enmities. The scene came off without added sparks and, consequently, when the picture found its release, not much was said about it. Nevertheless it received a good rating in its class.

Seventy - five - thousand - dollars richer Johnny went

straight into yet another Tarzan feature; thus it came as a surprise to him when his business manager suddenly decided to put him on an allowance hardly befitting his status in life.

"Weissmuller Has Trouble Living on $50 a Week", Bob Thomas wrote for the Citizen News, "If you see Tarzan climbing a tree to grab bananas, he is not acting — he is hungry. Takes lots of food to fill that big frame of his, and food prices are up, compared to his bankroll."

Somewhat astonished the reporter further commented about Jane's protector not being a millionaire. He hinted that Weissmuller, after all, had earned a fortune but had seen little of his monies because his financial diet was supervised by his business manager.

Bö Roos, in turn, claimed that Bobbe and Lupe had cost Johnny a tidy sum, and that his settlement with Beryel was still pending. He warned Johnny about her exorbitant demands, convincing him that under the circumstances it seemed wisest to employ frugality.

Meantime, other entertainment pages sampled items of Johnny's romantic interests, leaving the impression that he collected women in rather the same fashion as a croupier raking in the chips.

Only sports editors like George T. Davis of the Los Angeles Herald-Express maintained complimentary reviews: "Swimming records are being broken almost daily, but the greatest merman of all time — without even a rival, in the opinion of experts — is still Johnny Weissmuller.

"A group of us were talking at Lakeside the other day— including Fred Cady, Pat McCormick, Maurie Luxford, John Farrington, Bob Ford, Tom Russell, Dutch Smith and Jimmy

McLarnin — and Cady, probably the greatest swimming authority in the world, commented: 'They broke the mold with Weissmuller. He was Mr. Swimming himself and there's never been anyone like him. I don't care whether his records are broken or not, Johnny was by far the greatest of 'em all. He had power, form and competitive ability to a greater degree than any swimmer of all time and ranks in his sport along with such other champions as Bobby Jones, Bill Tilden, Babe Ruth, and Jack Dempsey.' "

This statement was seconded by John Maynard, who wrote, "Johnny Weissmuller, for the benefit of any junior readers in the audience who may consider him simply Tarzan, was one of the bonafide jewels of what is recklessly known as the Golden Age of Sports.

"He was in the top drawer, along with Jones, Hagen, Dempsey, Ruth, Nurmi, Tilden, Tommy Hitchcock."

But whether or not Johnny was as good as gold or as wicked, in his private life his affable countenance and super-masculine physique still prompted women to throw themselves at him. Wherever he went he invited trouble as femme hearts kept pounding and one of these palpitating little troublemakers belonged to a teen-age girl called Allene.

The daughter of Ward "3-Iron" Gates often played at the California Country Club where Johnny was part-owner, officer, with Bö Roos serving as vice-president. When Allene Gates first met Johnny he was still a married man, nonetheless, the girl, a devout Mormon whose family came from Ogden, Utah, could not take her eyes off him. The unsophisticated brownette, her hair sometimes covered with a self-wound turban secured with bobby pins on either side,

249

gave no heed to the kidding she received on the golf links that she was suffering from a bad case of puppy love, and paid little attention to the fact that many years separated her age from his. Her naturally scintillating youth shone even brighter when he happened to be near, and Johnny soon found himself noticing her freshly ironed blouse, her crisp appeal, her lithesome manner. When she challenged him to play in a mixed foursome, both won honors in the low gross.

Johnny discovered that he laughed more readily in Allene's company, escaping the melancholy of his last separation. He again became conscious of diversiform activities such as outdoor living as a pursuit of health and happiness. When she told him that she did not swim well, he gladly volunteered to teach her, even agreeing to conduct classes at Santa Monica in how to save people from drowning. Gossip in the C.C.C.'s Tee Tattler soon read, "Confidentially, and this is no rumor, but if Johnny Weissmuller and Allene Gates get any chummier, the C.C.C. will have to be hosts to a pre-nuptial party — and won't that make Bö Roos happy?"

Why, exactly, Roos should have consequently felt happy failed to register a clue with Johnny, but he thought that his business manager probably got satisfaction out of seeing him back in shape. Besides, Roos had never cared for Beryel and, possibly, was delighted to see the legal battle near end because of his new romance.

However, despite the constant urging he received from his friends to marry Allene, Johnny himself felt uncertain. Even if Allene had something more to offer him than his previous wives had, and granting that he was fond of the girl, her healthy neatness, her game of golf, her sunny disposition, there still remained the question of their ages. Her father, for whom he held a tremendous liking, was close to his own age. How could he ask Gates' daughter to share his declining years? He had not led an idle love-life by far. How then could he be sure this inexperienced girl held the key to mutual bliss. Was he willing to risk yet another failure? He even felt uncertain about his own contributing factors because he no longer possessed absolute emotional honesty; too much bitterness had besieged his heart to open all its chambers without reservations. He had loved too well in the past, lost too completely, been disillusioned too often. Just when his resistance was getting dangerously low, he was ordered on location. He packed his bags and flew to Acapulco, Mexico, leaving Allene's pretty face and the songs of praise his friends sang about her at a relatively safe distance.

"Tarzan and the Mermaids" discovered Linda Christian. Johnny wondered how the green-eyed beauty had gotten to play the other femme lead in his feature. Usually he was asked about his choice of co-stars, but Linda had successfully evaded the casting routine. He got the distinct impression that she was a woman who knew where she was going and how to get there. While rumors had linked Linda with el presidente himself before Tyrone Power appeared on the scene, Johnny's role never exceeded that of gentleman-escort who kept a lady safe when accompanying her to given parties. He never discovered the tantalizing mystery that surrounded her frail voluptuousness, possibly for the good reason that his mind was tied to, and filled with, Allene.

Between thoughts and working hours, however, Johnny went to see the fiesta brava. Years ago when he had first visited Mexico, he had stayed away from bullfights, found them repugnant, because he had always loved all four-legged creatures. He found it hard to understand that any living thing could be killed for sport alone. Then he had met a dark-haired, almost tubercular-looking man, with scars marking a face that harbored soulful eyes under slanted dark brows.

It had happened during a visit to a prominent breeder of bulls who had invited Johnny to witness the tienta.

When the young bulls and heifers have reached their second birthday, they are put through a bravery test. First, el derribo, when the young animal is cut from the herd and chased by two horsemen carrying garrochas, blunt-tipped lances. Then comes the trial in the ring where the mounted picador pricks each with a sharp-tipped lance. The beasts are judged by their performance: whether they are looking for war — buscando guerra — or not. The brave heifers are marked for motherhood. The brave young bulls are destined for the arena. The cowardly ones, however, are discarded, castrated, and eventually butchered.

The tienta always presented an excuse for a fiesta attended by a variety of guests, gentlemen toreros, aspirant matadors, socialites, foreigners, and on this occasion one Manuel Rodriguez. When Johnny first met "Manolete", he realized little that this man was the finest matador ever to have graced the sands of the plaza de toros. He considered him as just a Spaniard whose love for the bull ring clashed with his own feelings.

Johnny spilled his emotional, personal opinions, calling the display in the arena barbaric, nonbefitting civilized men. Manolete listened, his grave eyes searching the other's face. When he spoke in turn, he gave an eloquent speech.

"My friend," he said. "You call it a sport as many do who cannot understand. It is not a sport. It is a ritual. It is an art. It is a tragedy. But it is not a sport! Let me try to explain ... The ritual dates back to ancient days when the Persians revered the bull god, when the Cretans practiced games with bulls, exposing themselves to danger by acrobatic leaps over their backs. The history of the bulls runs in four stages: the divine came first. Then, when gods assumed human form, they made the bulls the highest sacrifice, holy in its own right. Thirdly, the bulls became objects of chase by tribes who wanted to destroy their enemies' symbols and tear down their superiority. Finally, the last stage, the actual fighting of bulls, found its origin in Spain. This combat between man and beast presented an evolutionary step of human courage against brute force, but deeply buried in it there might have still been hidden the subconscious struggle of man against the idols he had helped to create and which had outgrown him, surpassing his power.

"It is a struggle of man's weakness against the unknown power of fear. You call a bullfight cruel, barbaric, uncivilized. It is true that the bull never has a chance. He is doomed. But — is it not better to die in glory, than under the ax in a slaughterhouse? Is it not better to go down fighting mad, than to yield meekly to a merciless executioner? Meat is just meat when you eat a juicy steak; you never think about its source. Yet when a bull is killed in the arena, it is his meat that supplies nourishment to many hungry peasant families, free of charge. It is even a charity . . ." He paused, and drew a long breath. "Yes, a charity. Do you know why many boys become novilleros? Because they are hungry! Because their families are starving, or selling their very pride in some . . ." Manolete's hand brushed across his eyes as if he were suddenly very tired. He continued in a moment. "I also said it was an art. At the age of four — five — the bull weighs at least one-thousand pounds. He is taught to charge anything that moves. He is faster than a race horse, quicker on his turns than a polo pony, much more dangerous than a lion. A matador needs great skill to meet him who has been bred for his one and only performance, in the plaza de toros. The matador must run eight miles a day, rehearse endlessly with the capote, the banderillas, the muleta, so he can draw the horns closer and closer to his body . . . to his body that is a vulnerable, outer shell to his great, living, inner fear. Yet the matador masters this fear because he must, because he cannot permit man's image to crumble in the face of a brave bull, because he himself has willed it thus to show superiority over the beast."

A dark cloud fell over the speaker's face, his eyes deepened their impression of sadness. "Of course, it is mostly a tragedy. A great tragedy that such a beautiful, wild, lethal brute should die at all in his prime of life, and by the hand of a dismounted man he has never before encountered. Nevertheless when the bull faces his hora de verdad, the man who delivers the kill knows its meaning only too well because — because the matador himself feels his own moment of truth coming closer . . ."

Manolete remained silent for long; when he looked up his expression had changed, become almost amused. "No, Tarzan, protector of animals, the festival of bullfighting does not merely represent a pastime, or a question of morality — at least not to those who understand it."

Their talk had been noticed by the host. "Juanito," the gentleman-rancher addressed Johnny, "I see you've met Manolo . . ."

Manolete!

No one else. A boy like himself, once born to poverty, ignorance, fighting his way out of the "Dunkelheit" as he, Johnny, had in his youth. In America there were many means of becoming great; he had chosen swimming. But in Spain, only bullfighting supplied the desired result. Suddenly he understood. Suddenly he knew. Suddenly a passion was born in him . . . Los toros!

Johnny became an aficionado whenever he visited Mexico. He dropped gold watches, dollars into a torero's montera as a token of appreciation. The matador often reciprocated, at one instance tossing a bull's ear to Johnny in friendship. The gesture spurred the crowd to keep up their waving of handkerchiefs, and their shouts of "Oreja!" filled the arena until the other ear, too, was awarded the victor in honor of his performance. He was picked up by his most ardent admirers, carried on their shoulders around the ring, by-passing Johnny who smiled, holding up the ear in spite of its dripping blood all over his brand-new white jacket. It mattered little. He was filled with a kind of elation

255

that left him breathless, feeling part of the man who had grafted fearlessness on his audience and part, too, of the throes that had befallen the brave bull.

Olé!

Mexico's season of corridas formales, the big fights, was from November to March. During the summer the novilladas, featuring apprentice fighters, took place. Johnny's present stay encountered the latter.

As he seated himself on the shady side of the arena, the appointed hour struck, with the band playing the dramatic "Virgen de la Macarena" and "Cielo Andaluz". He watched the colorful parade file into the ring, each matador dressed in his traje de luces, accompanied by his three banderilleros who belonged to his cuadrilla, and followed by the unpopular mounted picadors two of whom belonged to his team, ending with the drag mules bringing up the rear. The crowd cheered until all bullfighters had bowed to the presidente. The picadors and the drag mules left the ring, and the matadors and banderilleros slung their ornate dress capes up to friends in the first row.

And Johnny donated yet another watch!

Then, the arena cleared, the kettledrums rumbled, the trumpets blared, a sudden quiet settled over the spectators as all eyes turned in the direction of the Puerta del Toril, whence the first bull of the afternoon assaulted the open.

There is an erroneous belief by some that the beasts are kept in the dark so as to blind them by the sudden exposure to sunlight. This is not the case; the sudden light only serves to lure them into making a quick exit from the dark enclosure.

Nostrils wide and steaming with the breath of his fierce temper the beast galloped at an amazing speed around the empty circle, lowering his head before hooking toward the barrera, which he rammed with his horns. Then, he charged back again into the center where he stood, snorting in protest, as the banderillero approached with caution, flinging out his cape in front.

Normally the prelude was but a brief test of the bull's habits, giving the matador a chance to size him up. However, on this occasion el toro had decided to use his imagination, and lend a little humor to the bull ring. As the man advanced, the beast suddenly made a U-turn, stampeded in the opposite direction, crashing through the gate that led straight into the parking lot, next to which a lazy river murmured.

"The bull he is taking a swim in the river!" someone sitting close to Johnny suggested. But the man, next, trumped him, "The bull he is not willing to let Tarzan call the elephants." Giving a semi-toothless grin he lifted his sombrero in a greeting.

The crowd had broken into indignant hisses, loud boos at the novel turn of events in the bull ring. Johnny laughed. His American sense of humor got the best of him. "The bull he is plenty smart!" he cracked.

"But, señor, it is a cowardly thing to run away!"

"Si! If tragedy lifts the corners of its lips, it becomes comedy."

The message was lost . . .

Johnny returned to Acapulco. As he climbed the stairs to his suite, he saw a light burning in his window. He hastened to open the door and, finding it unlocked, entered.

Allene got out of an easy chair. "I came as soon as I read this," she said and handed him a newspaper clipping.

"Dive Kills Double for Johnny Weissmuller," the caption disclosed. "Acapulco: Angel Garcia, doubling for Johnny Weissmuller, was killed today during filmization. Garcia had just completed a spectacular dive when a wave dashed him against the rocks at the base of the cliff from which he leaped. The swimmer was dead when pulled from the surf."

"Hora de verdad!" Johnny murmured.

"What did you say?"

"Nothing." But Johnny thought about the moment of truth, how it sometimes comes when least expected. The mask of comedy at the bull ring earlier had again turned its expression into tragedy. In every way of life, in every situation, in every profession, for every living thing, small or great, puny or powerful, there comes a moment of truth no one shall escape in the long run. "I shouldn't have gone to watch the bullfights," he said. "I didn't know they planned to shoot this sequence. If I'd been here . . ."

"You might have been killed!" Allene protested. "You, with your foolish notion that you can still perform all your own stunts. Johnny, you need someone to watch over you!"

Doesn't everyone? Johnny thought. Yet no vigil could prevent the inevitable, the hora de verdad arrived sooner or later, touching plant, mineral, fish, fowl, reptile, animal, man — man most dramatically on the blood-stained sands of the arena.

On August 27, 1947, upon his return from the land of the Aztec, Johnny learned that his friend had died in

Linares, Spain. Manolete and a brave bull named Islero had killed each other. The tragedy of the bull ring was complete. They had died because the bull was not permitted to withdraw from the fight unless he turned cowardly, and the matador was too proud, too valiant to quit as long as his audience demanded an encore. Johnny pondered for many long hours about the "why?" In the end, he knew — he still understood.

After seventeen years, Tarzan, Weissmuller style, ceased. "Tarzan and the Mermaids" closed down the sensational orbit that Johnny entered at the start of the Thirties. At about this time, Louella O. Parsons wrote in her column:

"If Johnny Weissmuller is willing to pay a minimum of $600 a month and 25% of his earnings he can have his divorce from Mrs. Beryel Scott Weissmuller, from whom he has been separated almost two years. But yesterday, Johnny refused to sign. He thought Mrs. Weissmuller's demands too exorbitant, but her attorney, Charles Katz, is holding out firmly for that amount, while Frank Belcher, representing Johnny, said the demands are out of all reason.

"According to Bö Roos, who manages Johnny, Mrs. Weissmuller has been given a counter-offer of 25% of his earnings with all doctor bills for the children taken care of, and the house and furniture. Johnny hasn't a job, said Bö, so how can he pay $600 a month?

"Johnny wants the divorce so he'll be free to marry Allene Gates, but Mrs. Weissmuller said yesterday, 'I won't give him his freedom unless he supports the children and me.' "

True, Allene was getting restless. The girl felt that she had waited for Johnny long enough; it was a ripe time to get married. While Johnny's income had ceased momentarily with the end of his Tarzan films, he had already been invited to appear in a water show at Blackpool, England. Allene believed this voyage offered them an opportunity for a perfect honeymoon. Johnny, too, wanted to settle the affair once and for all.

But Beryel refused to talk alimony in person and insisted the issue should be left to their respective attorneys. She held no grudge against Johnny but remained firm.

"If I don't get the money," she once told Johnny, "Bö Roos will take all. At least, your giving it to me will help make secure the children's future."

"But you're taking me to the cleaners!" Johnny argued.

Beryel shrugged. "We shouldn't even have talked that much; let our lawyers slug it out. There's no reason why we should fight."

"You win!" thought Johnny. "So will Allene!" Ever since Acapulco, he had had no desire to alter his intentions. Allene was to be the fourth Mrs. Weissmuller, regardless of consequences.

She got her wish on January 29, 1948, at Reno, Nevada, where, with a fresh signature affixed to his divorce papers, Johnny walked from one office to sign his name on a marriage certificate in the next. The entire transition took place within minutes, leaving the bride beaming with joy, the group of well-wishers happily contented, and the groom beyond all pain as he escorted his new mate to the wedding reception.

Spring comes early in England. Suddenly, almost overnight, green grass grows in a morning breeze that awakens sleepy trees and, while they still stretch their branches to a lazy melody of the blues trying to get used to a miracle that so swiftly has changed the gray and uneventful yesterday into a today of sunshine and warmth, tiny leaves appear, promising enchantment.

Soon the parks were filled with couples walking hand in hand under a shady foliage, stopping now and again to smile at the orators who had climbed atop self-constructed pulpits, or gazing after some wild ducks that took off in flight, never singly but always in pairs, like the lovers who had come to spend their honeymoon in London, prior to the husband's engagement at Blackpool.

In any season London Town exhaled an air of magic from Covent Garden in the morning to the Savoy at night; from Buckingham Palace to Trafalgar Square, the Old Vic, Piccadilly Circus and Oxford Street — to Soho, even Elephant & Castle; the Embankment, Westminster Abbey, the Thames ... And Big Ben chiming away the hours that added to the search for wisdom, the love for art, the surrender to music, while the statue of Queen Victoria smiled upon Albert Hall.

Johnny took his young bride on a tour of the city he knew so well, awakening memories of by-gone days. The war had marred but little of the grandeur that represented the seat of the United Kingdom. Claridges still continued as the foremost hotel, but Johnny kept away from its yawning portal. They stayed in a flat overlooking Hyde Park, and often strolled through the Marble Arch, taking a taxi to

Chez Boulestin where French waiters served the most delicate cuisine for dinner.

It was the first time that Johnny had found himself a honeymooner at leisure. His basic need to feel happy made him almost forget past disappointments as he enjoyed watching Allene's bubbling excitement; she had never traveled from the American West, and everything she saw was a new, thrilling experience. However, Johnny had passed through too many phases to ever again be entirely carefree; for that he had lived too long. Even his outlook on the film capital was tempered with his feelings as, when asked about it by British friends, he replied, "There's nothing to say about Hollywood. It's still the same old place, with just a lot of movie stars." This to British cinema fans sounded like heresy, but the average Englishman, who held himself above such trivia, applauded the statement as a decisively sound observation.

Despite the fact that the newspapers had referred to Allene as the NEW Mrs. Weissmuller, it often happened that some mentioned Johnny's domestic status as "married and the father of three children" all in one breath. This subjected his bride to embarrassing cross-examinations which her youth resented and seldom answered with tact. At about the time when Allene tired of London and the nonhumorous assaults on her age, they were ready to leave for Blackpool. The holiday had come to an end. As it turned out, even their aloneness had ended with their honeymoon. Henceforth crowds waylaid their passage and, upon their return to the United States, Allene's odd number of many relatives made a habit of frequenting their home.

Meantime, another complication had arisen from their union. California's law challenged the legality of Johnny's Nevada divorce and remarriage. Thus it came about that he found it wisest to take Allene to Scottsdale, Arizona, where a second ceremony was performed to insure the validity of the first. To further complicate matters, Roos suggested Johnny might try and sell his shares in the California Country Club, basing the idea on the State's community property law by which Beryel was entitled to half. Johnny recouped his original investment but little did he know that later the same shares would sell for much . . . very much . . . more! Looking back it would have been cheaper to buy out his ex-wife's interest with funds obtained elsewhere, but again Johnny had lacked financial wizardry and insight, whereas his business management shrugged off a client's loss.

Johnny moved into an apartment in his own building on Almont, in Beverly Hills. Between occasional swimming exhibitions he played golf at the Riviera Country Club, where one day he received an urgent life-or-death call from his wife. Rushing up the hill to the telephone, wondering what this was all about and almost suffering from nervous prostration, he learned that Allene had just won the Lakeside Women's Championship and, as a prize, a cocker spaniel named Lucky. Johnny's building had hitherto forbidden tenants to keep pets because of the neighborhood regulations, but with Lucky moving in, all renters followed suit and, soon, picket lines were forming in front of his property in a march of protest, with signs that read: "Tarzan Permits Beverly Hills to Be Turned Into a Zoo!" Johnny's only alternative besides surrendering Lucky or throwing out his tenants was to sell the building. He hired Roos' construction firm to build him a house on Lorenzo Drive, near the Rancho Country Club in West Los Angeles. Moving into the new house with its Olympic-size swimming pool, one of their first visitors turned out to be Duke Kahanamoku who had come to Hollywood to support John Wayne in the "Wake of the Red Witch."

Kahanamoku liked what he saw, and commented. "My friend, I envy your good fortune. As you see I'm trying again to break the same ice which you broke many years ago crashing into the movies. But I'm not playing a very athletic role," he added mildly, "I'm the faithful retainer serving the lady of the household — Gail Russell."

Johnny wished him luck. "A pretty young woman, Gail. She reminds me of Maureen." But he thought: "Luck indeed! With all the pictures I've made, I still need to find some permanency in life. Romances I might have possibly conquered - - - but finances? I guess, old man, we were both better off swimming!"

As it happened in later years, Kahanamoku, too, began to think about having his biography written and, following the pattern, he remembered with most kindness the era of his aquatic feats.

Much water has flowed down the river of time. Kahanamoku's leading lady, Gail, for one, was destroyed by Hollywood as were Johnny's Lupe, Carole Landis, Marilyn Monroe. These beautiful, talented young ladies all succumbed to bitterness when their hearts became bruised in the pro-cess of having their beings glamorized. Which, perhaps, verifies the strength of the masculine persuasion, for no major leading man was ever found lacking in the lust for life to such an extent where suicide alone presented the final answer, with but one notable exception — and he called himself Superman.

As Johnny spent more and more hours at home watching television, or plunging into his spacious pool, Allene decided that the time was ripe for her, too, to be glamorous. Her first step was to tint her natural brown hair blond, her second — to buy a new wardrobe befitting her marital position. As she stood in front of the full-length mirror, admiring her outfits one by one, Johnny wondered quietly whether or not her infatuation for him had originally been mixed with her desire to bear his name. Even during the honeymoon in London, he had glanced at Old Bailey and thought if their love were balanced right, or if the importance of his fame weighed in on a slightly heavier scale. No matter! She was his wife.

Johnny, too, had found good cause to think of his own appearance. He had received an offer to play Jungle Jim in the motion picture series. The extra poundage he had gained over a period of idleness had to go. He started the battle of the bulge. A glass of lemon juice with hot water in the morning before light exercises was followed by breakfast which consisted of two eggs, but not fried, two slices of lean, crisp bacon, coffee with skim milk and saccharin, a piece of dry toast. For lunch, he ate a lamb chop, stewed tomatoes, perhaps jelly for dessert. A small steak for dinner for sure, but no cocktails to whet the appetite with, instead more coffee, preferably Sanka, assorted vegetables, or a salad and some fruit. Complemented with vitamin pills, the diet worked wonders, especially since Johnny helped it along by daily swimming. He lost 36 lbs. in a very short period of time. Once more in shape, he increased his activities by accepting a part in a water show at the Duquesne Gardens in Pittsburgh, Pennsylvania. Coincidentally, the Businessmen's Association invited him to visit his birthplace, Windber.

The Welcome Home Testimonial Luncheon was arranged at the New Palace Hotel in Windber, at noon sharp. The menu sported such palatable dishes as tomato juice, radishes, celery, olives, Palace Swiss steak with mushrooms, fluffy mashed potatoes, natural gravy, buttered peas, Palace salad, rolls, coffee, and . . . Ice Cream a la Weissmuller! — Need one say more about his waistline? And yet more festivities followed in the beginning of the Fifties. Among them was one that crowned all his past achievements.

The Associated Press, the nation's sports writers and broadcasters voted him by an overwhelming margin of 132, against 102 for all other swimmers and divers, "The Greatest Swimmer of the Past Fifty Years."

At the same time Helms Athletic Foundation, founded by Paul H. Helms, a Southern California sportsman and philanthropist, on October 15, 1936, had created a "Swimming Hall of Fame Trophy," with his name deeply engraved upon it. This trophy was to enhance Helms Hall, the sports shrine of the foundation whose purpose was serving the interest of wholesome athletics, with the thought of contributing to their programs and striving to award those deserving of special recognition.

On the trophy's wooden stand small plaques were attached citing all the "Swimmers of the Year," among whom

Johnny had won the nonrepetitive award in 1922. The following were named:

1900 — E. C. Schaeffer	1925 — Harry Glancy
1901 — J. Scott Leary	1926 — Walter Spence
1902 — Harry Lemoyne	1927 — George Kojac
1903 — Charles Ruberl	1928 — Walter Laufer
1904 — Charles Daniels	1929 — Clarence Crabbe
1905 — H. J. Handy	1930 — Maiola Kalili
1906 — A. M. Goersling	1931 — Albert Schwartz
1907 — L. B. Goodwin	1932 — Leonard Spence
1908 — L. G. Rich	1933 — Jack Medica
1909 — Chambers	1934 — Edward Lee
1910 — Harry Hebner	1935 — Ralph Flanagan
1911 — J. H. Reilly	1936 — Adolf Kiefer
1912 — Duke Kahanamoku	1937 — John Higgins
1913 — Perry McGillivray	1938 — Peter Fick
1914 — Michael McDermott	1939 — Steven Wozniak
1915 — L. Langer	1940 — Otto Jaretz
1916 — Herbert Vollmer	1941 — Kiyoshi Nakama
1917 — Norman Ross	1942 — Bill Smith, Jr.
1918 — W. L. Wallen	1943 — Alan Ford
1919 — Leo Geibel	1944 — Keo Nakama
1920 — Ted Cann	1945 — James McLane
1921 — Warren Kealoha	1946 — Joseph Verdeur
1922 — John Weissmuller	1947 — Walter Ris
1923 — Harold Kruger	1948 — Alan Stack
1924 — Robert Skelton	1949 — Robert Gibe

Many of these names are familiar to the reader who became acquainted with them in the earlier pages of this biography.

Those honored were chosen by the Helms Hall board, whose members, authorities in their field, were George T. Davis, Alex Kahn, Robert Myers, Rube Samuelsen, Al Santoro, Ben Woolbert, Sid Ziff, Paul Zimmerman, W. R. Schroeder, and Paul H. Helms, Jr. All selections dated back to the first modern Olympiad, in 1896. But the above mentioned belonged to the first half of the twentieth century, in which Johnny received his trophy.

Entering the building on 8760 Venice Boulevard in Los Angeles, a visitor walks among tall, stately pillars supporting Hall of Fame trophies including those from the ranks of baseball, football, track and field, golf, tennis, boxing, basketball, automobile racing, swimming and many other recognized sports. The Olympic Flag Room displays the national emblems of the nations that have served as Olympiad hosts since the very beginning. A most complete library embraces all divisions of sports and the magnificent Helms World Trophy, made of solid silver and gold, glistens from light slanting down through the high window beside which it stands in proud splendor. A tribute paid to all whose names appear there in engraved script ... all of which leaves the deepest impression with the guest in transit.

Johnny's big night arrived on March 8, 1950, when a testimonial dinner was held at the California Country Club. The stag party was supervised by Frank Borzage, famed Hollywood director, a brilliant golfer and Johnny's beloved friend. As the evening shadows fell on the Wednesday in question, the speaker's table seated men like Leo Durocher, Fred Cady, Jimmy McLarnin, Ellsworth Vines, Bob Waterfield, Luke Appling, Dutch Smith, Jack Dempsey, Ben Hogan, Lloyd Mangrum, Joe Novak — representing the various sports ... George Davis, Robert Myers, Tommy Harmon, Sid Ziff ... representing the radio and press ... W. R. "Bill" Schroeder, managing director of Helms Hall ... Charles Coburn ... Leo Carrillo ... notables like Maurie Luxford, Tony Pereira, Fred Ussher, Leonard Roach ... many more. Scores of telegrams arrived, among them greetings from Governor Earl Warren, Phil Harris, Hoagy Carmichael who cabled: "Made every effort to be with you and dip into that pool of blue jello on the table but can't make it. Anyway you are my boy. Suggest that we take you, a fan dancer, and Frank Borzage with that handicap (golf) of his and tour Texas. Congratulations." And Fred Haney's P.S. read, "Personally, I like Esther Williams."

It was a sentimental, speech-and-fun-filled, roaring night Johnny never forgot. As he accepted the honors bestowed upon him, a tear in his eye, holding in his hand a gold watch engraved with "To JOHNNY WEISSMULLER, World's Greatest Swimmer, 1900-1950. From his Friends, March 8, 1950," he remembered his youth with all its victories . . . its peace of mind. Bachrach had telephoned him earlier. The old coach had wanted to fly over, but his health would not permit the trip. He blessed Johnny as ever and wished him well. Later that night, Allene showered him with kisses, affectionate pride.

But not all who knew him shared in the elation. When daylight dawned and Los Angeles' early risers were reading about the gala affair, a little girl ran from the side of her ailing brother to the window, through which peered a strange face. Her tiny feet quickly retraced their steps to her sister's side.

"Wendy!" she called. "Who's that man looking in?"

Wendy glanced up and took hold of Heidi's hand. "Silly," she said. "That's father!" And the children went to admit Johnny, who had rushed over the moment Beryel had telephoned him about his son's appendicitis.

"Win any medals lately, Dad?" John Scott asked him as he bent down, taking the boy's small hand into his huge paw.

For a long moment Johnny's look lingered on the child's face; he remained silent. When he sat down beside his first-born, the words were still locked in his throat.

TARZAN VS. JUNGLE JIM

19

LIKE THE MOON Axel Munthe scolded in his "Story of San Michele," the camera's lens spied on Johnny, but instead of finding him in the arms of a lovely countess, it saw him in the company of the *panthera leo, panthera tigris, panthera pardus,* or with rare luck, even a *felis concolor.*

A special cage resembling a medium-sized trailer had been built to harbor crew and equipment in safety, while wild beasts prowled about the sound stage with Johnny running loose at their side. This cage was fashioned with an opening for the camera to protrude through the wire mesh reinforced with iron bars, and it included an emergency entrance for the director just in case his animal thesps did not go for his artistic delineation of a scene. Whenever Johnny spent his time "caged out" with the big cats, he suffered from a peculiar sensation of the extraordinary: — Before the era of unions, super taxes, and free-lance actors, cages had personified the trapped — omitting honest folk. Nowadays, when people were gradually finding themselves more and more fenced in, it stood to reason that the original beasts of creation should roam the world in freedom. But he remembered the animals in Chicago's zoo, and how re-

271

laxed they were in minding their own business behind bars. These humans, however, seemed really nervous despite their protection, with their business minding his! Confused, but not Confucian.

It had all started after a conversation with Sam Katzman back in 1948, when Katzman had asked, "How about playing Jungle Jim?"

This familiar King Features comic strip character, basically, was a Tarzan with clothes on. The sale of comic books alone reached 500,000 copies with each issue, as distributed by the Dell Publishing Company. Syndication had embraced over 150 newspapers with a combined circulation of more than forty million. Katzman's choice held all the advantages publicity-wise, as well as a pre-sold market of fans.

The William Morris Agency closed the deal for Johnny. Columbia Studios began to revamp one of their sound stages to resemble a jungle setting, while in wardrobe the mistresses in charge started sewing exotic outfits for the players, including sarongs for a long line of pretty starlets. Katzman had promised: "A different leading lady in every new adventure."

When Tarzan dropped his loincloth and donned a pair of tropical dungarees he became Jungle Jim. The filming got underway on the North Gower Street lot, but not before scribes had dreamed up story plots that surpassed even the "cage-builders" in imagination.

These tales, for instance, ranged from a blond doctor searching for rare drugs in a great African pyramid — complete with a free-for-all entanglement with native witchcraft colleagues — to men disguised as gorillas guarding gold hidden in a game preserve, notwithstanding the charms of a local princess. As a switch, the next installment told about a colony of real gorillas helping their pal Jungle Jim recapture the treasure of Dzamn. (Of course if anyone cared to subtract the "z" from "Dzamn," it could become evident that the collaborators must have passed through a period of relative frustration when writing the screenplay!)

Then a Wac living with pygmies got mixed up in a search for fiber necessary to America's stockpile of strategic materials, obviously too secret to define. Solving a legend about a leopard woman came next (yes, not only Tarzan but Jim had one too!) and, a cache of gold at the bottom of the Lagoon of Death, the film's hero discovering all the mysterious circumstances, including the fact that a decidedly female leopard could belong to white parents. While in another episode enslaved natives worked a dangerous synthetic diamond mine, with Tamba (filling Cheetah's role) blowing the whole caboodle, and Bob Waterfield as an army officer lost during a wartime mission, throwing a number of self-styled bombs. When a smuggler posing as a police inspector searched for an unique animal whose glands secreted a powerful narcotic fluid, plenty of primitive Amazons flitted about. Or then there was a Nazi war criminal fleeing with French art treasures who had to escape in a government plane but, alas, only to find dancing girls and a tiger aboard? Whatever happened to "The Lady or the Tiger?"

Giant people, a tribe of million-year-old man-monsters fought for their rights with a handful of unscrupulous ivory traders thrown in as a bargain ... Mineral deposits, oil, head hunters, an unexplained heroine ... A site of an atomic test, saboteurs, and another female doctor inoculating the natives

... A diamond smuggling ring; white hunters' experiments on animals producing a vicious drug for use in warfare and, if that were not enough, a half-human giant killer ape! ... Pygmy Moon Men — Pygmy MOON Men??? And Jungle Jim agreeing to become their high priest!!! Then back to more government investigations of thefts of cobalt; natives, foreign agents and a wicked female ward ...

Fire worshippers; a ritual altar in a forbidden land; a missing scientist; another professor but with a beautiful daughter; fabulous treasures in sapphires; a group of renegades—all this before a volcano errupted molten death! Quite a lot of action to pack into some 70 minutes of running time.

Still, the leading ladies were all young and of a pretty variety, a pity only half of them could act! The rest of the casts, too, were composed of a mishmash of some old pros and rank amateurs thrown together to stew in the same pot.

But the critics did compare the swimming with a Minsky ballet!

Nevertheless the younger generation liked all the offerings, even some adult crowds soon began cheering the adventures despite their weakness in opus caused by usual budget problems. The result was, perhaps, not top flight drama, but definitely entertaining, profitable programming.

Had it been up to Johnny, his suggestion might have changed at least one of the features, possibly the introduction, giving it a self-explanatory story line and title: "Tarzan vs Jungle Jim," a dual role with its definition reading, "Prince vs Pauper" — an apparent never-never idea between Pygmy Moon Men and Dzamn!

Oh, w(h)ell ...

However, Columbia Studios at the same time was putting out also a different kind of entertainment, like "The Wild One," starring enigmatic Oscar nominee and, later, winner of the coveted award, Marlon Brando.

Adjacent to Johnny's jungle stage, Marlon's supporting gang dressed in fashionable blue jeans, leather jackets marked with a motorcycle insignia of indefinite design and the slouchy black leather boots characteristic of the breed. The movie bore down upon the afflictions of misunderstood adolescents nursing individual psychoneuroses. All participants showed great promise in acting out Stanislavsky's method under the skilled leadership of their star, whereas neighboring Johnny inflicted the teachings of society's idiosyncrasies only upon one, as yet, unclad individual, and born method actor, named Tamba. Whether or not a parallel existed between both Darwinian branches could run into a difference of opinions — for men born apes could equal apes born men almost as A plus B equals B plus A in algebra.

Tamba, descendant from a long line of Cheetahs, but modernized with the times, one day decided that the jungle environment really presented a setback to civilization and mechanics. The ape's deep urge to explore this latter field prompted him to sidetrack to where the motorcycles roared. He fled straight into Marlon Brando's somewhat hairy arms.

All of this happened in the lunch hour; Tamba felt hungry. He settled for a bite from The Wild One's sandwich. Liking the taste he puckered his lips, then whispered something into Brando's ear. Brando laughed and whispered back. The chimp began an unintelligible harangue composed of a great variety of noises; also, he twiddled his pinkies. Brando looked astonished. "He's so much like people, I can't get over it. This guy actually understands me!" he exclaimed in wonderment. Henceforth, Brando settled down for a daily powwow with the chimp on the set next door; canceling any outstanding engagements, he kept his midday break reserved.

After the feeding time, often, the actor glared at Tamba in silence, a sullen expression on his face. The ape in turn lowered his puss between his arms, emitting a forlorn, morose sound of woe. "That's right, Tamba!" Brando came out of his trauma, "You've got the feeling. That's just how I shall act this afternoon in the scene where no one cares what happens to me."

Tamba tilted his head, nodded, bared his gums in an approving smile. Marlon sighed, handing him a leftover cooky. "Want to take a ride on my motorcycle?"

All ape now, Tamba began jumping around, sounding off in his natural dialect, "uh-uh-uh-uh-uh!" Then, rushing to the man's side he planted an affectionate smack on his cheek.

Johnny arrived to claim the chimp for an early scene. "Tamba really loves you," he said knowingly. "Like the first Cheetah used to care for me."

"It's a strange, fulfilling relationship," Brando commented.

When Brando's picture came to an end, he asked the chimp's trainer to sell Tamba to him. He offered $5,000. But the Jungle Compound to which the ape belonged refused to part with their property.

"The chimp's under contract for five years," they said.

A sample of Sam Katzman's promise . . . or Johnny between a panthera pardus (Anita Lhoest) and a panthera tigris.

Johnny fights a tiger. (Columbia photo by Christie)

Johnny fights a lion.

Johnny fights a hippopotamus. (Columbia photo by Van Pelt)

Johnny fights a native witch doctor.

The star of the Minsky water ballet!

With Brando gone, Tamba returned to Johnny and the filming of a fishing scene.
(Columbia photo by Van Pelt)

. . . And once I knew a parrot! (Columbia photo by Crosby)

Old Acquaintances! Cheetah I has nothing but love for his old pal Tarzan, now Jungle Jim. (Courtesy of Columbia Pictures Corp.)

Cheese! (Columbia photo by Lippman)

Jackie the lion's son following up on the "love routine." (Columbia photo by Coburn, Jr.)

"He's worth more than five grand. Sorry! Even if you upped your price there'd still be legal entanglements. Forget him!"

"Why don't you choose another?" Johnny suggested.

Brando sadly shook his head. Only this one had caught his fancy. Only Tamba belonged in his life. He walked to his car, the chimp at his heels. As he drove from the lot, Tamba ran alongside his automobile, begging to be taken for a ride. Johnny caught up with him as he carried his pursuit through the studio gates past the guard, who tried to stop him in vain.

Poor, heartbroken Tamba! How he missed his luncheon companion! But, a disciplined performer, he returned to Johnny and the filming of a fishing scene.

"The Wild One" was released in 1954. The same year brought Brando an Academy Award for his performance in "On the Waterfront."

However, Johnny, the star of the so-called Minsky water ballet, also attracted attentions of a different kind when the USSR seemed anxious to offer him a medal. A mysterious, nameless, hatless, English-less visitor turned up in the studio, accompanied by an interpreter. As the translation revealed, the Russians offered Johnny the position of head coach for the Soviet swimming team.

"You will train our swimmers to win. Name your own price. Our boys will do what you say!"

Johnny remembered Japan, in 1928! He declined the offer with thanks. "I'm an American," he said simply, "I've seen our flag in the place of honor atop Olympic arenas. I believe in fair contests and sportsmanship, but also in national pride. I'd train our boys anytime, but I couldn't train their opponents. It's against my nature."

After the Russian had learned about Johnny's answer he sneered, "In the Soviet Union you could teach until you die of old age. Mark my words, Gospodin Weissmuller, the capitalists will put your talents to rest the moment your income ceases." Before Johnny managed to utter an angered reply, more foreign sounds spurted from the Russian's throat into the interpreter's speech. "We believe in the national image of our motherland just like you. If you change your feelings, you can always contact us. Here . . . " The spokesman handed over a calling card.

Johnny studied the card. After the affair with the chauvinistic Japanese swimming coach, the one who ordered one of his swimmers to make a Kamikaze dive into the swimming pool, Johnny had become increasingly aware of an undercurrent to be found deep under the smooth surface of water sports.

True enough, the sports pages were filled with photos of beautiful, lithesome girls on water skis, of skin divers in frogman suits catching rides on whales, of surfers on their sleek boards plunging ahead of mountainous waves.

But . . . ! In other sections of the daily newspapers were other stories.

In Europe, not so long ago, swim fins had suddenly disappeared from the shops, were completely off the market . . . and rumor had it that a large, militaristic nation had its order in for 15,000 more pairs.

Shortly after the disappearance of the fins, a Scandinavian fisherman, in the Baltic Sea, near the Gulf of Finland, was working close to shore in his dory. Looking up, he was surprised to see an attack transport suddenly appear over the horizon, steam up and drop anchor by a nearby island, put landing nets over the side, drop several hundred frogmen into the sea who disappeared, came up on the island, then returned to the sea and the ship.

The entire practice maneuver was completed with such ease and speed that the fisherman just sat in his boat, flabbergasted, watching the ship quickly disappear over the horizon.

Johnny shook his head hard.

When he had bade farewell to the Soviet emissary and his mouthpiece, he walked away, deliberately tore the card into quarters and dropped the remnants into a nearby wastebasket.

Ever since he had reached voting age Johnny had fulfilled his duties as a citizen come election time. Yet he had never sided with any political party, simply observing basic Americanism, casting his ballot for whom he thought the better man. His deep devotion to the common cause had been rooted within his spirit, strengthened by his athletic endeavor to excel in sports for the glory of his land. In contrast, with almost childlike fervor, he had despised the enemies of his country. Unlike many sophisticates who claimed to find some good or interesting theories in obverse doctrines, he never wavered in his opinions. When Tarzan defeated the Nazis, Johnny was enacting his personal belief. When Jungle Jim fought Communist infiltration, Johnny again was behaving true to his code. Complicated internal issues or Democratic or Republican platforms interested him little because he knew without concern that both political affiliations had the good of the United States foremost in mind. He looked upon their differences as a healthy competitive force, a rivalry beneficial to the nation's welfare. When, once in a while, he appeared on behalf of some candidate, he did so purely out of personal friendship and the respect that sprung from such a relationship. Otherwise, the intricate political machine passed him by, without altering his convictions.

Working in the Jungle Jim films, Johnny passed his fiftieth birthday with no one the wiser. He still managed his own stunts: swam, wrestled, fought, ran, jumped. His physique had suffered none through the years; he had kept fit and even-tempered, but his schedule between pictures and watercades had slowed down considerably, with his free time spent at home with his wife, Allene.

"Erstwhile Tarzan Still Jungle Guy," the Los Angeles Daily News headline read above Edith Kermit Roosevelt's column: "Johnny Weissmuller said today that he's one of the happiest men in the world — he's found a way to make money with almost no work. Johnny, who's starring in a Jungle Jim series for Sam Katzman, says he works only a month and a half of each year. The rest of the time he loafs. He throws his leftover salary into real estate, sits back and lets his business agent do the worrying and make money for him."

Johnny had clung to Bö Roos with stubborn loyalty. He trusted him. Besides, Johnny really had had no experience in managing his affairs without advice, and because he hated change, he stuck with Bö. Since he had married

Allene, the latter never inveighed against Roos as Beryel had done. Thus, Johnny, simply kept the status quo.

Actually Johnny worked a good deal more than the press story implied. His employment lasted through three to five months a year, with two to four pictures scheduled annually. He also appeared in Las Vegas, at Wilbur Clark's Desert Inn which featured as a novelty a spectacular Aqua Fair.

On opening night, Red Skelton looked him up in the dressing room. The two friends put their heads together and, as all the lights were turned up for the show, Red came rushing over to Johnny to shake hands. Missing him on purpose he walked right into the pool, clothes, cigar and all, much to the delight of the fashionable, outdoor, dinner audience. Yet there was plenty of time left over for leisure and he, with Allene, traveled to the major golf tournaments across the country, going on to foreign lands, some as near as Cuba, others as far as Egypt.

Second only to baseball, golf had entered the big league with its long list of competitive events, such as the Bing Crosby National Pro-Amateur Golf Championships at Pebble Beach; the World Entertainment Golf Championships at Long Beach; the Celebrity Pro-Amateur Tournament of Champions at Las Vegas; the 500 Festival Indianapolis Pro-Celebrity Tournament; the Frank Borzage Motion Picture Golf Tournament; the Golden Gate Open, and many, many more too numerous to mention. With the emphasis on Southern California, throughout the entire land new recreational areas were being developed, up to and including desert golf courses with 27 holes! And speaking of these, classed as good birdie holes for long knockers; tough holes into the wind during afternoons; slicers-beware holes; long-tee-shot-and-pitch holes; water-for-the-hooker holes; traps-on-both-sides holes; large-green-to-approach holes, or easy holes — all distributed like the pieces of a jigsaw puzzle about the course, a word of advice might easily be welcome to the fan who, a novice on the golf links, plans a visit.

If you arrive after the tournament has already begun, because traffic on the freeways moved along at the speed of a snail, it would be wise to stick with the teeing-off party. At least you can enjoy the game's progress from stage to stage. In searching for a particular celebrity along the fairways, trudging across greens, eyes focused on the far horizon where — east, west, north, south — tiny dots no larger than pinpoints represent the players, your chances of finding your party are poor, so very poor! Holes four and five may be as distant from each other as an orbiting 1963 satellite from the moon. By the time you reach the next tee, exhausted, the lost players may have moved onward, easily transported by fast go-carts to tee number ten, right next to the clubhouse, which beckons to you like an oasis. A trip to this promising place, however, has a habit of tempering all golf enthusiasm. Arriving weary, nursing a near bump on your head caused by a flying ball that shaved your skull because you failed to duck when somebody shouted "Fore!", thirsting for only a cooling refreshment such as a scotch with soda perhaps, anyone is likely to forget all about the tournament after more of the same, caring less if the sought-after player made the 18th hole at all! The freeway home, providing you can even find it, leads eventually straight into a police trap. After all that, unless you care to practice putting around and through the bars of a cell, it is doubtful you will ever become an absolute supporter of the sport, without harboring just the slightest trace of reservations . . .

Ah, yes: all this, with the exception of the sad conclusion, happened to the writer of Johnny's biography while trying to gain knowledge as to how he had won his hundred or more golfing trophies throughout the years.

Nonetheless, observing the game from the beginning to end never failed to develop new golfers, with the game per se as hard to shake as the habit of eating sunflower seeds.

While Allene motored a short distance to Griffith Park to play in, and win, the City Championships, Johnny journeyed to an exclusive country club popularly referred to as the Cherry Hillsdilly, in Denver, Colorado. As it happened, a great American who pursued this particular sport with fervent vigor often visited the links. On these occasions many somber-looking fellows were seen loitering in the vicinity, either driving golf carts, hauling zipped-up bags, or sitting around the clubhouse in rolled-up shirt sleeves. If, however, someone mistook them for caddies, and offered a day's wages, each declined, all just waiting about like coiled springs.

Johnny's tee-off time was scheduled in twenty minutes as he strolled from the clubhouse. He felt tired of conversation and ready to brace himself for the game. He breathed in the fresh summer air, took a seat on an empty cart, and for a moment closed his eyes. Suddenly he experienced a sensation such as comes when someone is staring at a person and, glancing up, he noticed several strange men scrutinizing him from close at hand. Since none of them seemed familiar to him, he once again shut his eyes, but a spooky feeling had settled in his mind. It stubbornly persisted, so he looked up once again. The ranks had closed in, joined by a few others. His observations cleared away all doubt. These men certainly were not his fans. As the circle tightened around him, he smiled asking, "Nice day, eh? How are you, guys?"

"Swell, John." "Swell, John." "Swell, John." "Swell, John." "Swell, John." Each one of them, in turn, echoed the monotonous chorus.

He felt decidedly uneasy by now. What was this all about? He narrowed down his attention first on one, then onto another. These men were not ordinary caddies, this much was certain! They were not players, either! Their golf bags sagged on their shoulders as if something weighed too heavily within them.

"Good God!" he thought. There was a submachine gun hidden in at least two of the bags! No doubt remained, the contours were easily identifiable through the thin disguise . . .

But this was America in the Fifties, and not the Twenties!

Suddenly someone tapped his shoulder; he swerved aside, ready to defend himself if need be!

"Hi, Johnny!" a pleasantly familiar voice said. "You're sitting on my cart. Do you mind if I take it?" Johnny looked up . . . right into President Dwight D. Eisenhower's smiling, friendly face. Jumping to stand at attention, he managed to stammer his apologies, after overcoming his initial surprise.

"It's quite all right, Johnny," the President said. "I'm just watching today. My confounded nursemaids won't let me play." He motioned to the camouflaged, armed set. "They say, without a fence they can't give me ample protection. Isn't that silly! What will they think of next! Well," Ike settled in his cart, "see you!"

The Secret Service agents had, in the meantime, come out of their lethargy and begun flitting about. Before making his departure, the President again leaned closer to Johnny. "Let's see them catch me!" he chuckled and took off.

Johnny saw the Federal boys conjure up walkie-talkies out of nowhere. "He's coming down Fairway 14; get him on Green 15!" the word went out.

When Johnny took his drive, Ike watched. The ball flew some 200 yards, and disappeared from sight. "You're in the chicken coop, Johnny Weissmuller," the President was amused. "Confidentially, that's where I go all the time. But don't tell anyone!" Johnny had heard that President Eisenhower was a natural hooker, always hitting to the left.

"We'll see," Johnny said, and went to investigate. He found his ball had hit the coop and bounced onto the fairway. He selected a nine-iron and got it onto the green.

"What a ricochet!" Ike declared. "I'd have sworn this wasn't your golf ball but a mislaid egg." And he watched Johnny putt.

He did — a "lovely" birdie!

On this day Johnny shot a 76 low-gross and 67 net. The next time he had reason to recall this Presidential meeting happened when he was invited to an international pro-celebrity tournament in Cuba at the period when Fidel

Castro's guerrillas were hiding in the hills and shooting government troops full of holes less than 50 miles from Havana. Along went Hoagy Carmichael, Bill Gargan, Bob Crosby, Robert Sterling, Buddy Rogers and other golf naturals. The party was assigned bodyguards upon arrival to prevent possible kidnapping, which, President Fulgencio Batista y Zaldivar worried, seemed a likely rebel scheme to bring worldwide attention to their cause.

As the golfers drove toward the Villa Real course, rebel soldiers suddenly leaped from the bushes, surprising and disarming the guards and, taking them prisoners, they closed in around the famous guests with pointed tommy-guns.

There was no time for panic! To the contrary! All passengers froze in their vehicle seats, except — Johnny. His mind swiftly reviewed the message he had previously received: that uneasiness caused by circumstantial evidence, such as his mistaking United States Secret Service agents for gangsters, could possibly belie the action of these guerrillas . . . who might not wish his troupe harm at all.

Still — this was Cuba in the Fifties, and not the Twenties!

He stood up in the car, giving everyone a moment to get accustomed to his appearance; then, he boldly began beating his chest, letting loose his penetrating, famous jungle yell.

The soldados' petrified reaction soon changed into an earsplitting commotion of enthusiastic acclaim: "Tarzan! Tarzan! Bienvenida! Ah, Juanito! Welcome to Cuba!"

Johnny shook the outstretched hands on the left and on the right, answered questions about Jane, signed autographs. The rebels discarded their weapons, crowding around him for still more. It was Tarzan all the way! No one worried or wondered about a character named Jungle Jim. Only after the man who had played both explained that his party was already late for the tournament did they disperse, but they sent along an escort to make secure a truly safe passage for the celebrities.

Arriving at the golf links they were met by a visiting Errol Flynn. Somehow, he already knew about the incident.

"Johnny, old man," Flynn greeted him. "I hear you got through the roadblock on the strength of your immortal half-roar!"

"What are you doing in Cuba?" Johnny wanted to know.

"I'm a mercenary," Flynn suggested with a twinkle, "or maybe I'm hiding in the hills so my business manager can't tip off my creditors!"

"You're kidding!"

"No, honest! But I'm also starting a movie with cute, cuddlesome lady guerrillas — and that reminds me — I've always meant to ask you about the habits of the mountain male ... gorilla, that is ... does he beat his chest before or after the mating act?"

"Now wait a minute! Sure, me Tarzan but ..."

Flynn interjected before Johnny managed to end his protest, "Listen, I'm serious! When does a gorilla beat his chest? Before or afterwards?"

Johnny burst into loud laughter, he shook his head. "If you must know — only afterwards! He's satisfied and wants to be left at peace. Besides, the bull ape really only tries to advertise the completed deed, he isn't merely a phony braggart! Gorillas are not like monkeys or humans; sex is a minor matter to them. When a big male begins to drum his chest with both hands and starts his hooting, females and infants escape to a safe distance."

"Makes sense," Flynn nodded. "None of that Hollywood stuff for them!"

"Gorillas are actually peace-loving creatures, their tastes run to a select variety of tender vegetation; they sometimes have breakfast in bed, and when they sleep, which they quite frequently do, they never snore. All their frightening habits are part of a normal ritual, not rage but masculinity."

"If they're as nonchalant about sex as you say," Flynn said mockingly, "the *gorilla gorilla beringei* must put on a noisy, dust-throwing performance just for the sake of emotional relief."

"Well, now that you know — good luck!" Johnny snickered. "But don't scare your cute lady guerrillas out of their wits!" He left Flynn to join his partners at the tee off.

When the star golfers boarded their return plane, (with Buddy Rogers happy to "Hail Mary" himself home with the others), a dense throng of Cubans bade them a rousing farewell. Flynn, too, was there to shake hands with Johnny, who never knew that this was to be the last time he saw his friend alive. As the aircraft ascended, Flynn returned to his hotel. He packed his satchel and took to the hills. His revolutionary spirit had selected "Cuban Rebel Girls" as his last, and final, feature.

THE TROUBLE WITH TRUST

20

WITH THE advance of television, Johnny's adventure series changed format, becoming half-hour shows produced for home viewing by Columbia's arm of this medium, Screen Gems. But after some 29 episodes had been canned, the sponsors cancelled out, and Johnny found himself joining the ranks of the unemployed.

He went to claim his last paycheck in person. "So that's what the little rascals look like," he said eying it. "I just want to find out for once if they're worth as much as it says here..." He pointed to the round figures and, thereafter, made a straight dash to a jeweler where he blew the whole loot. He bought Allene a star-sapphire ring worth some $4,000.

"That's for the rainy days, Honey," he said as he presented the elaborate gift to his wife, smiling at her pleasure. "Now we've got something to pawn besides your minks if we ever run into trouble!"

Allene slipped the ring onto her finger, held it up so that the gem's blue hidden flame sparkled in the light, and vowed never to part with it under any circumstances. Her husband put his arm around her and assured her such sacrifice was entirely uncalled for. He reminded her of their realty interests on the Channel Islands; the part ownership of Los Flamingos Hotel in Acapulco; Mother Elizabeth's house in Palms; their own home in Cheviot Hills; bonds; sundry other investments; cars and valuable knickknacks; also his continued 25% cut in residuals from foreign and domestic sales of the Jungle Jim films. And surely another job would follow shortly, just let her wait and see; his name would take care of that! There was no need for Allene to worry her pretty, blond head about financial matters. He certainly did not worry himself! Why should he? when he had Bö Roos' Beverly Management Corporation to take care of everything. In 1955, his income had amounted to $94,919.27! When it had dropped the next year it still showed a comfortable circa $39,000. They were in fine shape.

However, as time and more time passed without his finding a job, Johnny found himself in need of cash despite Roos, who supposedly took care of all his running expenses, in turn continuing to receive Johnny's re-run monies the way he had always received his salaries.

Johnny's notorious habit of never looking at anything he signed had not changed with the years. Just as he had the time when Bachrach turned him into a pro, Johnny signed first and asked later, and often did not ask at all. Thus, whenever he visited the business office he was handed little white slips of paper which he initialed. IOU piled atop IOU. Even the ninety-five-thousand-dollar year showed on Roos' accounts as a year in need of a substantial loan. But throughout Johnny's money-making career he had, unfortunately, been unaware of exactly how much he owned, owed, or whether or not the payments on his properties were kept up or needed mortgaging? Had some payments become delinquent? What taxes were due and when? He had always maintained that these were problems for which he had initially hired a business manager, and after these many years, Roos certainly knew his finances better than himself. As long as his salaries had supplied additional funds he had had little trouble listening, for the simple reason that no one ever bothered to tell him about anything except, perhaps, his costly divorces and an occasional larger loss, such as the Deauville fiasco. Now that he no longer belonged to the high income bracket, however, it came as somewhat of a shock when he found himself sued by Beryel for back-alimonies amounting to $5,750.

When Johnny questioned Roos, the latter told him that his funds had become limited, which made payments impossible. When Johnny asked why he had not been told of this before, Roos replied that Johnny never cared to listen to advice, that he had lived too extravagantly, that it was his own fault of which he, Roos, washed his hands.

Beryel, who had since remarried, said when Johnny called her that she only knew he had made a lot of money. She could not understand why he withheld the payments from his own children. It was for their benefit, after all, that she had sued. If things were as black as Johnny stated, he should have communicated with her, informed her about the circumstances.

The truth of the matter was that Johnny had never been aware of owing them monthly support. Not even in his wildest nightmares could he have visualized this turn of his financial affairs.

The case was settled in court, cutting his alimony payments almost in half, and reducing a $16,000 trust fund to 65% of its total.

Yet in spite of his pecuniary downbeat, Johnny managed to keep up his front with interviews he gave about a new deal he had closed in the business world. An outfit manufacturing portable swimming pools made of "Bakelite Krene" offered to make him a partner in return for the use of his name. Constructed right on the job, these pools sold for less than the cost of a family automobile.

"Last year," said Johnny, "over $625,000,000 worth of swimming pools were installed in the country, and that was supposed to have been a recession year. This year, the goal is $900,000,000, and I wouldn't be surprised if the industry goes over that mark." This was a broad statement of overall numbers as told to him by the people who wanted to sell pools, using his name. He added, too, that while the backyard swimming pool was not as commonplace as a radio or television set, it was rapidly becoming as popular as an air-conditioned home. "And, I'll bet that by the end of next year there will be at least 250,000 of them in the country." Possibly the swimming pool rate equaled his estimate, but it certainly did not verify his high hopes for personal profit. He made some money, but it was soon discovered that the so-called super materials used in the manufacture of the pool were at fault, and when his fan-buyers started complaining, Johnny bowed out of the association at once.

Still, the magic of his name made him good copy for

the newspapers. While the articles as always glowed with his past glory, pictures were beginning to appear illustrating how he once looked and now, with captions reading — "Young Weissmuller Olympic Champ in 1924, and, Old Weissmuller as he appears today." Despite his still handsome looks it was inevitable, for such is human nature, that the "old" title hurt, especially in Hollywood where it brought along another and more ominous sounding tag within the industry itself — that of has-been. There were no job offers now and no promise of any in the future. To add insult to injury, some promoter came up with the idea of making a wrestler out of him, of capitalizing on his name in the ring.

Just when the strain was bearing down heavily on Johnny, a visitor arrived from the east who, aged but ageless in his support, handed him a ticket to confidence. Big Bill Bachrach, completely bald by now, his reddish tobacco-stained mustache shaved off, shook hands with his former pupil and his fourth wife.

"Return to the people who love you, the people in sports," he told Johnny. "You always wanted to teach. Well, now is your time! There are thousands of kids who want to learn swimming, some could develop into Olympic material. Think of Hollywood as a phase of your existence — good while it lasted! Sure you were the best Tarzan who ever swung on those vines, your fans still acknowledge that when your yell reaches them through television. But acting is not your only profession. Your real self lies in athletics! Think of all the medals you've won!"

"I've been thinking," Johnny said bitterly, "I've been thinking — here I was, with all those medals and a scrapbook that would cave in an ox, but the medals were no good to eat, not even with ketchup, and if you think the scrapbook could get me on a streetcar, you're crazy!"

Bachrach long studied the man who as a boy had been like his own son. "Then I feel sorry for you," he finally said. "If Hollywood has managed to change you in that way, then I must give you my profound pity. Have you forgotten that you're a champion, made from the material champions are made of? You were the best! Tops all the way! You never cried in your soup. You took the challenge no matter what the odds. You always won! You can, again, you know!" It was the last lesson Bachrach ever gave Johnny and, perhaps, the most important.

Bachrach died at the age of 82. The memory of this wonderful Jewish gentleman, the fabulous American swimming coach, however, remains part of the era in which he lived, to which he lent greatness through his teachings, and it will remain part of the people, like Johnny, to whom he gave so much of his self.

Johnny pondered about the words of his old coach for some time. He knew Bachrach had been right, as always. What kind of a man was he to sit around watching television, looking at swimming and golf trophies, waiting for better days, meanwhile accepting "alms" from his business manager.

He approached his agency about getting a daytime program on TV where he could demonstrate his sport, instruct, teach youngsters and oldsters alike. They thought it was a great idea, but between programming seasons it was a slow grind to interest sponsors on the spur of the moment. He began giving classes, to train Olympic hopefuls at a swimming school in San Diego. He taught his former Hollywood buddies' kids how to swim. He took a beating in pride, but then, false pride belonged only to one of the original seven sins of Marlowe's Tragedy of Doctor Faustus; whereas a pride in one's work served as a partial cure for a man's spiritual decay.

At the same time Johnny saw more of his son. Convinced that the boy would make a champion, he perfected his swimming strokes, especially the American crawl, the stroke which had made him famous. But John Scott, who had won the city championships at the age of 13, landed a movie role and quit swimming. His actual reasons, however, lay in the behavior of other school mates who, with the typical cruelty of youth, never failed to rub it in that he was not as good as his illustrious father had been. Almost twenty, young Weissmuller went to live with his grandfather in San Francisco, where he joined a small theatre group to learn his trade. He had grown to resemble his dad, surpassing him in height by two full inches. As Johnny saw his offspring lacking in interest, he began to hope that producers would recognize the potentials of an adventure series starring both father and son. But the old-timers were on their way out of the industry; many had retired; others death had reaped. Talk flared up, but subsided again before anything came close to basic negotiations with studio, sponsor or network. There was also some discussion about reviving Jungle Jim, but that, too, remained up in the air. Then Masquerade Party invited him as a guest, teamed with Buster Crabbe; some money trickled in, but too little and too late to fill the holes dug.

But the greatest harm was caused by gossip that spread once it was rumored not all was well with Weissmuller's revenues. When he had to sell his membership at Lakeside to raise cash, the unkind stories spread and spread until all of the film capital was buzzing with hints and guesses. Allene, too, for whatever reason had joined the ranks of talkers . . . possibly because she found herself on the defensive, possibly because she no longer cared for her on-the-verge-of-bankruptcy husband. Whatever her motives, powder rooms became her confession chambers, whence her words were carried with an even greater speed than from the bars where some men had turned into cackling hens. After one of those powder room sessions, two ladies accidentally brushed hips against one another while making an exit. Before Allene returned to Johnny's side, she threw a sidelong glance at the blond stranger, who apologized in a faint accent.

Moments later respective hosts and hostesses introduced the Weissmullers to the thoughtful blonde. As her fingers touched the former Tarzan's strong hand, she felt nothing but contact. With clarity and a sense of compassion sprung from her knowledge that his wife had betrayed the trust of their marriage in the talk she had just happened to overhear, she knew that she was going to become closer acquainted with Johnny. She was a woman who stuck to her beliefs.

Called Maria, her full name read Gertrudis Maria Theresia Elizabeth née Bauman; German by birth, a titled descendant from the House of Wittelsbach; widowed; divorced; in the United States since 1949; citizen. This woman, whose large, light-blue eyes reflected a hint of past suffering, had seen but little happiness from the time of her first teen-age marriage prior to the outbreak of World War II. Yet her lips parted in a bright smile that made her small nose crinkle slightly upward in her tanned face framed by hair the color of champagne, leaving a deceptively pixyish impression. In reality, however, her heart was often melancholy, searching to forget her own history.

No sooner had she become a bride than her first husband was drafted and sent to the Russian front, where he was killed in action, leaving her the mother of a baby girl. Bewildered by her loss, unable to grasp her widowhood, her youth met up with a dashing flyer. When he proposed marriage she consented, but again their union was short-lived. He was shot down eight months later. The time they had spent together had amounted to mere days. A lawyer friend of the family often visited her and little Lisa, her daughter, until one day he and all his relatives were arrested and, after a brief trial, hanged, accused as underground workers in the resistance movement.

Maria, too, was taken prisoner and questioned by the Nazis. They detained her until, finally, they had to release her for lack of evidence. Still haunted by this experience she had learned about life the hard way. She knew about human nature, about pride and the loss of it once it had been destroyed by constant brainwashing through whatever cause — tyrannical, financial, lovelessness. When after the war she had come to live with her uncle in Santa Barbara, she had tried marriage again, moved to Los Angeles, but it had not worked out. Her troubled heart was freed by divorce. She had, nevertheless, managed to put her daughter through the best of schooling. The girl had met and married a judge and moved to Indianapolis. What Maria had missed in happiness, Lisa had found without reservations. The mother felt grateful for that.

On this late afternoon, Johnny's thoughts were involved with his own affairs, among which Allene played a major part. For some time he had noticed a cooling in her affections, spiked with hints about a separation. He attributed this to his finanacial losses and, which perhaps hurt most, to the difference in their ages. They were drifting apart and he felt helpless to remedy the situation. Then, suddenly, Allene had packed her bags and moved in with her mother. She had returned shortly, however, and at present their relationship rested on a status quo. As he recuperated from his initial perplexity, he hardly paid abundant attentions to Maria. But fate willed it that mutual acquaintances would invite them together again.

He began to see her more often, and her understanding of his problems soon warmed their meetings. He began to feel that whereas his wives had always taken from him, giving little in return, Maria gave, accepting him for himself as he was now, helping him to find security in the loyalty of her friendship. When he discovered that Allene had been seeing other men, he became even closer with the other woman. After thirteen years of marriage, four tries that had left him none the wiser what love was all about, Allene separated from him on July 28, 1961. Johnny moved from his Lorenzo Avenue home, placed his personal possessions into cellar storage at the Bryson Hotel on Wilshire Boulevard where he took a room for address purpose only, while he stayed with friends.

Then a famous restaurateur on the Strip sent a couple of collectors to impound Johnny's Cadillac, to pay for an outstanding account amounting to some $200, a bill Johnny had never received because all were sent to Roos' office. After this treatment that needed no illustrating description, and after he got his car back suffering grievous embarrassment, Johnny called Roos.

"Listen, Bö!" he said, totally heartsick. "What are you doing to me? I've made millions throughout the years, where did the money disappear to? I haven't lived that high . . . You're my business manager . . . you're wealthy . . . Tell me, Bö: why is it I don't have a quarter?"

"What do you want from me, Johnny? Do you want to give me a heart attack? I'm a sick man! And you make me nervous. I'll talk to you tomorrow!" But the tomorrow never came because time after time the same song and dance continued, while Johnny, naively, still thought him a friend. "I can't hate the guy," he said to the party listening in on the extension phone, "I know he's ruined me, but we've known each other for so long. I was one of his first clients! I can't understand how he could do this to me!"

John Wayne understood. Red Skelton understood. They had their own reasons.

As things went from bad to worse, Johnny thought about declaring bankruptcy. He telephoned Mickey Rooney to ask him for advice. Rooney, the boy-wonder who had shared his early MGM days, had found himself in an identical dilemma and had previously taken this step. However, after more consideration Johnny decided against the issue. He was going to pull himself out of the rut no matter how difficult it seemed at present. He was open to suggestions. He made a business trip to Chicago, which promised to restore some of his income.

Maria, whose daughter was expecting a child, accompanied him part of the way, stopping by at Lisa's home in Indianapolis. Johnny's youngest girl, Heidi, was also pregnant. She had married a young man, Michael Husa, serving his enlistment in the Navy. As Maria offered her motherly guidance and knowledge to Lisa, she told her that she planned to marry Johnny as soon as his divorce became final. She confided gaily that both of them were going to be grandparents almost simultaneously, "At least he can't call me Granny — it's happening to him, too." She expressed her hopes about Lisa coming to the wedding in the spring, maybe Heidi could make it as well and the two young mothers could show off their babies and compare notes.

With Johnny's stay in Chicago coming to an end, Maria kissed Lisa farewell and left for the Windy City; they had planned a return flight together. She arrived in his hotel while Johnny was out. As she waited in his room, the telephone rang. She went to answer. She felt herself growing numb as she listened.

It had only been a little ring on the phone — the voice had belonged to a stranger and sounded vague across the thousands of miles of wires strung between the two distant cities. Was she awake? Was it a nightmare?

For a long while Maria sat staring into empty space, her hand still clutching the receiver after the line had been disconnected. She could not accept what she had just heard.

When she finally hung up, she dialed the airport to make immediate reservations for a passage back to the West Coast. The least she could do was see to it that they arrived in time for the funeral. Then she braced herself for the sad task . . . to tell Johnny the bitter news.

Young Heidi, 19, had been killed while driving her husband and a friend back to the naval station in San Diego after a visit to her mother, Beryel. According to the California Highway Patrol, Heidi had gone to sleep at the wheel and her car flipped over, tossing Michael Husa to the pavement, while their passenger in the back seat escaped injury. The accident occurred on November 19, 1962, (yesterday, Maria thought), near Laguna Beach on Highway 101. When an ambulance rushed the victims to a hospital, Heidi and her unborn baby were dead on arrival.

Thank God he did not find out yesterday, Maria thought again and again; he would have been alone, so much alone with his grief. Perhaps now he could share it . . . even a little.

As the double-edged sword of spiritual pain cut into it, the heart of Heidi's father was no different from that of any parent who had lost a child. Only the lapse of time itself helped to give some kind of remedy to his sorrow, a sorrow that words could never describe. But at the moment when Johnny learned about the accident time stood still.

Allene glanced at the star-sapphire on her finger. She picked up a pen and signed the divorce papers. Her settlement called for $2,000 payable in two years, and a life insurance policy naming her the beneficiary for $10,000.

She remarried a few days after the divorce became final, choosing a manufacturer to replace the swimmer-actor.

Johnny busied himself with getting his life back into shape. There were things to attend to — a list of items on his agenda.

Johnny, named "Greatest Swimmer of All Time" by Associated Press, 1950, holding Helms Athletic Foundation Swimming Hall of Fame Trophy. (Photo by Tampone-Clark: Courtesy of Helms Athletic Foundation.)

Receiving Helms Hall of Fame Awards — Helms World Trophy. (Left to right—
W. R. "Bill" Schroeder, Ralph Flanagan, Duke Kahanamoku, Johnny Weiss-
muller.) Photo by Douglas G. Kilgour: Courtesy of Helms Athletic Foundation.

Duke Kahanamoku teaching Johnny the real hula-hula.
(Photo by Douglas G .Kilgour.)

Hi Johnny
Ed Sullivan

After a B'nai B'rith Annual Awards and Bill Corum Memorial Dinner in New York, Ed Sullivan's program invites a lively backstage gathering of notabilities. (Left to right: Vincent Richards, Mrs. Babe Ruth, Jack Dempsey, Gene Sarazen, Ed Sullivan, behind whom Edward Eagan and a dignitary are paying court, Gene Tunney, Johnny Weissmuller, Douglas Fairbanks Jr., Clarence De-Marr, and The Four Horsemen — the greatest four football aces of Notre Dame.) Photo by: Jerry Saltsberg & Associates.

Joe E. Brown coaxes Johnny into asking Bing Crosby to lay down a bet. (Photo by Joe Rosenthal)

With Rocky Marciano — a golfing pal.

Tom Culligan greets John Raitt with Johnny in the rain at the Annual Culligan Invitational — Olympic Club at Lakeside — 5/23/60. (Albert "Kayo" Harris & Assoc. Photographers)

*Johnny drives at the World Entertainment Golf Championships.
(Photo by Lester Nehamkin)*

*Among Friends. (L. to R. Forrest Tucker, Pete de Paolo, Maurie Luxford, Johnny,
General Omar Bradley.)*

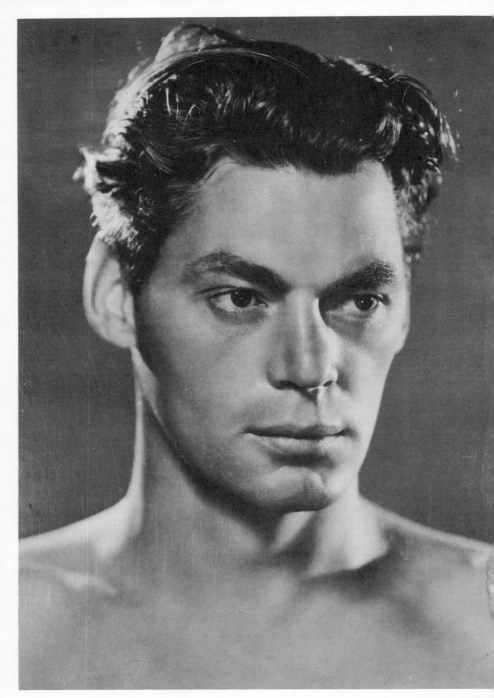

Father and .

. . Son

On a trapeze with the greatest of ease . . . Johnny keeps in shape for his new picture, TARZAN AND HIS MATE. *(MGM Photo by Clarence Sinclair Bull)*

An all-around athlete.
(Photos by Cronenweth)

*Young flyers — The U.S. Air Force greets Johnny as Col. Gilbert L. Curtis' sons
(Gilbert Jr., John, Charles, Robert, James) say "hello", and Andy Cannon, son of
Col. Cannon (in white shirt), introduces two little girl friends.
(Official U.S. Air Force photo by R. A. Carlisle.)*

Maria and Johnny. (Photo by Lee Wenzlick)

ITEMS ON THE AGENDA

21

P.o.d. form #4416, a small white slip of paper imprinted with United States Post Office, Direct Package, All for Firm on Face — read as hand-written: To Johnny Weissmuller, (present address).

Six days a week these letter-parcels arrived, tied with paper string and bearing the Postmaster's tenderly reluctant signature, reluctant because it took more than mere psychic talents to unscramble the puzzle spelling the addressee's identity. As the television tube kept sending Tarzan's yell and Jungle Jim's running feet into millions of living rooms throughout the country, the hard-working postal echelon was faced with a colossal, rising mountain of inadequately addressed mail that still somehow managed to reach Johnny, just when he most needed the support of his fans.

To illustrate this classic battle of the U. S. Post Office Department and the mailmen, the following samples show the writings on outer envelopes (provided, of course, that there were outer envelopes. Stamps often sealed but folded stationery) . . . or like one young fan wrote: "Postman, Postman, don't be slow . . . be like Tarzan, go man — go!"

1) Tarzan, One
   Of Western World, Kenya, Africa.
   Hollywood.
2) Johnny Weves Muller,
   406 California.
3) Tony Was A Miller, U.S.A. (Tarzan)
4) Father of Boy, Johnnie,
   A Metro-Goldwyn-Mayer Picture.
5) Westmiller, filmstar.
   Calva Citi.
6) Apelephantmuller, Tarzan.
7) Tommy Wisemiller, c/o Swimming Pool Co.,
   West Coast.
8) Olympic Swimmer, Tarzan,
   Local, California.
9) Jorn Weis Miler,
   Culliver, World.
10) Mr. Weissmuller, Black Sands Subdivision,
    Mainland Office, 16 W. Erie St.,
    Chicago 10, Illinois.
11) John W., Champion Swimmer and Actor,
    Hollywood.
12) Johnny Wiscier, RKO Picture,
    Pasadena.

... To quote a few together with a selection of other orthographic errors like Johonny Weissmiiler, Jock Waysmiler, Johnei Weisermueller, Tommy Weismullrir — Weesalmoor, Wellsmullar, Weisomula, Wersnuller, Wosmulleriscondir, Weissmulled, Wiceniller, Wailsmular, Wissmaler, Woswallor, Was Smiler, Wesmulla, Weismeler, Wesomler,

Wessmyllar, Was Moral, Wessimulare, Smallerweis... all designed to reach Johnny — all filled with admiration or pleas.

"Dear Sir, May you kindly despatch me your fine snapshot to be added to my album. I want to be your pen friend. Awaiting reply. Yours faithful..." a card from Ghana read, and mail from Ghana was as plentiful as to elect Johnny President if he had cared to run!

"Dear Mr. Weissmuller, This letter is mainly to ask you to come to our Century 21 Exposition which is here in Seattle. I am a great fan of yours and would be honored if you would stay at my house. I realize how busy you are but with all the celebrities coming, the greatest Tarzan (you of course) would be a welcome sight."

"I want to help a youngster from my home town, I think he has Olympic possibilities in fancy diving. Can you suggest a course of training and where he should start to get into competitive events?"

"Mother is writing this letter because I'm only five. But you are my first big crush! P.S. I like elephants and monkeys too!"

"Well, Johnny — I can do the Tarzan yell just like you. It took a bit of practice but I finally made it!"

"Please send me your repair kit with a large supply of patches for one of your swimming pools."

"How about a good Italian dish of Maccaronis at my house?"

"I want to be Tarzan some day but — I am a girl, so in that case I will be Jane. Oh, I almost forgot... Valerie wants to be Tarzan too!"

"Have you published any specific information about

swimming, the use of the arms, leg kick, how high you swim above the water and how you achieve that power stroke? I want to become an Olympic swimmer, I'm very interested in this sport."

"I know your age but I don't care if you are eighty! And the only reason I have not written before is because you were married."

"Please answer Air Mail, it is so much faster than Sea Mail."

"Dear Mr. Weissmuller, what is your contribution to the following movements: Abolishing the Electric Chair. End Colonialism Now. Raise Wages and Relief 100%. Free Africa. Newberry Library Pickets. Washington Park Forum and Square Soap Box. End British Martial Over Kenya — ?"

"Would you please send me your autograph (by pen, not reproduced). I collect them. I am a Lutheran minister and especially interested in sports personalities."

"Please, Tarzan, be my friend. I have no one. They all think I'm a stupid little boy. Will you be my friend? I will write to you at least once a week."

"Bravo! Just heard you telling about a TV swimming series you are preparing for children. But please give us active oldsters a concise underwater exercise program as well. I am 57 years old; obviously I can't walk 50 miles, or even keep up with regular exercises. But I know that many, many of us will be swimming in pools or at the good old beach resorts this summer maybe with our grandchildren. If only we could know some fun exercises to help us stay fit. The water is always so buoyant and seems helpful. Might even take off unwanted pounds. It sure would be nice. Best wishes to you."

"I want to come to California. The only thing that stops me is money. Send cash and address and I'll visit you."

"Are you interested in investing in land?"

"If you're here at Thanksgiving, drop in for dinner. Mother will have a big turkey and one more or less doesn't matter. Besides, you can show me how to climb trees without falling off."

"Can you send me general data about physical fitness?"

"I'll go to Africa next year. I have a friend, a wild man who swings through the vines and I'll be his lady Jane."

"Dear Mr. Weissmuller, My 11 year-old son is making a Tarzan scrapbook . . ."

"For two years now my greatest wish has been to become an Olympic swimmer. I'm a member of a swimming team here and have been beaten only twice in competition. I was hoping you might tell me how to go about training. Could you suggest any books that might help me? Perhaps your own? I would also like to know more about how old you are and were, when you began to swim."

"Please don't think I'm just another starry-eyed teenager. I've seen you since I was nine and my feelings haven't changed. I'm eighteen now — love swimming, boating, water skiing and golfing. I just read where your wife divorced you and I can't imagine anyone ever leaving you. Someday, some way I hope to meet you and if I get to California, I want to get your address and come to see you."

"If you come to Red Bluff I'll repair your car for nothing. I'm a good mechanic."

"Please send me a tape with your Tarzan yell."

"Please send me your loincloth."

"Please send me your big knife."

"Please ask Cheetah to send me a banana."

"If I don't get any pictures or little movies from you I'll die! Color, not black and white. Color!"

"I want to teach my wife and young child how to swim and not be afraid of the water. Can you send me the information?"

"We are interested in your Tarzan and Jungle Jim series and would like some information: A synopsis of your life story in detail, also — our parents think a lot about physical fitness. We are teen-agers. Please tell us what to do first and if YMCA swimming lessons are sufficient to excel in this healthy sport."

"I always wanted to be an adventurer and swimmer like you, but it didn't work out that way. Maybe this note will bring you a bit of warmth. God be with you!"

"What about the care, maintenance, heating of your pool?"

"I have a boyfriend who resembles you in his love of life and ability in sports. He doesn't have a mean bone in his body. I can't imagine you having one either."

"Dear Friend, I am very happy to write you this letter. Please kindly send me one of your best photographs which I will keep to remember you. Please — I will drop my pen here . . ."

I will drop my pen here . . .

From the world over they arrived! These letters written in many languages, bearing stamps issued in sundry corners of the globe. People interested in their idol, asking questions, desiring facts, collecting paraphernalia, autographs: praising, loving, wanting to be acknowledged. They wrote and wrote to addresses that never existed, to those old and time-worn, to fan clubs, the Motion Picture Academy, Screen Actors Guild on 7750 Sunset Boulevard in Hollywood, incidentally the most direct way of reaching an actor. To the studios crisscrossing the area where motion pictures rolled, from MGM to Twentieth Century Fox, Columbia to RKO, Paramount to Walt Disney. To CBS, NBC, ABC, the local stations. Even one they called Amalgamated Studios! It was impossible for Johnny to answer them all, that would have taken at least several secretaries, hundreds of dollars in postage, photographic reproductions, stationery; not to mention office space; expenses he could not afford in his present circumstances. But he read the letters, finding solace in their messages of goodwill, their feeling of trust. Then he sat down and wrote to those inquiring about physical fitness. They had a right to receive an answer because they had turned to him for information and help.

Johnny had always stuck to the theory that the body needed and craved healthy activity, that it could not wait. To exercise or to wither remained the individual's critical choice. You use . . . or lose. The building up of a young body from the teen ages to the thirty span supplied the necessary energy which later, re-aligned, helped to create a functional life of success. Utilized in daily routine the thus-won vitality was channeled to the brain, helping its mental development by the general conditioning of the physique. Just as a building on a solid foundation withstands the storms of time, the human body needs early fitness to grow into strong and enduring adulthood. And then there is the constant and proper maintenance . . . of man and building, alike.

He had noticed how the old, time-tested and worn dwellings in Europe stood for centuries, while modern structures in the new land crumbled. And he was quite concerned with having observed in Europeans a greater urge to pursue physical culture than was normally practiced by Americans. Yet he recognized that the well-being of his fellow citizens largely depended on a coordination of all faculties in times when man's strength and competitive force were most challenged, because the nation found itself involved in a race for survival of the fittest and supremacy in arms. Thus Johnny found himself preaching and giving advice to those who cared to listen.

His diagnostic procedure revealed man's self to be his own worst enemy, constantly submitting to basic laziness. Granted that not everyone could play soccer, football, tennis or golf, or join a baseball team, ride a horse or even find enough water to swim in, but all could incorporate simple gymnastics into their daily routine, as well as avail themselves of a kind of hydrotheraphy such as is possible under a shower or in a plain bathtub.

Throughout his years Johnny had been an all-around athlete, whether he tackled his own sport in the water or any other given medium. He was as much at home on the horizontal bar as in the boxing ring, had used trapeze and flying rings for working out and definitely favored free exercises, including the Turkish towel. Long before The Twist became a national dance craze, he had used the towel in conjunction with the pendulum, woodchopping, a standing kick, the trunk twist, all-around, knee-bend, tendon stretch with the foot, the ferris wheel and bunny hop or just massaging, which essentially represented The Twist on the dance floor. Starting with the neck, upper and lower back to cross back and finally the hips, he even used it as an ankle, foot and leg stimulator much in the way a person dries himself after a bath. Vigorous rubbing, stretching, bending, all supplied some activity in the physical education curricula without actual strain on the body or its parts. Stretching the towel behind the neck helped to work out the arms at the same time it relaxed tense shoulder muscles and those leading to the back skull.

Gymnastics developed arms, shoulders, chest and abdomen. If a person were too senile for tumbling, leg muscles too could be developed by merely lying on the floor and simulating pedaling a bicycle, or turning from one side to the other and, in succession, lifting the leg up and down. This latter exercise worked well when, in a manner of a ballet movement, an arabesque was executed while standing to front, side and back. Touching the toes helped. Reaching for the ceiling added to the posture. Doing an all-around rotating circle with the arms set in motion like the blades of a helicopter — up, around, down — helped decrease the size of the waistline. Calisthenics produced grace as well as organic vigor. He stressed the importance of rhythm and the necessity of starting at an easy pace, gradually increasing the output of strength but keeping it down to an effortless level at all times. The moment exercises became too difficult to handle for a layman, it showed that

311

the body was not yet sufficiently conditioned to undergo the effort and, therefore, had to return to the more easy-going beginner's early course.

Any unbalanced figure could improve itself through diet plus exercise. Johnny never believed in the use of drugs or reducing pills, but definitely in ordinary massage and hydrotheraphy, a brisk walk in a non-smoke-filled atmosphere, even a goose-step or bringing the knees up high with each movement. Lying in a tub of warm water, the athlete found, tense and fatigued muscles relaxed. If circulation needed stimulation, reducing of certain fatty tissues could be accomplished through applying a shower to back, stomach and hips, with the full force of the needle shower hitting these parts of the body, alternating between hot and cold. The water turned on thus brought about the desired effect in shaping, in helping to eliminate fatigue of the blood stream, harmful toxins, at the same time opening pores and releasing perspiration for a better skin texture and complexion. A hot bath helped to relieve aches and pains, to relax. A cold one served as a stimulant. Alternating the two gradually obtained — step by step — a greater resistance to common colds.

But Johnny's purpose was not just to give specific training which, without the aid of illustrations, was a difficult, if not impossible, task. His intent was to make the people aware of the necessity of seeking out such places where gymnastics could be performed under expert guidance, or the pointing out of books on these subjects as supplied by public libraries without charge. He taught the individual correspondents to appreciate the importance of what it meant to have all ligaments, the connecting ties holding organs and bones in place, work with perfection and how, consequently, it brought about agility, flexibility and offered proper balance.

The stressing of fundamental principles involving physical education, however, was not only expressed by men like Johnny, by trainers of sports or by doctors, but also by the leaders of the nation.

President Eisenhower called a conference on the fitness of American youth in 1956, but he directed attention toward this problem at a time when Russian Sputniks caused science and mathematical levels to overshadow this issue. When President Kennedy was elected to office, his new administration laid down the plans for a health program with emphasis on the body's strength.

In the White House news release dated February 14, 1963, President John F. Kennedy sent a Special Message on Our Nation's Youth to the Congress of the United States: paragraph VIII, in part, read:

"Finally, good physical fitness is essential to good physical and mental health. If our young men and women are to attain the social, scientific and economic goals of which they are capable, they must all possess the strength, the energy and the good health to pursue them vigorously. My Council on Physical Fitness has given leadership and

Note: The excerpt of President John F. Kennedy's Message is used with the permission of The White House. When the author requested a statement in regard to the above subject matter, Ralph A. Dungan, Special Assistant to the President, submitted a series of suitable quotations. His letter included the President's best wishes. It is with deep sadness and regret that the author cannot herewith thank the late President.

direction to programs aimed at achieving this goal, and with a heartening response."

As Johnny's thoughts became more and more involved with the requests of his fans, another item was included on the agenda that represented yet another cycle of his life.

"I want to have my biography written while I'm still around to censor it — nuts to a post-mortem!" Johnny decided, talked to this writer and revealed his plans. "A book that would cover the story of my life, at the same time serving to answer the questions I'm constantly asked. I've turned down several authors who wanted to get their hands on all the told and untold bits that happened to me . . . the scandals with Lupe . . . everything connected with that long forgotten jazz once I received my introduction to Hollywood. Heck, I'm no actor — I'm an athlete! I've never entered a race prompted by mere gossip. I want this book to be eligible reading for three generations, but I also want to tell the truth as it happened, without embroidery either way." He sat ready to transfer a piece of barbequed steak from a fork into his oral cavity as the first interview began.

"What are you thinking about?"

The meat remained stationary on the prongs. Johnny grinned, glanced at it and licked his lips. "Food. One has to remain a child at heart to appreciate the better things in life, like eating after a long swim." He swallowed the piece with relish.

In March, Johnny appeared on NBC's First Impressions, with host Bill Leyden and a panel of three who questioned him with unfinished sentences for the purpose of guessing his concealed identity. After listening to the following, the panelists agreed on Johnny as the mystery celebrity.

Q. I can go overboard when buying . . .
A. Hats.

Q. It takes courage to tell a woman . . .
A. To go away.

Q. I have a strong opinion about . . .
A. How I look.

Q. Give me a woman who . . .
A. Loves children.

Q. It's a mistake not to teach children . . .
A. To swim.

Q. All I need to be happy is to . . .
A. Go to the movies.

Q. When I meet a woman she thinks I'm . . .
A. Kind of corny.

Q. I feel best . . .
A. When I'm alone.

Q. I want to re-live . . .
A. My background.

Q. If possible, I would like to bring back . . .
A. The Foxtrot.

Q. I'm not the man who . . .
A. Cheats on my wife.

With the exception of "I feel best . . . when I'm alone" Johnny's answers ran true to character. And, perhaps, even this reply had sprung from the depth of his hitherto concealed subconsciousness, because despite his constant search for companionship, the many faces that had become familiar to him, and others that had smiled at him from a distance, he had basically remained alone through most of his personal life. Never more so than since fate had turned over the ugly side of its profile within the past few years.

The show had been taped earlier but was aired on the 22nd; thus it came about that the same night found Johnny on yet another program, the Tom Duggan Show on local Channel 13, talking about his dual careers and plugging Kevo-etts, a vitamin supplement designed to boost energy between meals. This latter advertising was hardly a full-time job but it paid and, besides, the interview was conducted in a manner far removed from a straight commercial blurb.

One thing leading to another, he received a phone call from a studio executive. "How would you feel about a role similar to Bogart's in 'The African Queen?'"

"But I'm no actor." Johnny was hesitant.

"That's a lot of hooey! In your own rights you're a Barrymore! After all, picture him swinging on the vines." The voice on the other end continued, "You've got sincerity, a good sense of humor; that's what this part needs! A skipper of a trading junkey. Maybe we'll even get John Huston to direct. Tell you what, I'll send you the screen play as soon as it's in somewhat respectable shape."

"That's okay with me." Johnny said and hung up.

His business transactions with Kurt L. Stier, an expert in the field of pre-fabricated pools, also were closed, resulting in The Johnny Weissmuller Steel Porcelain Pools by Alpoa.

Aileen Covington, publisher and editor of a magazine

called "Golf Life", expressed interest in partly sponsoring a TV series dealing with educational sports, with Johnny playing host.

Then Robert C. Wian suggested a position as public relations director at his Big Boy Franchises, Inc., with an annual salary that continued between cross-country tours for other subsidiaries. Johnny had first met Wian some seven years ago at Lakeside, where he had spent time at the pinnacle of his career. When the latter learned about his troubles from trusty friends like Al Dean, Maurie Luxford, Jim Raymond, and Forrest Tucker, all of whom in turn had assisted Johnny in various ways during his latent need, he immediately took action. "Tell me if you hurt," he said. "And if it's true, look me up tomorrow morning. I've got a job for you." As it turned out his idea produced a mutual boom.

Thus the business world Johnny had shunned, even during his brief association with B.V.D. Swim Suits, had again found an opening for him. His prospects on an upswing, he placed a call to Major Riddle, president of The Dunes Hotel in Las Vegas.

"I'm getting married," he said. "How about fixing up a bridal suite." At which a loud crash announced that Maria had heard the news and, taken by surprise, had dropped the earthenware pot containing a tasty concoction of Chili-Con-Carne she had just prepared for dinner.

317

BIOGRAPHICALLY GAMBLING

22

THE MORNING of April, the 23rd, dawned with sunny skies as two cars coming from the Weissmuller residence on Roscomare Road sped through the valley toward the Highway 6 turnoff. Then, taking a short cut to Victorville, they hit Route 91 and headed for the desert.

In spite of the warmness of the day, occupants of both automobiles kept comfortably cool as the streamlined Olds equipped with its air-conditioning led the way for a small MGA that followed faithfully like a miniature shadow sans its convertible top. Whenever a traffic light blocked their immediate passage the driver of the first vehicle was seen flashing a broad smile at occasional strangers who happened to stop alongside. As the tall, dark-haired man with the familiar face acknowledged congratulations voiced in his direction, the blond woman beside him clung to his arm, smiling almost shyly as she stole a kiss off his cheek before turning to wave at her one-motored caravan.

The pair in the trailing sports car, however, seemed in comparison rather nonchalant. As news broadcast on the radio revealed the purpose of their trip, producer George Virand and his wife talked about little but trivia, in which their cat left at home in the care of trusty neighbors played a major part. The couple had been married for exactly 3,808 nights, not to mention the days, and all future excitement that was to unite their friends in wedlock still lay in the blue haze of distance, across the Nevada border.

But even these two world travelers had underestimated the speed with which events of the day were to pass. At the same time as the nervous bride had hugged her groom, a jet had taken flight from far Indianapolis, bringing westward Maria's daughter and her eight-week old baby girl, while a private plane carrying Johnny's best man, Forrest Tucker, was en route from San Francisco. Tucker had previously asked Johnny to stand up for him on his former nuptial occasion; this was a gesture of reciprocity on his part.

At their destination, Major Riddle had left distinct instructions for his staff to accommodate the wedding party and fill their respective suites with flowers. They were to be treated as his guests. District Judge David Zenoff planned to preside at the afternoon ceremony. And Phil Harris, entertaining at The Desert Inn where his shows drew enthusiastic crowds, had left word for the Weissmullers to visit his nightly domain.

Reporters and loyal fans crowded both sides of The Dunes' portals and they took over the moment the two-car echelon finally arrived. Surrounding Johnny, they kept shaking his hand and asking for autographs until Maria suddenly found herself facing her new grandchild in Lisa's arms.

"Schnuckeline!" she called out, using a pet name. "Schnuckeline! What a place to see my grand-baby for the first time - - - in a parking lot!" The women exchanged hurried embraces as the dashboard clocks reminded all to make haste.

After a quick retreat to their suite, the wedding party returned to the Oldsmobile, and its owners began searching for City Hall. As they departed, a taxi pulled into the open spot.

"Paging Cary Grant!" a doorman hollered. Minutes later the ever-youthful, charming star checked out. Questioned by the newsmen at hand as to why he did not remain for the festivities, Grant said he had not been invited because he could not swim! Meantime the swimmer and his mermaid "crawled" up the steps that led to a room with a long desk, behind which a bespectacled matron was filling out marriage licenses.

"Name, please." The femme civil servant asked matter-of-factly, without wasting a glance at the couple.

"Weissmuller — Peter, John."

The woman's head flew back with a jerk as her jaw dropped open. "Tarzan!" she gulped. "Tarzan!" Her hand began to tremble so violently that she almost upset a vase containing a single red rose atop the writing area. "I've loved you all my life!"

"Thanks!" Johnny grinned. "Meet my bride . . ."

The rose found its proper place in Maria's hand.

When they returned to their hotel suite, they were lost in a crowd of bellboys and waiters setting up tables for the reception that was to take place immediately after the ceremony at 6 o'clock.

Johnny took one look at the massive flower arrangements. "Looks like a funeral parlor!" he quipped, while Maria telephoned her daughter to come down and help her get dressed.

"If Tuck calls, tell him to meet me at the lanai bar," Johnny instructed before making his escape to quieter spheres. On his way he was stopped by a stranger.

"You here to gamble, Johnny?" the man asked.

"Haven't you heard? — I'm getting married."

A loud guffaw accompanied a hearty wallop on his shoulder. "Same thing, isn't it, Pal?!"

The festive mood that had hitherto been manifest left Johnny, he oriented his steps to the bar near the center pool where he ordered his customary light Bacardi with water and an added drop of non-caloric sweetener. He started cracking his finger knuckles as his answers to the bartender's chatter revealed his fidgety disposition.

He began to brood.

He hated to admit it, but the stranger was right. Marriage was a gamble and no one knew it better than himself. Those impressive, felt-covered gaming tables in the adjoining enclosure gave a man some kind of odds. What odds had he drawn throughout his married affairs?

His thoughts took him back through the years. "It seems like an eternity since I took the first step with Bobbe . . . almost as if I had been a different man! But Bobbe preferred ten grand and walked out of my life. And Lupe, dear Lupe! Our fights made history with one K.O. after another, and our victories split in the middle. How we enjoyed the time between the rounds! Then came Beryel . . . She is free

321

again; her second try, too, ended in divorce. Allene? I was happy with her until the years took their toll."

He was aware of the bartender's chatter but his ears remained deaf to the words.

"Here I go again," his thoughts continued, "for the fifth and last time. If something happens to this marriage, I don't think I'll have the strength or the will power to carry on. I have always desired a lasting union. It's funny, but I still hope for five-to-one in my favor. I've grown older . . . outwardly I belong to the third generation . . . but inside, I guess, my feelings haven't much changed. I still believe in the ideals that accompanied my early swimming career. Maybe not all of youth's purity had washed off after all . . ."

He glared at the drink in front of him.

His mind trailing back to the days of his youth, awakening other memories in him — memories about his children. Where were they today? John Scott . . . Wendy . . . Heidi . . . Little Heidi, so gentle, so loving, so unspoilt. Now she was dead. A strangely lingering sadness crept through his being, a yearning to listen to their blessings on this day.

He acknowledged a passer-by whose face seemed vaguely familiar.

"Where are my friends?" he wondered. "Most drifted away when I left the roster of wealthily independent entertainers. Relations once hot turned luke warm, and some iced. Like ships on the sea, most of my friends have passed me by at a near view but they soon disappeared from sight and, now, no longer belong to my horizon. The new faces I see are relative strangers. Only a few have remained steadfast - - - good, old Tuck! He's always chartered a course in my direction regardless of time or circumstance or convention or material consequence or..." No matter! It was not quantity but quality he counted best.

He felt tired of this rat race called fame. "I want to spend my declining years in peace, security not necessarily bordering on wealth but coupled with companionship only a mate who is both wife and friend can give. Maria!"

Again he felt himself wondering how many cycles a life could hold in store. Was he yet to be granted a new beginning? He realized all the mistakes he had made in his past but somehow the reasons remained hazy in his mind.

His fingers touched the glass, it felt cool and inviting.

Then, suddenly, a strange feeling befell him, as if his little late daughter were present — for sweet angels travel lightly and brush against one's cheek with soft, invisible wings. "Little Heidi — you have come after all ..."

Johnny pushed aside his untouched Bacardi, and his steps carried him back to his temporary quarters.

Alike a shadow descends along a mountain with the breaking of yet another dawn, Johnny's outlook on the future began to brighten. He had lived a full life. He had forsaken much in favor of Hollywood, but the film capital had in return given him everything a shell could produce in artificially cultivated pearls. Even his marriages had been part of this capricious oyster bed. It would be different now.

Later, Johnny stood beside Maria, listening to the judge's words. He looked into her eyes and saw tears running down her cheeks as she repeated her wedding vows with faltering language. At this instant his own heart was swept by emotion. This then was his love.

Soon after champagne flowed, hors d'oeuvres were served, the party moved downstairs to the Sultan's Table where violins serenaded them at a special dinner.

That same night, too, saw them at the Desert Inn. Throughout his performance Phil Harris kidded Johnny — his name, his swimming, crawling, making whoopee! Suddenly at a given moment in the midst of Phil's song, Johnny let go his Tarzan yell.

A quietness that lasted for several seconds descended on the crowded theatre restaurant, then applause set in, reaching its crescendo in a standing ovation. The shafted spotlight flicked across the room and onto Johnny's face as he stood taking bows, his white teeth bared in a smile, his eyes moist, his looks belying his age. He was still Johnny Weissmuller — beloved champion, and star.

And as the show on the stage continued, life inevitably went on.

APPENDIX

JOHN WEISSMULLER
His Swimming Records and Achievements
Compiled by W. R. "Bill" Schroeder,
Managing Director Helms Athletic Foundation

OLYMPIC GAMES
GOLD MEDALS WON — NEW OLYMPIC RECORDS

1924, AT PARIS, FRANCE
100-Meters Freestyle champion 59.0
400-Meters Freestyle champion 5:04.2
800-Meters U.S.A. Relay Team champion 9:53.4

1928, AT AMSTERDAM, HOLLAND
100-Meters Freestyle champion 58.6
800-Meters U.S.A. Relay Team champion 9:36.2

SPECIAL INTERNATIONAL AND NATIONAL AWARDS

1922 — American Swimmer of the Year
(Chosen by Helms Athletic Foundation)
Non-repeat award. Weissmuller, if eligible, might have also won in
1923, 1924, 1925, 1926 and 1927.

1923 — Helms World Trophy Winner (Athlete of the Year, North America)

1949 — Helms Swimming Hall of Fame
(Elected by Helms Hall Board)

1950 — Greatest Swimmer of the First Half-Century — 1900-1950
(Chosen by Associated Press)

NATIONAL CHAMPIONSHIPS

OUTDOOR			INDOOR		
EVENT	YEAR	TIME	EVENT	YEAR	TIME
50-Yards	1921	23.2	50-Yards	1923	23.6
50-Yards	1922	23.0	50-Yards	1924	24.0
100-Yards	1922	52.8	50-Yards	1925	23.2
100-Yards	1923	54.6	100-Yards	1922	54.0
100-Yards	1925	52.0	100-Yards	1923	54.8
100-Meters	1926	59.6	100-Yards	1924	53.8
100-Meters	1927	58.0	100-Yards	1925	52.2
100-Meters	1928	57.8	100-Yards	1927	51.4
220-Yards	1921	2:28.0	100-Yards	1928	50.8
220-Yards	1922	2:22.4	Pentathlon	1922	
440-Yards	1922	5:16.4	Pentathlon	1923	(Tied)
440-Yards	1923	5:37.4	220-Yards	1922	2:17.4
440-Yards	1925	5:22.5	220-Yards	1923	2:22.0
440-Yards	1926	5:21.8	220-Yards	1924	2:14.8
440-Yards	1927	4:52.0	220-Yards	1927	2:10.8
440-Yards	1928	4:58.6	220-Yards	1928	2:10.4
			500-Yards	1922	5:46.8
			500-Yards	1923	5:43.6
			500-Yards	1924	5:50.4
			500-Yards	1927	5:28.4
			500-Yards	1928	5:35.0
			150-Yards Backstroke	1923	1:42.0

NATIONAL CHAMPIONSHIPS (Continued)

OUTDOOR			INDOOR		
RELAY	YEAR	TIME	RELAY	YEAR	TIME
880-Yards	1923	10:05.4	300-Yards Medley	1927	3:06.2
880-Yards	1924	(No Time)	300-Yards Medley	1928	3:05.6
880-Yards	1925	11:12.0	200-Yards	1922	1:39.2
880-Yards	1926	9:43.0	200-Yards	1924	1:38.8
880-Yards	1927	10:22.2	400-Yards	1922	3:43.6
880-Yards	1927	9:35.0	400-Yards	1923	3:42.0
880-Yards	1928	9:32.6	400-Yards	1924	3:41.4
			400-Yards	1925	3:45.0
			400-Yards	1928	3:32.6
WATER POLO		1924	WATER POLO		1927

WORLD RECORDS — 20-YARD POOL

EVENT	LOCATION	DATE	TIME
100-Yards	Chicago, Illinois	Nov. 21, 1921	52.6
100-Yards	Minneapolis, Minn.	March 19, 1923	51.8
150-Yards	Chicago, Illinois	April 6, 1922	1:25.4
200-Meters	Chicago, Illinois	Jan. 4, 1923	2:14.0
220-Yards	Honolulu, Hawaii	May 26, 1922	2:15.6
220-Yards	Chicago, Illinois	Jan. 4, 1923	2:14.0
400-Meters	Chicago, Illinois	April 6, 1922	5:05.2
400-Meters	Chicago, Illinois	Feb. 1, 1923	4:51.4
440-Yards	Chicago, Illinois	April 6, 1922	5:05.2
440-Yards	Chicago, Illinois	Feb. 1, 1923	4:51.4
500-Yards	Chicago, Illinois	April 6, 1922	5:46.8
500-Yards	Chicago, Illinois	Feb. 1, 1923	5:42.0
150-Yds. Bkst.	Chicago, Illinois	April 4, 1923	1:42.0

WORLD RECORDS — 25-YARD POOL

EVENT	LOCATION	DATE	TIME
50-Yards	Columbus, Ohio	Aug. 1, 1922	22.8
100-Yards	Honolulu, Hawaii	May 27, 1922	52.6
100-Yards	Miami Beach, Florida	Feb. 17, 1924	52.4
100-Yards	Ann Arbor, Mich.	April 5, 1927	51.0
100-Meters	Brighton Beach, N.Y.	Sept. 27, 1921	1:00.4
100-Meters	Culver (Ind.) Mil. Acad.	May 2, 1922	59.4
100-Meters	Miami Beach, Florida	Feb. 24, 1924	57.4
150-Yards	Brighton Beach, N.Y.	Sept. 27, 1921	1:27.4
150-Yards	Pittsburgh, Pa.	Dec. 7, 1925	1:25.4
200-Meters	Honolulu, Hawaii	May 26, 1922	2:15.6
200-Meters	Ann Arbor, Michigan	June 5, 1927	2:08.0
220-Yards	Honolulu, Hawaii	May 26, 1922	2:15.6
220-Yards	McKeesport, Pa.	Dec. 9, 1925	2:15.2
220-Yards	Ann Arbor, Michigan	June 5, 1927	2:09.0
300-Yards	Philadelphia, Pa.	March 25, 1922	3:16.6
300-Yards	Chicago, Illinois	June 17, 1927	3:07.8
300-Meters	Philadelphia, Pa.	March 25, 1922	3:35.2
500-Yards	Great Lakes, Illinois	June 27, 1923	5:50.4
500-Meters	Milwaukee, Wisconsin	Sept. 30, 1922	6:24.2
100-Yds. Bkst.	Milwaukee, Wisconsin	Nov. 4, 1922	1:05.4
100-Meters Bkst.	Milwaukee, Wisconsin	Nov. 4, 1922	1:12.6
150-Yards Bkst.	Milwaukee, Wisconsin	April 20, 1922	1:45.4

WORLD RECORDS – 100-YARD OR 100-METER POOL

EVENT	LOCATION	DATE	TIME
100-Yards	Honolulu, Hawaii	June 23, 1923	52.8
100-Yards	Seattle, Washington	Aug. 1, 1925	52.0
100-Meters	Alameda, California	July 9, 1922	58.6
100-Meters	Amsterdam, Holland	1928	58.6
440-Yards	New Haven, Connecticut	March 6, 1923	4:57.0
440-Yards	Honolulu, Hawaii	Aug. 25, 1927	4:52.0
400-Meters	New Haven, Connecticut	Mar. 6, 1923	4:57.0
880-Yards	Honolulu, Hawaii	Aug. 27, 1927	10:22.2

WORLD RECORDS – OPEN WATER

EVENT	LOCATION	DATE	TIME
100-Yards	Honolulu, Hawaii	June 23, 1922	52.8
150-Yards	Atlanta, Georgia	Sept. 9, 1922	1:27.8
200-Meters	Honolulu, Hawaii	June 24, 1922	2:17.2
220-Yards	Honolulu, Hawaii	June 24, 1922	2:18.4
300-Meters	Honolulu, Hawaii	June 22, 1922	3:45.0
400-Meters	Honolulu, Hawaii	June 22, 1922	5:06.6
440-Yards	Honolulu, Hawaii	June 22, 1922	5:07.8
500-Yards	Honolulu, Hawaii	June 22, 1922	5:47.6

AMERICAN RECORDS – 20-YARD COURSE

EVENT	LOCATION	DATE	TIME
50-Yards	Chicago, Illinois	Jan. 8, 1925	22.8
100-Yards	Chicago, Illinois	Nov. 21, 1921	52.6
100-Yards	Minneapolis, Minnesota	March 13, 1923	51.8
100-Yards	Omaha, Nebraska	May 10, 1924	51.4
100-Yards	Chicago, Illinois	Dec. 3, 1925	51.2
100-Yards	Cleveland, Ohio	Jan. 29, 1926	51.2
100-Yards	Chicago, Illinois	Jan. 6, 1927	49.8
120-Yards	New York City, N.Y.	Sept. 27, 1921	1:08.4
150-Yards	Chicago, Illinois	April 6, 1922	1:25.4
150-Yards	Homestead, Pa.	Dec. 10, 1925	1:25.0
200-Yards	Chicago, Illinois	Feb. 10, 1926	1:58.4
220-Yards	Chicago, Illinois	Feb. 2, 1922	2:18.4
220-Yards	Chicago, Illinois	Aug. 13, 1922	2:18.4
220-Yards	Chicago, Illinois	Jan. 4, 1923	2:14.0
220-Yards	Chicago, Illinois	Jan. 7, 1926	2:10.4
220-Yards	Chicago, Illinois	Feb. 3, 1927	2:08.6
300-Yards	Chicago, Illinois	Jan. 3, 1924	3:12.4
440-Yards	Chicago, Illinois	April 6, 1922	5:05.2
440-Yards	Chicago, Illinois	Feb. 1, 1923	4:51.4
400-Meters	Chicago, Illinois	April 6, 1922	5:05.2
500-Yards	Chicago, Illinois	April 6, 1922	5:46.8
500-Yards	Chicago, Illinois	Feb. 1, 1923	5:42.0
500-Yards	Chicago, Illinois	April 8, 1927	5:28.4
100-Yds. Backst.	Chicago, Illinois	Dec. 7, 1922	1:05.6
100-Yds. Backst.	Chicago, Illinois	Feb. 4, 1926	1:01.8
150-Yds. Backst.	Chicago, Illinois	April 4, 1923	1:42.0
Relay (400 Yds.)	Chicago, Illinois	Mar. 2, 1922	3:42.4
Relay (400 Yds.)	Chicago, Illinois	Mar. 1, 1923	3:39.6
Relay (500 Yds.)	Chicago, Illinois	April 3, 1928	4:28.2
Relay 300 Yds. Medley	Chicago, Illinois	April 5, 1927	3:06.2
Relay 300 Yds. Medley	Chicago, Illinois	April 4, 1928	3:05.6
Relay (400 Yards)	Chicago, Illinois	April 3, 1928	3:32.6

AMERICAN RECORDS – SHORT COURSE

EVENT	LOCATION	DATE	TIME
100-Yards	Honolulu, Hawaii	May 27, 1922	52.6
100-Yards	Miami Beach, Florida	Feb. 17, 1924	52.4
100-Yards	San Francisco, Calif.	Aug. 10, 1925	52.0
100-Yards	Ann Arbor, Michigan	June 5, 1927	51.0
100-Meters	Brighton Beach, N. Y.	Sept. 27, 1921	1:00.4
100-Meters	Culver (Ind.) Mil. Acad.	May 2, 1922	59.4
100-Meters	Chicago, Illinois	Nov. 7, 1923	59.2
100-Meters	Miami Beach, Florida	Feb. 24, 1924	57.4
150-Yards	Brighton Beach, N. Y.	Sept. 27, 1921	1:27.4
150-Yards	St. Louis Missouri	July 2, 1925	1:26.3
150-Yards	Pittsburgh, Pa.	Dec. 7, 1925	1:25.4
200-Yards	Ann Arbor, Michigan	May 4, 1927	1:56.8
220-Yards	Honolulu, Hawaii	May 26, 1922	2:15.6
220-Yards	McKeesport, Pa.	Dec. 9, 1925	2:15.2
220-Yards	Ann Arbor, Michigan	May 4, 1927	2:09.0
200-Meters	Culver (Ind.) Mil. Acad.	April 15, 1922	2:16.0
200-Meters	Honolulu, Hawaii	May 26, 1922	2:15.6
200-Meters	Ann Arbor, Michigan	May 4, 1927	2:08.0
300-Yards	Philadelphia, Pa.	March 25, 1922	3:16.6
300-Yards	Milwaukee, Wisconsin	Nov. 11, 1925	3:14.0
300-Yards	Chicago, Illinois	June 17, 1927	3:07.8
300-Meters	Philadelphia, Pa.	May 25, 1922	3:35.2
300-Meters	Chicago, Illinois	Oct. 24, 1927	3:31.0
440-Yards	Milwaukee, Wisconsin	Sept. 30, 1922	5:08.0
440-Yards	New Haven, Connecticut	March 6, 1923	4:57.0
400-Meters	Maui, Hawaii	June 1, 1922	5:08.2
400-Meters	New Haven, Connecticut	March 6, 1923	4:57.0
500-Yards	Maui, Hawaii	June 1, 1922	5:52.0
500-Yards	Great Lakes, Illinois	June 27, 1923	5:50.4
500-Meters	Sacramento, California	July 10, 1922	6:42.6
500-Meters	Milwaukee, Wisconsin	Sept. 30, 1922	6:24.2
100-Yds. Bkst.	Milwaukee, Wisconsin	Nov. 4, 1922	1:05.4
100-Yds. Bkst.	Detroit, Michigan	Jan. 30, 1926	1:03.4
100-Meters Bkst.	Milwaukee, Wisconsin	Nov. 4, 1922	1:12.6
150-Yards Bkst.	Milwaukee, Wisconsin	April 20, 1922	1:45.4
150-Yards Bkst.	Chicago, Illinois	Jan. 18, 1924	1:44.8
Relay 200 Yds.	Brooklyn, New York	April 1, 1922	1:39.2
Relay 200 Yds.	Milwaukee, Wisconsin	March 17, 1923	1:37.2
Relay 400 Yds.	New York City, N. Y.	March 29, 1922	3:43.6
Relay 500 Yds.	New York City, N. Y.	March 29, 1922	4:41.8
Relay 250 Yds.	Milwaukee, Wisconsin	March 17, 1923	2:02.6

AMERICAN RECORDS – LONG COURSE

EVENT	LOCATION	DATE	TIME
50-Yards	Columbus, Ohio	Aug. 1, 1922	22.8
100-Yards	New York City, N.Y.	Sept. 24, 1921	53.2
100-Yards	Indianapolis, Indiana	Aug. 10, 1922	52.8
100-Yards	Seattle, Washington	Aug. 1, 1925	52.0
100-Meters	Alameda, California	July 9, 1922	58.6
100-Meters	Amsterdam, Holland	1928	58.6
100-Meters	Honolulu, Hawaii	Aug. 24, 1927	58.0
100-Meters	San Francisco, California	June 7, 1928	57.8
150-Yards	Honolulu, Hawaii	Nov. 14, 1928	1:26.0
200-Yards	Detroit, Michigan	Aug. 4, 1927	2:01.2
220-Yards	Geauga Lake, Ohio	July 11, 1926	2:17.0

AMERICAN RECORDS – LONG COURSE (Continued)

EVENT	LOCATION	DATE	TIME
220-Yards	Honolulu, Hawaii	Aug. 26, 1927	2:13.6
200-Meters	Coral Gables, Florida	Jan. 3, 1926	2:16.2
200-Meters	Honolulu, Hawaii	Aug. 26, 1927	2:13.6
300-Meters	Coral Gables, Florida	Nov. 29, 1925	3:42.2
400-Meters	New Haven, Conn.	March 6, 1923	4:57.0
400-Meters	Honolulu, Hawaii	Aug. 25, 1927	4:52.0
440-Yards	New Haven, Conn.	March 6, 1923	4:57.0
440-Yards	Honolulu, Hawaii	Aug. 25, 1927	4:52.0
800-Meters	Honolulu, Hawaii	Aug. 27, 1927	10:22.2
880-Yards	Honolulu, Hawaii	Aug. 27, 1927	10:22.2
Relay 880-Yards	Honolulu, Hawaii	Aug. 26, 1927	9:20.2

AMERICAN RECORDS – OPEN WATER

EVENT	LOCATION	DATE	TIME
100-Yards	Honolulu, Hawaii	June 23, 1922	52.8
150-Yards	Atlanta, Georgia	Sept. 9, 1922	1:27.8
200-Yards	Honolulu, Hawaii	June 24, 1922	2:03.8
200-Meters	Honolulu, Hawaii	June 24, 1922	2:17.2
220-Yards	Honolulu, Hawaii	June 24, 1922	2:18.4
300-Yards	Honolulu, Hawaii	June 22, 1922	3:23.6
300-Meters	Honolulu, Hawaii	June 22, 1922	3:45.0
400-Meters	Honolulu, Hawaii	June 22, 1922	5:06.6
440-Yards	Honolulu, Hawaii	June 22, 1922	5:07.8
500-Yards	Honolulu, Hawaii	June 22, 1922	5:47.6
500-Meters	Decatur, Illinois	July 4, 1923	6:55.0
Relay 400-Yards	Chicago, Illinois	Aug. 27, 1921	3:51.0

NOTEWORTHY PERFORMANCES – 20-YARD POOL

EVENT	LOCATION	DATE	TIME
40-Yards	Buffalo, New York	Dec. 1, 1922	18.0
50-Yards	Chicago, Illinois	Jan. 8, 1925	22.8
60-Yards	New York City, N.Y.	March 31, 1922	29.6
80-Yards	South Bend, Indiana	Oct. 26, 1923	40.8
100-Meters	Buffalo, New York	Dec. 1, 1922	1:00.8
100-Meters	Chicago, Illinois	Dec. 6, 1923	58.6
100-Meters	Chicago, Illinois	March 1, 1928	57.0
110-Yards	Buffalo, New York	Dec. 1, 1922	1:00.8
110-Yards	Chicago, Illinois	Dec. 14, 1923	59.2
110-Yards	Chicago, Illinois	March 1, 1928	57.0
120-Yards	Chicago, Illinois	March 1, 1928	1:02.6
200-Yards	Chicago, Illinois	April 5, 1923	1:59.2
200-Yards	Chicago, Illinois	Feb. 10, 1926	1:58.4
300-Meters	Chicago, Illinois	March 6, 1924	3:34.0
400-Yards	Chicago, Illinois	Feb. 7, 1924	4:30.6
Relay 160-Yards	Chicago, Illinois	Feb. 2, 1922	1:16.0
Relay 160-Yards	Chicago, Illinois	Dec. 7, 1922	1:14.8
Relay 160-Yards	Chicago, Illinois	Feb. 2, 1928	1:14.2

NOTEWORTHY PERFORMANCES – SHORT COURSE

EVENT	LOCATION	DATE	TIME
110-Yards	Kansas City, Missouri	July 15, 1922	58.4
120-Yards	Kansas City, Missouri	July 15, 1922	1:06.4
200-Yards	Philadelphia, Pa.	March 25, 1922	2:05.2

NOTEWORTHY PERFORMANCES — (Continued)

EVENT	LOCATION	DATE	TIME
200-Yards	San Francisco, Calif.	Aug. 10, 1925	2:00.2
200-Yards	Ann Arbor, Michigan	May 4, 1927	1:56.8
220-Yards	Honolulu, Hawaii	May 26, 1922	2:15.6
250-Yards	Philadelphia, Pa.	March 25, 1922	2:41.0
250-Yards	St. Louis, Missouri	April 30, 1924	2:37.0
400-Yards	Milwaukee, Wisconsin	Sept. 30, 1922	4:40.0
100-Meter Backst.	Toledo, Ohio	Jan. 28, 1926	1:10.4
Relay 300-Yards	Milwaukee, Wisconsin	March 17, 1923	2:28.4
Relay 600-Yards	New York City, N.Y.	March 29, 1922	5:39.6

NOTEWORTHY PERFORMANCES — LONG COURSE

EVENT	LOCATION	DATE	TIME
50-Yards	Columbus, Ohio	Aug. 1, 1922	22.8
80-Yards	Indianapolis, Indiana	Aug. 10, 1922	40.6
200-Yards	Detroit, Michigan	Aug. 4, 1927	2:01.2
75-Yards Backst.	Columbus, Ohio	Aug. 1, 1922	46.6
Relay 800-Meters	Newark, New Jersey	Sept. 9, 1923 Open Water	10:05.4
Relay 880-Yards	Newark, New Jersey	Sept. 9, 1923 Open Water	10:05.4
Relay 880-Yards	Philadelphia, Pa.	July 31, 1926 Pool	9:48.6

330

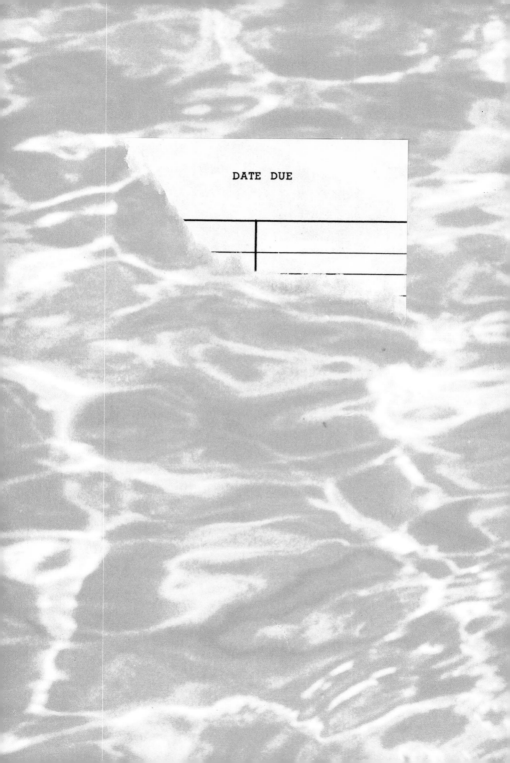

DATE DUE